ST MARTIN'S
TRUE CRIME
CLASSICS

"I HAVEN'T FORGOTTEN YOU."

ONLY HOURS after Tim Boczkowski discovered his wife Maryann's lifeless body floating in their backyard hot tub—and upon learning that Tim's first wife had died suspiciously in the bath tub four years earlier—Allegheny County, PA Police Detectives Jim Cvetic and Kevin McCarthy placed a call to North Carolina authorities.

"Is that so?" Greensboro, NC Police Detective Ken Brady said after being told of Maryann's death.

Brady had never stopped believing that Tim had gotten away with murdering his first wife Elaine. And he had been sure to let Tim know that he wasn't giving up. Every December, Brady sent Tim a Christmas card with the inscription:

"I haven't forgotten you."

**St. Martin's True Crime Library titles
by Fannie Weinstein**

and Melinda Wilson
THE COED CALL GIRL MURDER
WHERE THE BODIES ARE BURIED

and Ruth Schumann
PLEASE DON'T KILL MOMMY!

PLEASE DON'T KILL MOMMY!

FANNIE WEINSTEIN

AND

RUTH SCHUMANN

St. Martin's Paperbacks

PLEASE DON'T KILL MOMMY!

Copyright © 2001 by Fannie Weinstein and Ruth Schumann.

Cover photographs © AP Worldwide

All rights reserved.

For information address St. Martin's Press, 175 Fifth Avenue, New York, N.Y. 10010.

ISBN: 0-312-97720-4
EAN: 978-0-312-97720-7

Printed in the United States of America

St. Martin's Paperbacks edition / April 2001

10 9 8 7 6

For Maryann Fullerton and Elaine Pegher

ACKNOWLEDGMENTS

I owe many people my deepest gratitude.

First, thanks to my agent, Jane Dystel, and my editor at St. Martin's, Charles Spicer, for their continuing encouragement and guidance.

To St. Martin's assistant editor Joe Cleemann for his invaluable editorial input.

To retired Allegheny County (PA) Detective Jim Cvetic, Guilford County (NC) Assistant District Attorney Randy Carroll, and Kevin Rochford, for being so generous with their time, and insights, both personal and professional.

To Sister Pat Baker, Gay Barbiaux, Eileen Datt, Wes and Sue Semple, Shirley Marks, Kara Ruffin, and others who asked not to be named, for the assistance they provided.

To Paul Engstrom, for his photographic contributions.

To Meg Grant, for her unparalleled editing skills.

Lastly, special thanks to all of the friends who supported me in every way possible throughout the arduous task of completing this book.

F.W.

I co-wrote this book to honor the memory of my niece, Maryann Fullerton, and Elaine Pegher. It could not have been written without the help of Gay and Bob Barbiaux, Eileen and Chuck Datt, Shirley Marks, Sister Pat Baker, Sue and Wesley Semple, Dr. Maryanne Davis, Dr. Tom Brown, Kay Falkenhan, Bob Eddins, Pat Martino and others who asked not to be mentioned by name. I would especially like to thank Gay and Eileen, who have become dear friends.

I thank my sisters, Donna, Eleanor, Madeline and Claudia, my nephew, John Fullerton, and my other nieces and nephews, especially Jean Zappa, who I called so often that she began to recognize my ring.

I am also grateful to Randy Erwin for his willingness to testify, and paramedics Stacy Tamburo, Scott Long and Carmen Hart for their professionalism.

My deepest appreciation goes, too, to the detectives, police officers and prosecutors who I came to know, especially Detective Gary Waters of the Ross Township (PA) Police Department, retired Allegheny County Police Detective James Cvetic, and ACPD Detective Kevin McCarthy, all of whom deserve medals for their devotion to their work and for putting up with me, and to Allegheny County Assistant District Attorney Ed Borkowski for continuing the diligent effort begun by former Allegheny County District Attorney Chris Conrad. From North Carolina, I'd like to thank retired Greensboro (NC) Police Detective Ken Brady—I'll never forget your kindness towards me and your concern for Maryann's family—and Guilford County Assistant District Attorney Randy Carroll, for fighting to bring Elaine Pegher's murderer to justice.

I thank my immediate family, my husband, George, my sons G. Michael, Eric and Christopher, my daughters Beth, Gwen and Karen and my daughter-in-law, Annette, for their unending support over the years it took to bring this book to fruition.

Finally, I thank—and my heart goes out to—my sister, Pat, and my brother-in-law, Lew, who experienced the greatest loss two people can suffer.

R.S.

AUTHOR'S NOTE

The material in this book derives from personal interviews, public records and news reports from the *Greensboro* (NC) *News and Record*, the *High Point* (NC) *Enterprise*, the *North Hills* (PA) *News Record*, the *Pittsburgh Tribune-Review*, and the *Pittsburgh Post-Gazette*.

Documents, courtroom testimony and personal recollections were used to reconstruct dialogue.

Pseudonyms were used for four individuals, solely at the author's discretion.

Finally, neither monetary inducements nor editorial promises were made to any source in exchange for information.

CHAPTER 1

IT WAS nearly 1:30 a.m. on Sunday, November 4, 1990, by the time 34-year-old Elaine Boczkowski climbed behind the wheel of her 1985 Chevrolet Celebrity, which was parked outside St. Paul the Apostle Catholic Church in Greensboro, NC. The dance Elaine had attended at St. Paul's Saturday night had ended around midnight, but she'd volunteered to help clean up the hall for Sunday morning Mass. Elaine's 35-year-old husband, Tim, had been at the dance, too, but he had left sometime earlier. He was playing in a church golf tournament Sunday morning and was determined to get a good night's sleep.

Elaine and friends Kevin and Marianne Rochford, who had also stayed behind, finally left the church at around 1 a.m. Once outside, the two women, best friends since meeting shortly after Elaine and Tim moved to Greensboro in 1986, stood in the parking lot and chatted away. After about twenty minutes, Kevin convinced Elaine and Marianne to say goodnight.

"Guys, I'm tired," pleaded Kevin, who knew all too well that, if left to their own devices, the pair might talk until sunrise. They had before. Elaine and Marianne, in fact, spent so much time together that Kevin used to kid Elaine that it sometimes felt like he had a second wife.

After bidding Kevin and Marianne goodbye, Elaine began walking towards her car.

"Elaine," Kevin shouted upon realizing just how late it was. "We'll wait here and follow you out."

Moments later, Elaine started her car, then maneuvered it to the aisle where her friends sat with their car idling. Kevin assumed that Elaine would continue directly to the exit. Instead, she pulled to a stop. Her face illuminated by the glare of Kevin and Marianne's car's headlights, Elaine flashed what Kevin would later describe as "the biggest smile I ever saw her give." She then waved goodbye and drove off into the cool Greensboro night.

It would take Elaine maybe five minutes to reach the townhouse apartment where she and Tim lived with their three young children, Randy, Sandy, and Todd. As soon as she walked in the door, she was greeted by Michelle Rotante, the children's teen-aged babysitter. Tim had paid Michelle, but because he didn't want to leave the children, who were asleep, alone in the house, he left Elaine with the task of taking the sitter home.

Though thoroughly exhausted by the time she returned from the twenty-minute round trip to Michelle's northwest Greensboro home, Elaine decided to draw herself a bath in the upstairs hallway bathroom. Tim would later say he was asleep when Elaine got back, having drifted off while listening to music on his Walkman. But sometime around 2:30 a.m., he said, he was awakened by a thud. At first, he thought nothing of it. Maybe Elaine was still up and had dropped something. Thirsty, he got out of bed and lumbered downstairs, where he poured himself a glass of water. At one point, Tim glanced around the first floor. There was no sign of Elaine. Then, as he climbed back up the two zigzagging flights of stairs that led to the second floor, it dawned on him that he hadn't heard any other noises since the one that had woken him up.

Upon reaching the landing at the top of the staircase, Tim noticed that the door to the bathroom was shut tight. Puzzled, he walked towards it and knocked softly.

"Elaine?" Tim called. "Elaine?"

There was no answer.

Tim returned to the master bedroom. Moments later, he went back out to the hallway. For a few seconds, he stood in front of the bathroom door. He knew Elaine didn't like to be bothered when she was taking a bath. At the same time, he had a sinking feeling something wasn't right.

When he couldn't open the door by turning the knob—it was locked from the inside—Tim ran and grabbed a screwdriver. He stuck the tool inside the lock and began jiggling it. When that didn't work, he tried to pry the lock off the door. He eventually succeeded. Tim then pushed the door open and stepped inside. Much to his horror, he found Elaine completely submerged in a bathtub full of water.

Tim dropped to his knees by the side of the tub and pulled Elaine's head forward. He then took her nightgown, balled it up into a pillow, and placed it behind her neck. Ever so gingerly, he pushed on her stomach. Vomit oozed from her mouth. He pushed a second time, then a third. The result was the same. After managing to grab a firm hold of Elaine's wet body, Tim pulled her out of the tub. He turned her over on her stomach and draped her across the side of the tub so that her head was hanging over the water. He pushed on her back in the hope of clearing her throat. When that didn't work, Tim turned Elaine onto her back on the bathroom floor and again tried pushing on her stomach. Again, vomit spewed from her mouth. Finally, Tim ran for the phone and called 911.

It was approximately 3 a.m. when two firemen from Greensboro's Fire Station No. 12 arrived at Tim and Elaine's apartment. They found Tim upstairs, attempting to perform CPR on Elaine. The firemen squeezed their way into the average-sized bathroom and immediately checked to see whether Elaine was breathing. She wasn't. They couldn't detect a pulse either.

Seeking more room to work, they moved Elaine into the carpeted hallway outside the bathroom. Moments later, two paramedics from Guilford County Emergency Medical Services rushed up the stairs. With the firemen's help, they carried Elaine downstairs. There they connected her to a heart monitor, but the only reading they ever obtained was a flat line, an indication of no heart activity whatsoever. The paramedics then started an IV and began pumping a variety of cardiac drugs into Elaine's lifeless body. When she failed to respond, they placed a call to Greensboro's

Wesley Long Hospital. The doctor they spoke to, after being apprised of Elaine's condition, instructed the paramedics to transport her to the hospital immediately.

As the paramedics loaded Elaine into the back of their ambulance, a frantic Tim began pounding on next-door neighbor Liz Maple's door. Maple, who was sound asleep at the time, woke up and rushed down from her upstairs apartment.

"Something happened to Elaine," a shirtless Tim, his chest still covered with vomit, told Maple once she opened the door. "I have to go to the hospital. Can you watch the kids?"

Randy, Sandy, and Todd, clad in their pajamas, stood huddled around their father.

"Sure," replied a startled Maple.

At 3:25 a.m., Elaine was rushed into Wesley Long's emergency room. Within minutes, Dr. Elizabeth Stewart, a local family doctor whom Elaine had visited a number of times, arrived on the scene. Dr. Vincent Cheek, one of the physicians on duty, had called Stewart after being told by one of the paramedics that Stewart was Elaine's doctor. As an anxious Tim waited outside the emergency room, Cheek and Stewart attempted a number of potentially life-saving measures in the hope that one might cause Elaine's heart to start to beat again on its own. None did, and, at 4:16 a.m., Elaine was pronounced dead.

Stewart broke the news to Tim. She also told him that, because it was unclear exactly why Elaine had died, an autopsy would have to be performed. Tim said he understood.

By this time, Greensboro Police Officer Steve Goode had arrived at the hospital, too. When an emergency call like Tim's comes in to Greensboro's 911 system, standard operating procedure requires that a city police officer be dispatched to monitor the injured party's condition. In this case, the job fell to Goode, a veteran of ten years with the Greensboro force. Goode spoke briefly with Stewart, who told him she thought it was possible Elaine had choked to death on her own vomit. A short time later, Goode approached Tim and asked if he'd be willing to come down to police headquarters to answer some routine questions. Tim, knowing Randy, Sandy, and Todd were safe at Liz Maple's apartment, readily agreed.

Later that day, Dr. Deborah Radisch, associate chief medical examiner for the state of North Carolina, performed an autopsy on Elaine. Radisch's exam was thorough and exhaustive, but in the end, shed no light on the precise cause of Elaine's death. As a result, when it came to filling out Elaine's death certificate, Radisch, in the space following the words "immediate cause of death," had no choice but to enter a single word: "undetermined." She then forwarded her findings to the Guilford County Coroner's Office for final approval.

In time, Radisch's report would be amended. But it would take some four years before the puzzle that was Elaine Boczkowski's death was solved. Four years—and another watery demise.

CHAPTER 2

THE NORTH Hills is a sweeping term used to describe a region of twenty-nine Allegheny County boroughs, municipalities, and townships north of Pittsburgh, PA. Timothy Boczkowski (pronounced Boss-cow-ski), the youngest of Kieran "Buc" and Rose Boczkowski's four children—he was preceded by sisters Pat and Joan, and by brother Ron—was born and raised in Ross Township, a working- and middle-class suburb of roughly 33,000, situated some seven miles north of the Steel City. Throughout Tim's youth and beyond, the Boczkowskis lived in a three-bedroom, red brick, ranch-style house on Sprucewood Drive that was typical of most of the homes built in the area in the decade following World War II.

By all accounts, Rose, a homemaker, was warm, soft-spoken, and eager to please. "She always wanted everybody to be happy," said Mark Crendall, a longtime friend of Tim's.

Buc, on the other hand, had a somewhat gruff disposition and made no apologies for it. "Buc was Buc," Mark said of Tim's machinist father. "It's not that he wasn't easy to get along with. But if he didn't like what you were doing, he made sure you knew it."

Tim attended St. Sebastian, a Catholic school, through the sixth grade, then transferred to the local public school system, spending grades seven through nine at Ross Junior High School.

"Tim was outgoing," said Mark, who met Tim when both were seventh-graders at Ross. "He never had any trouble making friends."

In the fall of 1969, Tim, or "Boss," as his high school

pals nicknamed him—think the first four letters of his last name—began his freshman year at North Hills High School. He was an above-average student, earning mostly *B*'s and a smattering of *A*'s. He labored hard outside the classroom, too. Throughout junior high and high school, Tim worked afternoons and weekends at a family-owned fruit and produce market that was within walking distance of the Boczkowski home. He used the money he earned to cover typical teen-age expenses—Saturday night dates, clothes and records. At one point, he saved enough to buy a Harley-Davidson motorcycle. Buc owned a Harley, too, and on weekends, after Tim got his bike, the two would take to the road, riding in and around Pittsburgh. Father and son hunted and fished together, too.

The young Tim was slim, tall, and reasonably athletic. He played a year of volleyball at North Hills and was also a member of the school's physical fitness club. But contact sports were out of the question because of a congenital heart murmur doctors discovered when Tim was six, after a fall from his bicycle led to his being hospitalized.

"He couldn't get a doctor's okay to play basketball or football," Mark said. "They didn't want to take a chance on something happening to him on the court or on the field."

Thus, despite his relative athleticism, Tim was never a jock, per se. In fact, he was never really a part of any particular clique.

"One year, the school gave out this survey," remembered Mark, who remained Tim's best friend through high school. "You were supposed to say whether you thought you fit in with one group or another. But we weren't part of the in-crowd, and we weren't hoods and weren't into drugs. And even though we played sports, we weren't jocks either. We were just sort of on the fringe."

One of 744 members of North Hills High School's Class of 1973, Tim, for a time at least, planned on attending college. But a lengthy teachers' walkout in the fall of 1972, and lingering hostilities between the faculty and the school's administration after the strike was over, made for a difficult senior year for Tim and his classmates. Most of the annual senior class activities they'd been looking forward to were canceled. As a result, Mark recalled, "by the end of the year, a lot of people had had it with school." Tim was one of them.

But Tim was also ambitious and determined to make a success of himself. After graduating from North Hills, he explored a variety of career possibilities. Eventually, he stumbled across the dental products business. Convinced the field was a potentially lucrative one, Tim enrolled in a local trade institute where he learned to make bridges, dentures, crowns, and other dental appliances. After completing the program, he took a job with a firm in his hometown of Ross Township. Eventually, he went into business for himself, setting up shop in his parents' home, where he had continued to live following high school. Leaving the safety of a secure, well-paying job was inherently risky. But according to Mark, Tim was never the type to shy away from taking a chance.

"Back in high school, there were a lot of people who said they were going to start their own businesses," Mark said. "But when it came time to put their money where their mouths were, very few of them did. Tim was one of the exceptions, one of the few who had enough confidence to actually do it."

Once his business, which he named Boczkowski Dental Laboratory, was up and running, Tim turned his attention to another goal: meeting a girl and settling down. Although he hadn't had a serious relationship with any one girl during high school, he did date regularly. "He always had a girlfriend," said Mark. "We'd go to school dances, games, movies."

Mark and Tim continued to hang out together after high school, spending more than a few Friday and Saturday nights trolling Pittsburgh area dance clubs in the hopes of meeting women. Neither, however, had much luck finding someone with whom he could envision spending the rest of his life. "Tim wasn't looking for someone who was real wild," Mark said. "He wanted to meet someone who was, well, more on the wholesome side."

Tim came up with a way to be more selective about his search. He had been an active parishioner at St. Sebastian Church over the years and, in the winter of 1976, with a small group of fellow twenty-somethings from other local Catholic churches, helped to organize the North Hills Singles Club. Tim, then 20, envisioned the club, which met at St. Sebastian's, as a way to help young, professional, single Catholics from Pittsburgh and the surrounding area meet other young, professional, single Catholics. Some thirty people turned out for the club's initial meeting. Among them was a 21-year-old secretary named Mary Elaine Pegher.

A petite, 5'2" blue-eyed blonde, Mary Elaine, who was known simply as Elaine, was one of three children adopted as infants by James Pegher (pronounced Peg-ger), a prosperous water well drilling business owner, and his homemaker wife, Carmella. Elaine had grown up and was still living with her parents in Wexford, a rural community some thirty miles north of Pittsburgh.

Elaine graduated from North Allegheny High School in Wexford. After high school, she enrolled at Allegheny Community College in Pittsburgh, where she studied accounting and business. At the time she met Tim, she was working as a secretary at Westinghouse's Pittsburgh headquarters.

After attending the first meeting of the North Hills Singles Club, Mark had decided he could take it or leave it. But for Tim, who was immediately smitten with Elaine, it was another story entirely. "I didn't want to go back," Mark would later recall. "But Tim was all excited. All he talked about was Elaine. He liked everything about her. He thought she was the greatest." (Despite his initial lack of interest, it was through the club that Mark ended up meeting his wife, Maria.)

At the club's second meeting, Tim was elected president.

"You could just tell he'd be a good president," said Maria Crendall, explaining why she cast her vote for Tim. "He was really enthusiastic and was open to everyone's ideas. He really seemed to be on the ball."

"He wanted to be in a leadership position," added Angela Di Marco, who met husband Paul through the club and who eventually became close friends with Tim and Elaine and Mark and Maria. "I remember Tim having all these ideas. He was really fired up."

Elaine, on the other hand, was a little harder to read, as Angela would later recall. "She was kind of quiet," Angela said of Elaine, who was drawn to Tim from the outset, just as he was to her. "But once you got to know her, you realized what a great person she was."

Elaine had a sense of style, too. According to Angela, although Elaine always struggled with her weight—she was 151 at the time of her death—"she always looked good. I wouldn't say she was extremely stylish, but because of her job, she had the money to buy nice clothes and accessories for herself."

At the same meeting at which Tim was elected president, Elaine was elected secretary, and Mark and Maria, co-treasurers. Despite their immediate mutual attraction— "You could tell by their body language that they were interested in each other," Maria said—Tim and Elaine both, for a time, actually dated other club members. But it didn't take long for them to begin seeing each other exclusively. From that point on, the club became the center of Tim and Elaine's social life. Oftentimes, they'd double-date with Mark and Maria and the foursome would spend entire evenings planning club activities.

In many ways, Tim and Elaine were very much alike. Both were easy-going and were perfectly happy to go with the flow. As Mark once put it, "If they were on a date and they got a flat tire, it was no big deal. They just looked at it as an adventure."

Within six months, Tim and Elaine were a serious item. According to Angela, the turning point in the pair's relationship came in the summer of 1976 when she and Elaine took a week-long trip to Fort Lauderdale. "Back then," explained Angela, "Fort Lauderdale was a swinging place to be, and we did go out every night. But we didn't really enjoy ourselves. Elaine had been dating Tim for some time, and I had been dating Paul for a while, and we both realized that we didn't want to be with anyone else. We actually ended up coming home early because we missed them."

Angela would later say that it made Elaine feel special that Tim, who she was convinced could have any number of women, had chosen her. "I think she was really flattered by that," Angela said.

It also pleased Elaine that Tim was as close to his family as she was to hers. She was thankful, too, that her parents took to Tim immediately.

James Pegher, according to those who knew him, was somewhat reserved. On the other hand, Carmella Pegher, who went by "Mitzie," was vivacious and outgoing. "People migrated to Mitzie," Mark said. "She and Tim were alike in that way."

Mitzie, in fact, sometimes acted more Elaine's age than she did her own. "I remember going to a pool party at Elaine's parents' house not long after Tim and Elaine started dating," Mark said. "Mitzie was like a kid. She'd come up and push you in the swimming pool. And if she got knocked in, that was okay, too."

Buc and Rose Boczkowski, meanwhile, eventually grew to love Elaine as if she were their own daughter.

Two years after they met, Tim asked Elaine to marry him and she excitedly agreed. "We all knew it was just a matter of time," said Maria. "I remember the first time I saw her engagement ring. It was a gorgeous solitaire diamond."

Tensions, however, began to flare as Tim and Elaine's wedding date grew closer. Mitzie, who could be as opinionated and controlling as she could be fun, thought her daughter and son-in-law should have the kind of wedding she wanted them to have. "The Peghers wanted something elegant," Mark remembered. "They wanted everyone to have limousines and all that stuff. But that's not what Tim and Elaine wanted. They wanted a buffet dinner at a fire hall. They wanted everyone to be able to relax and dance and have fun."

Eventually, the strain grew so intense that two days before the wedding, Tim and Elaine actually talked about calling it off. Tim ultimately put his foot down, telling Elaine that she had to choose between him and her parents. Although it wasn't really in Elaine's nature to challenge her mother, she ultimately sided with her future husband.

"I remember Elaine saying to her parents, 'You know what, Mom and Dad? This is Tim's and my wedding, and we're doing it our way,' " Maria said. "From then on, Tim and Elaine were a united front whenever it came to Elaine's parents."

On August 11, 1979, Tim and Elaine exchanged vows at St. Alexis Church in Wexford. A reception for some 400 guests followed at a fire hall in the northwest Pittsburgh suburb of Franklin Park. A rock band played both the top hits of the day and a selection of wedding standards, giving Tim the chance to show off some of the steps he'd learned at a dance class he'd taken so he could keep up with Elaine, who was an excellent dancer. Even the Peghers seemed pleased with the way the day turned out. "You can see it in the wedding pictures," Maria said of Tim's in-laws. "They're smiling from ear to ear."

Tim and Elaine honeymooned in the Poconos. Upon their return, Elaine, who had left her job with Westinghouse to work for her new husband, began managing Tim's dental lab, which he had moved from his parents' house to a location in Bridgeville in southwest Allegheny County. "They were excited to set up house and to get on with their lives," Maria would later recall, "and Tim was anxious to get back to work."

Tim and Elaine lived in a rented apartment for some months before buying a home in Claysville, a rural community about forty miles southwest of Pittsburgh. Split-level with three bedrooms, the house previously belonged to an older couple and needed work. But Tim and Elaine saw the required renovations as more of a challenge than a chore. Living in the country also afforded them much more space—inside and out—than they would have had in any Pittsburgh suburb. The house sat on about an acre of land and was bordered on one side by a working dairy farm. Tim even bought a tractor for mowing and gardening.

"They loved entertaining there," Maria remembered. "They were always inviting Mark and me and Paul and Angela to visit."

Tim and Elaine, according to Maria, also liked the fact that living in Claysville put some distance between them and James and Mitzie Pegher. It wasn't that Elaine didn't love her parents. She did. It was just that now that she was married and on the verge of starting her own family, she didn't appreciate her mother, in particular, trying to run her life. "Mitzie wanted to have a say in every decision they made," Angela said. "But Tim was adamant that they weren't going to live that way."

Tim and Elaine were thrilled when they learned shortly after celebrating their first anniversary that Elaine was pregnant. "Having kids was a big priority for both of them," said Maria.

On May 14, 1981, Elaine gave birth to a son she and Tim named Randy. Daughter Sandy followed a little more than two years later, on June 11, 1983. Son Todd was born about two-and-a-half years after Sandy, on November 12, 1985.

Tim and Elaine were as thrilled by Todd's arrival as they were by Randy's and Sandy's. But at the same time that they were celebrating the birth of their third child, they were struggling with another dilemma.

Because of his heart condition, Tim paid close attention to his health. Around the time Todd was born, he received some rather dramatic news from his cardiologist. Tim said the doctor had told him there was a chance he would have to have one of his heart valves replaced. If that were to happen, the doctor said, Tim would be out of commission work-wise for some time. Although Tim had taught Elaine how to make crowns and other dental appliances, she was not legally certified to do so. That meant there was no way Elaine could operate the business on her own.

Although Tim's cardiologist wasn't certain Tim would have to have the valve replacement, the prospect alone gave Tim pause. It also led him to start considering the possibility of a new career. After researching a number of business opportunities in a variety of locales, Tim and Elaine settled on opening a Dairy Queen–style restaurant and ice cream stand in Greensboro, North Carolina.

Tim believed he'd found a sure thing. Greensboro, at the time, was experiencing tremendous growth, and, as local business owners, he and Elaine would have the chance to grow with it. Tim, in fact, envisioned eventually opening two or three more restaurants in the Greensboro area. More importantly, the business was one Elaine could handle on her own should Tim have to undergo the valve replacement.

For both Tim and Elaine, the move to Greensboro meant leaving behind the only home either of them had ever known—and their respective families. But they'd grown tired of Mitzie meddling in their lives. "Whatever Elaine—and Tim—did, Mitzie knew better," Maria Crendall said, "whether it had to do with where they chose to live or how they raised their children."

In fact, Elaine wasn't even talking to her mother by the time she and Tim moved, in part because of her desire to find her birth parents. "Elaine had wanted to look for her birth family for a long time," Mark said. "But Mitzie saw that as a slap in the face and took it to mean that Elaine didn't love her. Mitzie just couldn't get over the fact that Elaine wanted to know where she came from and why she was put up for adoption."

In truth, Maria said, Elaine's wanting to find her birth parents had nothing to do with Mitzie. It had to do mainly with her wanting to learn about her biological family's medical history. She wanted to know what hereditary risks, if any, Randy, Sandy, and Todd might face in the future. "She even said to her mother once, 'Don't you want your grandchildren to know their background?' " Maria said. "But Mitzie didn't get it. Instead, she felt insulted."

Elaine, too, had begun to find life in rural Claysville somewhat isolating.

Just before Tim and Elaine left for Greensboro, Mark and Maria hosted a going-away dinner for them. "Both Tim and Elaine seemed excited about the move," Maria would later recall. "They saw it as a new beginning. Of course, we were all sad that they were leaving. But they kept saying, 'Come down and see us. The door will always be open.' "

CHAPTER 3

LOCATED AT the heart of a twelve-county region of central North Carolina commonly referred to as the Piedmont Triad, Greensboro was founded in 1808 and named after Revolutionary War hero Nathanael Greene. With a population of just over 200,000, it currently ranks as North Carolina's third largest city, behind only Charlotte and Raleigh. Long one of the nation's leading textile manufacturing centers, Greensboro, in recent years, has undergone an economic transformation. Although one-quarter of the city's employed residents continue to work in manufacturing, major employers now include American Express, Sears, and NationsBank as well. Moreover, during the late 1980s and early 1990s, when much of the country was in the throes of a recession, Greensboro was in the midst of a growth spurt. Many of the city's newcomers were, like Tim and Elaine, young couples with children who were attracted not only to Greensboro's Southern flavor and small-town charm, but also to its booming economy, which offered them a chance to thrive financially.

Upon arriving in Greensboro, Tim and Elaine moved into a small house on the city's north side. The rental property was only a temporary stop, the pair told friends back in Pennsylvania. They couldn't afford to buy a home in Greensboro right away because they'd poured all the money they had into their new business, which they'd built from the ground up and ultimately named King Kones. But if everything went according to plan, it wouldn't be long before they saved enough to build a brand new house of their own. Tim was sure of it. Tim was sure of everything.

Tim and Elaine quickly got down to the business of

making a new life for themselves. While Elaine set up the house and enrolled Randy and Sandy in school, Tim focused his energies on getting King Kones up and running. They also joined a church—St. Paul the Apostle—where they not only worshipped but also socialized and made friends. Elaine, in fact, soon had a best friend.

Marianne Rochford lived with her attorney husband, Kevin, and their young daughter, Madison, in High Point, a city of 76,000 some fifteen miles southwest of Greensboro. The Rochfords, like Tim and Elaine, were recent Greensboro transplants, having relocated from St. Louis. And they, too, had just joined St. Paul's.

Elaine and Marianne, who got to know each other through a number of church-based women's groups, hit it off immediately. Tim and Kevin met through their wives, but never became friends themselves. This was due, in part, to the respective demands of their jobs. Kevin, at that point, was a young associate with the High Point law firm of Wyatt, Early and Harris, a position that required him to put in extremely long hours. Tim, meanwhile, was consumed with making King Kones a success. But in reality, there was more to it than that.

"I didn't really like Tim at all," Kevin said unapologetically. "He wasn't very bright or very sophisticated. It's not like he was offensive or obnoxious. He was just kind of goofy. He was like a big, overgrown kid. Elaine, on the other hand, was well read and well spoken. I thought they were very much mismatched. I always thought, 'What is she doing with him?' "

It wasn't just Kevin, though, who had difficulty relating to Tim. The majority of men whose families attended St. Paul's were, according to Kevin, "typical guys," men who followed professional sports and enjoyed going out for a beer. "Tim was not that way," he said. "He didn't know much about sports and when you'd go out for dinner, he'd order a Shirley Temple."

Even so, Kevin said, "because people liked Elaine, they tolerated Tim."

Tim and Elaine also kept in touch with friends back in Pennsylvania. Although they'd exchange phone calls on holidays and other special occasions, they kept up mainly by mail. Elaine and Maria Crendall, in particular, exchanged letters regularly. According to Maria, Elaine's missives were chatty and dealt mostly with day-to-day life. Without fail, Maria said, Elaine would gush about the kids: how they were doing and what they were up to. On occasion, she'd mention the business, too. She'd describe how she and Tim would take turns manning King Kones and watching the kids. But in one letter, written not all that long after she and Tim had moved to Greensboro, Elaine conceded that the business hadn't taken off in quite the manner that she and Tim had anticipated. She was disappointed, too, that they were still living in the rented house they had moved into when they'd first come to town. But for the most part, Elaine, on the phone and in her letters, remained her typically upbeat self, confident that it was just a matter of time before the business and life in general took a turn for the better.

Still, the stress of getting a new business off the ground began to take a toll on Elaine. During the summer of 1986, Angela and Paul Di Marco visited Tim and Elaine in Greensboro. "Elaine seemed worn out," Angela would later recall.

Part of the problem, Angela thought at the time, was that King Kones demanded Tim's undivided attention. Back in Pennsylvania, Tim and Elaine's lives had, to a great extent, revolved around their children. Both, by all accounts, were devoted parents who doted on their kids. But in Greensboro, Elaine was forced to handle most of the parenting duties on her own.

Angela, upon her return to Pittsburgh, told Maria about her and Paul's visit to Greensboro. Because Elaine had kept Maria updated via her letters, Maria was already aware that Tim and Elaine were going through a rough patch. But Maria would later concede that she may well have underestimated just how difficult a time they were having, thanks in part to Tim's mood whenever he and her husband, Mark, spoke by phone. Tim, unlike Elaine, tended to downplay the problems at King Kones. Rather than conceding that things weren't exactly going as planned, Tim would make a point of noting that the business had just had a good week. As a result of the mixed messages Maria and Mark received, Maria said she was hardly prepared for the chaos she witnessed when Tim and Elaine and the kids returned to Pittsburgh over the 1986 Christmas holiday.

"Randy, Sandy, and Todd were totally out of control," Maria would later say, describing the night Tim and Elaine dropped by with their children. "They were running around and yelling, but it was Mark and I who had to keep saying, 'You guys have got to calm down.' Never once did either Tim or Elaine tell them to stop. It was almost as if they were tuning the kids out, which was really strange because before they moved to Greensboro, Tim and Elaine were so attentive. They lived for those kids. After they left that night, Mark and I were, like, 'What in the world is going on?' "

After they returned to Greensboro at the beginning of 1987, little changed for—or between—Tim and Elaine. The failure of King Kones to become a profitable enterprise remained a source of tension. Elaine admitted as much in a letter to Maria, yet, at the same time, maintained it wasn't entirely her and Tim's fault. Tim and Elaine had built King Kones on the northbound side of Highway 220, a then–two-lane road connecting Greensboro and Roanoke, VA. When they first opened the ice cream stand/restaurant, it was easily accessible to cars headed both north and south. But a short time later, a cement median was added to the roadway. As a result cars headed south had to drive past the restaurant and then double back if passengers wanted to stop at King Kones. The addition of the median, Elaine wrote, translated into an economic disaster for her and Tim's business.

Kevin Rochford, however, attributed the restaurant's problems to Tim's lack of business sense. He said Tim miscalculated when he chose where to build King Kones. The restaurant was actually north of Greensboro, near a city called Madison. Although Highway 220 is a heavily-traveled roadway, Kevin said even an inexperienced businessman would have realized that people would be more likely to stop at McDonald's or any of a number of familiar fast-food outlets in Madison or Greensboro than they would at Tim's less-than-lustrous roadside stand. "Their location hurt them," Kevin said. "I don't think you get a lot of repeat business on a road like that."

But according to Kevin, it was Tim's way of running the business that was the primary contributing factor to King Kones's failure. "He was oblivious to the kinds of things that keep people coming back or keep them *from* coming back," he said.

For starters, Kevin noted, Tim wasn't willing to put in the elbow grease required to keep the restaurant appetizingly clean. "The place was so dirty–grimy dirty—that I wouldn't let my family eat there," Kevin said. "Tim never mopped the floor, and there were straw wrappers and napkins all over the place."

The same problem extended to the homemade miniature golf course Tim eventually built next door to King Kones. "He thought, 'If I build it, they will come,' " Kevin said. But because Tim had already invested all of his and Elaine's money in King Kones, he couldn't afford to hire a professional designer to build the course. Instead, he constructed it himself with help from Kevin, his father, Buc, and his brother, Ron. In Kevin's eyes, this was another grave mistake. "There was nothing to it," Kevin said, describing the course. "Every hole was a straight-away. He just did not have any concept of what he was doing."

Moreover, Kevin said, Tim seemed to care little about maintaining the attraction. "The first time I played there," he recalled, "I put the ball in one of the holes and when I reached down to pick it up, I realized there was a mother spider and about five hundred baby spiders inside the cup. I went and told Tim and he said, 'Oh, it's just a few spiders,' like it was no big deal. He didn't pay any attention to the putting greens either. I remember saying once, 'Tim, if people are going to play, you have to keep the carpet clean. No one wants to putt over leaves and twigs.' He said it was too much effort to vacuum. That was his mentality."

As a result of the failure of King Kones to turn a profit, Tim and Elaine's dream of building a house of their own remained just that—a dream—and they were relegated to remaining where they were. The box-like one-story rental was quite a step down from their house in Claysville. An older home, it was desperately in need of structural repairs and a paint job. The carpets were filthy and, because money was so tight, Tim refused to let Elaine buy any furnishings he considered non-essential, including curtains and blinds. Moreover, because Elaine was putting in so many hours at King Kones, she was having difficulty keeping up with household chores.

"She tried as hard as she could to keep that house neat," Kevin said. "She worked herself to the bone."

Despite his disdain for Tim, Kevin said he never doubted Tim's devotion to Elaine and the kids. "That was a plus," he said. "He was very family-oriented."

But the fact that Tim was willing to let his family live in near-squalor, Kevin said, "offended me as a father . . . I couldn't believe he would let his wife and kids live in that dump."

IN THE summer of 1989, just when it seemed to Tim and Elaine that things couldn't get any worse, Elaine and the children were involved in a car accident. Elaine was heading north on 220, on her way home from King Kones, when the car directly in front of her pulled to a stop to make a left turn. Elaine stepped hard on her brakes, but when she did, she was rear-ended by the car behind her. Because that driver was traveling at a pretty fast clip, Elaine's car was, for all intents and purposes, totaled. Fortunately, neither Elaine nor the kids suffered any serious injuries, but they did suffer their share of bruises. Elaine somehow hurt her back and would later see a chiropractor for the pain.

According to Kevin, the accident would prove to be a

turning point for Elaine in that "life-flashing-before-your-eyes kind of way." In fact, she wrote about the accident and about how happy she was to be alive in a journal she had begun keeping in February 1989.

Sometimes Elaine wrote in her journal on a daily basis; sometimes only once every three or four weeks. But regardless of how often she turned to its pages, it was, by all accounts, something she held sacred. In fact, many of the entries were addressed, in a sense, to God.

On August 13, 1989, Elaine wrote about the accident, thanking the Lord for sparing her and the children's lives. She also thanked God for having been a pillar of support for her during the ups and downs of the previous several months. "You have been there for me," she wrote, "and I believe so strongly that you always (will.)"

Elaine's accident also led to a bizarre encounter between Tim and Kevin Rochford. On more than one occasion, Tim had tapped Kevin, informally, for legal advice. That, in and of itself, was not unusual for Kevin. Because he was a lawyer, friends and acquaintances often approached him about one situation or another, looking to gauge where they stood legally. But because of his low opinion of Tim, Kevin would not even consider accepting him as a client. What's more, Tim's questions tended to be the kind lawyers often hear from litigious types looking to make a quick buck off a lawsuit. Once, for instance, after the police caught and arrested a youth who had broken into King Kones, Tim asked Kevin if he thought he had a legitimate lawsuit.

"He wanted to sue not just the young man, for inflicting emotional distress," Kevin recalled. "He wanted to sue his parents, too." Tim, in other words, saw the act not as an unfortunate incident, but as a potential financial windfall.

Then, not long after Elaine had her accident, Tim sought Kevin out for another legal opinion. He wanted to know if Kevin thought he could sue the woman who had rear-ended Elaine because Elaine, since the accident, had become more demanding sexually. Tim thought he should be compensated as a result.

Money. It was always about money.

"His question was the strangest one anyone has asked me in my twenty years of practicing law," Kevin would later say.

Tim went on to tell Kevin that Elaine's personality had changed as a result of the accident, and that he didn't like the new, more sexually uninhibited Elaine. Kevin was dumbfounded. "I said, 'Tim, I don't think any lawyer could stand in front of a jury and argue that someone should be compensated because his wife wants too much sex.'"

Later, Kevin would mention Tim's question to some of his law partners. "They just laughed," he said, "and after that, the big joke around the office was that everyone was trying to figure out how to get their wife up to that stretch of road."

Tim's query cemented Kevin's belief that Tim was, for lack of a better term, an incompetent oaf. But as telling as Tim's query was about the kind of person he was, it also, Kevin believed, said a great deal about Tim and Elaine's financial situation. "If he was really serious about suing the woman who hit Elaine because Elaine, in his mind, wanted too much sex," Kevin said, "I knew their money problems must be pretty bad."

As time went on, the entries in Elaine's journal—a spiral-bound notebook, actually—contained more and more references to her unhappiness with Tim and their marriage. In an entry dated January 10, 1990, she wrote: "Tim wants everything resolved so our lives can go back to normal (but) . . . I'm growing and changing at such a rapid rate." At the same time, Elaine appeared to believe that her marriage to Tim would survive, and become even stronger once they addressed the problems they were having.

However, Elaine's optimism that her and Tim's marriage could get back on track proved to be short-lived. A little over two months later, she wasn't even sure that she wanted to remain married to him. She was angry about one incident in particular.

Tim had become acquainted with some members of St.

Paul's who sold Amway products. Moreover, he became enamored with the prospect of becoming an Amway representative and lining his own pockets with profits from sales. One night in March 1990, he decided to attend an Amway get-together but, prior to the meeting, was supposed to pick up the children's babysitter and drop her off at the house. Tim, however, had become so obsessed with the notion of becoming an Amway kingpin that he forgot about the babysitter entirely and simply went ahead to the meeting, leaving the children home alone. When Elaine, who was at work at King Kones, learned what had happened, she nearly exploded.

In a journal entry dated March 11, she wrote that her and Tim's relationship had reached the point where she was no longer sure whether it could be saved. She went on to accuse Tim of living in a "dream world," and expressed her anger over his having forgotten to pick up the children's babysitter. "I'm so suffocated that it frightens me so," Elaine wrote.

CHAPTER 4

Two weeks later, on March 24, Elaine wrote again in her journal about the problems she and Tim were having, bemoaning the fact that their marriage was beginning to mirror that of Buc and Rose, Tim's parents. She described how she and Tim had fought the night before over her wanting to go visit Kevin and Marianne Rochford. She dropped the idea, she said, after Tim told her not only that she could, but that she should stay there overnight. Elaine went on to write that the next morning, she apologized to Marianne for getting her involved. Marianne, of course, forgave her.

Elaine's friendship with Marianne had increasingly become a source of tension between Tim and Elaine. Tim felt that Elaine was spending too much time with Marianne and with other friends from St. Paul's, where she taught religious education classes, served as a lector, and helped out with secretarial work. But what bothered Tim most of all was the close bond Elaine had formed with one of the priests at St. Paul's—Father Jim Weisner. Father Jim was tall and slim with salt-and-pepper hair and a dark moustache: think the Marlboro Man with a clerical collar.

"I know there were dozens and dozens of ladies at the parish who had a crush on him," said Kevin Rochford. "They were enamored with his looks and personality." Father Jim, according to Kevin, was bright (before becoming a priest, he had attended law school), compassionate (he was always available to parishioners in need), and liked to have fun (his musical taste ran toward rock 'n' roll). "He was the perfect dinner party guest," Kevin said.

Tim's unhappiness over Elaine's relationship with Father Jim became clear one night in early April, during a phone call Tim made to Marianne and Kevin at their home in High Point. "He said that he was feeling enormously threatened by Elaine's relationship with both myself and Father Jim," Marianne would later say. "He didn't understand the changes in her."

But it went beyond Tim's inability to understand—or appreciate—the person Elaine was becoming. Tim, according to Marianne, was convinced Elaine was having an affair with Father Jim. When Marianne asked him what made him think that, Tim admitted he had read Elaine's journal and that she had written of her fondness for Father Jim. Feeling rejected, he seethed with jealousy.

Later that night, Marianne called Elaine and told her about the call she and Kevin had gotten from Tim. Elaine was livid. She couldn't believe Tim had read her journal. Marianne told Elaine that she had every right to be angry. She said she, too, would feel violated if someone were to read her journal without her permission.

It wasn't just Kevin and Marianne, though, with whom Tim shared his displeasure. The night of April 5, which also happened to be Holy Thursday, Tim went to St. Paul's to confront Father Jim. He found the cleric in the church library, sitting at a table with several church members.

"I need to talk to you," Tim told the priest.

"Can this wait?" Father Jim asked.

"No, I have to talk to you now," Tim insisted. "We need to talk about this situation."

Elaine, when she learned what had transpired, was devastated. In a journal entry dated April 6, she wrote of going to talk with both the therapist she had begun seeing, a Greensboro psychologist named Bill Springs, and Father Jim.

She described visiting Springs, then going to St. Paul's. "(I) was so devastated that I cried and cried," Elaine wrote of her meeting with Father Jim. "He hugged me and he cried, too." She noted, too, that when she asked Father Jim if he wanted her to back off, he said, "No."

Making matters worse, Tim and Elaine were still living in the rented house that had begun to seem all the more cramped, especially when they compared it to the spacious home they'd left behind in Pennsylvania. Elaine was unhappy, too, with the school Randy and Sandy were relegated to attending due to the location of the family's home. Finally, in the beginning of May 1990, at Elaine's insistence, Tim and Elaine moved to an apartment complex on the north side of Greensboro called Yester Oaks, renting a three-bedroom, two-and-a-half-bath, two-story townhouse.

"It was definitely a step up," Kevin would later say of Tim and Elaine's new home, Apt. 104 G. "It was cleaner, and there was a pool for the kids. Most of all, Elaine didn't have to be embarrassed anymore when people came to visit."

The move gave Elaine the space she'd been craving, both literally and figuratively. She finally felt like she was living in a real home again. Best of all, she and Tim weren't on top of each other all the time. In a journal entry dated May 28, Elaine wrote that the move to Yester Oaks had improved her outlook.

Even so, she and Tim continued to have their troubles. In that same May 28 entry, she wrote that they'd recently had "a few big blow-ups," in part over their sex life and her newfound confidence in the bedroom.

In yet another May entry, Elaine wrote, following a session with Bill Springs, the psychologist she had been seeing, "I'm very afraid of my own femininity and of expressing myself as a woman because I was taught to be controlled and to do as you are told."

Still, there were times when Tim and Elaine and the kids seemed very much your average American family, at least to Kara Ruffin. Ruffin lived next door to Tim and Elaine, in Apt. 104 H of Yester Oaks, with her mother, Liz Maple.

"Both Tim and Elaine were devoted to the kids," said Ruffin, who noted that during the summer of 1990, either Tim or Elaine, at any given time, could be found hanging out with the kids at the Yester Oaks pool. "Tim would do belly flops into the water just to make Randy, Sandy, and Todd laugh," Ruffin recalled.

Elaine, on the other hand, never ventured in deeper than her knees. "Occasionally, she would stand on the steps in the shallow end, but she never really went in," Ruffin said.

One day, Elaine explained her dislike of the water to Ruffin and Maple. "She said she had a younger brother who'd drowned," Ruffin recalled, "and that after that, she stopped swimming."

In fact, no one was quite sure how Elaine's brother, Jimmy, had died. One Sunday in December 1981, James and Mitzie Pegher received a call from the police telling them their 23-year-old son, who was living on his own in Holly Hill, Texas, at the time, had been found dead in his bathtub, an apparent drowning victim. But the very next day, the police called back and told the Peghers they had reached a different conclusion. This time, they told them that Jimmy had died after falling off the toilet and hitting his head, possibly after suffering an epileptic seizure. Mitzie, unhappy with both explanations—Jimmy, for starters, had no history of seizures—wanted to press the police for more information. But James, distraught over the death of his only son, convinced her that nothing would bring Jimmy back, and that it was better that they simply bury him. For Elaine, though, even the possibility that her brother might have drowned was enough to instill in her a deep-seated fear of water.

In the end, the move to Yester Oaks did little to repair the damage that already had been done to Tim and Elaine's marriage since their move to Greensboro—damage that was readily apparent to anyone who spent time with them. When Patrick and Irene O'Donnell, mutual friends of Tim and Elaine's and Mark and Maria Crendall's, returned from visiting Tim and Elaine in Greensboro in the summer of 1990, they told Mark and Maria they couldn't help but sense some underlying tension. "They said there was friction," Maria recalled, "and that Tim and Elaine didn't seem as together as they had before they'd left town."

Mark and Maria were struck by their friends' report, but weren't overly concerned. "You must have caught them on a bad day," Maria suggested to the pair.

Then, shortly after Tim and Elaine moved to Yester Oaks, Paul Di Marco paid a second visit to Greensboro, this time without wife Angela. He, too, returned to Pennsylvania thinking Tim and Elaine's relationship had soured. "He said it was like they just weren't the same Tim and Elaine, and that things seemed tense between them," Maria said.

Paul related one incident, in particular, that left Mark and Maria stunned. He described how Tim, at one point, asked Elaine if she would get him a drink. "Get it yourself," Elaine snapped back. Maria didn't know what to make of the exchange, which clearly suggested that Tim no longer controlled Elaine the way he once had. "That was totally out of character for Elaine," she would later say. "She had always been so compliant."

Paul told Mark and Maria, too, that Tim and Elaine's apartment was, for lack of a better term, a mess. "There were boxes everywhere," he said. "Nothing was in its place."

Elaine had never been someone Maria thought of as obsessively neat. Still, she found Mark's description of Tim and Elaine's apartment somewhat disconcerting. "I just couldn't picture her living that way," Maria said. "When they lived in Claysville, she kept the house neat. If you happened to stop by and she hadn't had a chance to straighten up, she would apologize."

Finally, Paul reported, Elaine had put on some weight. Maria, knowing Elaine as well as she did, knew this meant her friend was going through a hard time. After talking to Paul, Mark and Maria compared notes. Both, it turned out, had reached the same conclusion: Tim and Elaine were in trouble.

It wasn't until the end of the summer of 1990, though, that Tim and Elaine reached rock bottom. Eventually, so little money was coming in that Elaine confessed to Marianne and Kevin that she had applied for food stamps. Tim, for his part, begrudgingly conceded that King Kones was a losing proposition and, in August, entered into an agreement to sell both the stand and the miniature golf course.

Elaine became incensed when she learned Tim had signed a deal to unload the two properties, not because she thought they still held promise, but because Tim had agreed to the sale without consulting her first. In Elaine's mind, this was the last straw. Her marriage to Tim was beyond repair. Divorce, she reasoned, was the only option.

By all accounts, Tim was less than pleased with Elaine's decision regarding their marriage. But once he realized that Elaine had made up her mind, he reluctantly agreed to the split. Custody, for all intents and purposes, was not an issue. Although there would come a time when Elaine began to fear that Tim might fight her for the kids, she'd received assurances from Kevin and others that the chances that a judge would award custody to Tim were virtually nonexistent. Money was another issue entirely. Elaine didn't want any alimony from Tim. She did, however, want what she believed was rightfully hers: half of everything they had. But Elaine had long since stopped trusting Tim as far as their finances were concerned. The fact that he had unilaterally entered into an agreement to sell King Kones without consulting her first only cemented her conviction that if she didn't take matters into her own hands, she could end up with nothing. To ensure against that possibility, Elaine asked Kevin to act as a mediator between her and Tim. Kevin agreed, and, one Sunday afternoon in August, Tim and Elaine and Kevin sat down together in the conference room of Kevin's law firm for three hours. The purpose, in Elaine's mind at least, was to iron out the financial terms of their separation. She was still angry, though, about the deal for King Kones that Tim had made behind her back and had no qualms about letting him know exactly how betrayed she felt.

"What gave you the right to do that?" she asked her husband.

"No one's going to tell me how to run my business,"

Tim responded angrily. When it came to money issues, Tim didn't like anyone telling him what to do. But by the end of the meeting, Tim promised Elaine he wouldn't make any financial decisions that affected both of them without running them by her first.

Still, over the next month or so, Elaine's distrust of Tim continued to grow. In fact, in a journal entry dated September 25, she wrote:

> I'm very relaxed and calm now which only comes once in a while these days. It's so hard to try to be the person ... I know I can be, but I'm trying. I've been so afraid to write now because I can't trust Tim.

Elaine took further steps to protect her financial interests by retaining High Point attorney Lee Cecil. Cecil, a domestic law specialist who worked for the same firm as Kevin, had agreed to represent Elaine on a *pro bono* basis as a favor to Kevin, and had begun the process of drafting a separation agreement.

It was early in the fall that Tim and Elaine began sharing the news that they were separating with friends back in Pittsburgh. Angela Di Marco learned they were splitting up when she received a phone call from Elaine after not having heard from her for several months. But it wasn't just the news of Tim and Elaine's separation that left Angela concerned about Elaine's well-being. It was the way she sounded in general.

"She was all over the place," Angela would later say. "She was talking about things like how much she wanted to try skydiving. She said, 'I just want to experience everything. I want to try everything.'"

Tim, meanwhile, had called Mark Crendall and given him the news that he and Elaine were splitting up. When Elaine learned this, she sent a letter to Mark and Maria telling them she would have called, but felt it was better that the news came from Tim. She asked Mark and Maria to pray for her, Tim and the children.

This decision to separate is not made with haste or without much tears, pain, and sadness. The best way to describe all that has occurred is to say that Tim and I are like oil and water. Each one has a great value but to mix them just doesn't work.

Though Tim and Elaine's split wasn't entirely unpredictable, the news still caught Mark and Maria off-guard. "We were shocked that things had gone that far," Maria would later admit. "We knew they were having a tough time, but we didn't think it was anything they couldn't work out. We thought even if the business ended up going under, they'd bounce back."

After receiving Elaine's letter, Maria called her friend, and the two spoke for a good two hours. Elaine told Maria that because she and Tim had so little money, they were going to continue living together at Yester Oaks. They agreed for the children's sake, Elaine said, to stay there through the Christmas holiday. Then once the New Year rolled around, Tim would find a place of his own. Elaine also said that the tension between her and Tim had lessened somewhat of late. She attributed the change, in part, to Tim's having taken a night job as an MCI operator. As a result, they saw each other much less frequently.

Elaine assured Maria that she and the kids were doing just fine. Elaine's journal entries from around this time make it clear, however, that considering Tim's penchant for wanting to be in control, some days were definitely better than others.

"I'm worried that Tim is going to cause trouble," Elaine wrote in an entry dated October 27. "I just pray that he doesn't."

On the other hand, in an entry written the very next day, Elaine didn't even mention Tim. "What a beautiful day," she wrote on October 28. "I just can't imagine not being outside today. What an experience at Mass this morning. Jim's sermon was terrific, the songs and music beautiful, and I really felt so loved by you, dear Lord. I'm feeling so much better about myself, and I know I will be okay."

These entries, however, did little to placate Tim, who had begun making a habit of perusing his wife's journal. According to neighbor Liz Maple, one day in late October, Tim dropped by her fiancé's townhouse—he also lived at Yester Oaks—and told her and her fiancé that he had read Elaine's journal. Although he didn't say exactly when he had read it, he complained that in it, Elaine had written that she was unhappy with him. Maple recalled how Tim, who was sitting on the floor in front of her fiancé's coffee table, suddenly burst into tears. He was especially upset, he sobbed, about Elaine's relationship with Father Jim. He was convinced the two were having an affair. This, however, wasn't the first time Tim had complained to Maple about Elaine's "friendship" with the priest. One day the previous summer, while lounging by the Yester Oaks pool with Maple and her fiancé, Tim had insisted that Elaine and Father Jim were lovers. And, as he would in October, he sat there and cried.

CHAPTER 5

BY THE end of October, Tim and Elaine had settled into a routine. During the day, they went their separate ways. They remained apart at night, too, with Tim, when he wasn't at his night operator's job, sleeping in the master bedroom upstairs. Elaine, meanwhile, slept on the couch, downstairs. Considering the animosity that had festered between them for some time, it was a relatively civilized arrangement. At times, in fact, the split seemed perfectly amicable. As neighbor Kara Ruffin would later note, "They both seemed fine with it."

Especially Elaine. By all accounts, Elaine, at this point, seemed to be undergoing a kind of transformation. "She was more confident than I'd even seen her before," Ruffin said. "She was excited about starting a new job. She was excited about maybe having a new man in her life. She was really looking forward to the future."

But as long as Tim and Elaine continued to live under the same roof, Elaine's future remained on hold. Until the new year, when Tim and she had agreed Tim would move into his own place, she had little choice but to accept that he was still a part of her everyday life.

Around the townhouse, Tim's presence proved to be a non-issue. For the children's sake, Tim and Elaine did the best they could to maintain some semblance of normalcy. Every night, they and the kids ate together as a family. But just how Tim and Elaine would cope with their redefined relationship in the outside world was another question entirely.

Their first real test came the night of Saturday, November 3. That evening, for the first time since they'd met some

14 years earlier, Tim and Elaine attended a social function not as a couple but as individuals.

Tim spent most of that Saturday fishing with Randy, Sandy, and Todd at a local park. Elaine spent the early part of the day writing in her journal, in part about how she and Tim were managing:

"I've been sleeping on the couch for a couple of weeks," Elaine noted, "and on Halloween, Tim learned a lesson in doing things separate. I stood my ground, and we took turns taking the kids out for trick or treats."

Elaine also recounted how she'd woken up at 1:30 a.m. in a cold sweat after having a romantic dream about Father Jim.

In her dream, she described how she and Father Jim were enjoying themselves at a party, "as though we were just two people in a vacuum." Away from the other guests, Father Jim told Elaine that he was planning to leave the priesthood and open a religious bookstore. "I walked over to him and stroked his hair," Elaine wrote. "He said, 'Let's leave and head back to my house.'" They left in separate cars, and when Elaine got to Father Jim's home, he was already inside.

Elaine recounted finding herself in the living room of a familiar house where the furniture had been rearranged to make room for a Christmas tree. Father Jim was on the floor and she sat down beside him.

After talking for hours, Elaine continued, "all of a sudden, he started kissing me." Then, as she was stroking his hair, she asked the cleric, "Why now?" He told her that he was hurting, and that he needed her. After, they cried in each other's arms.

Elaine wrote that after hearing a noise on the second floor, she looked up and saw her children coming down the staircase. She told them they could have something to drink, but then should go back to bed. Moments later, Elaine noticed her mother at the top of the stairs. She said she was checking on the children.

Then Elaine heard her father's voice calling from upstairs. She was startled at first, she wrote, because she knew her father was dead. However, she felt comforted when he came downstairs, looked at her and Father Jim and told them that both they and the children would be fine.

Her father began to walk away, she wrote, and as he disappeared, she said she felt "an incredible warm feeling" come over her. She then sat up straight on the couch, and realized she was "all wet from sweating." Thinking back on her dream, unsure of its meaning, she began to cry. Then, once again, she turned to her faith. "I trust you, dear Lord, just as in the past," she wrote her in her diary. "You will guide me to the answer."

Later that afternoon, at about 4:45 p.m., Elaine went over to neighbor Liz Maple's townhouse. The two had a glass of wine each before Elaine returned home about forty-five minutes later. At around 6 p.m., Tim and the kids walked in the door. All five sat down to a chicken dinner. Afterward, Tim got both Randy and Sandy in the bathtub and took a bath himself. He then spent about twenty minutes playing cards with Sandy. At about 8:15 p.m., Tim left to pick up Michelle Rotante, the children's teen-aged babysitter. He arrived back at the townhouse at around 8:35 p.m. A few minutes after that, Tim and Elaine left for St. Paul's. Elaine drove in her car, Tim in his.

The dance at St. Paul's the night of November 3 had a Polish theme. A polka band from New York had been hired to provide the entertainment. Refreshments included traditional Polish foods such as kielbasa, or Polish sausage, sandwiches. Like most of the church's social functions, the dance drew a large crowd, perhaps as many as 250 people.

Tim proved, over the course of the evening, to be particularly open about the fact that he and Elaine were splitting up. "Did you know Elaine and I are going to separate?" he asked Chris Cheek, a good friend of Elaine's, after spotting her at the dance.

Tim's declaration was hardly news to Cheek. Cheek had joined St. Paul's after moving to Greensboro in 1986 and, like Elaine, regularly attended the church's 9 a.m. Mass on weekdays. Elaine would bring Todd, who was still too young for school, and Chris would sit directly behind them. Sometimes, following the service, Elaine would stop by Chris's church office—she served for a time as St. Paul's youth director—and the two women would drink coffee and chat. Eventually, their talks took on a more serious tone, particularly once Elaine became convinced that she could no longer stay married to Tim.

Tim, besides being very matter-of-fact about he and Elaine no longer being a couple, also had no qualms about advertising himself as a free man at the dance that night. "I'm available," he informed a small cluster of fellow church members at one point in the evening. "Any takers?"

Elaine, on the other hand, was for a time emotionally overwhelmed by the evening's significance. At one point, she started crying and was so upset that she had to step outside for a few moments with Marianne Rochford's sister, Gerri Minton, also a member of St. Paul's.

But for the majority of the evening, Elaine seemed to most of her friends to be in an up mood. Chris Cheek would later recall that Elaine was "her usual bubbly self." In fact, Cheek remembered joking around with Elaine and several other church members in the women's room at one point. They were laughing so hard, she said, they could barely stop.

When the dance ended around midnight, Elaine and Kevin and Marianne offered to help clean up. As they readied the chairs that had been set out for the dance for Sunday morning's first Mass, Elaine posed a question to her friends that caught them somewhat off guard.

"Will you guys take my kids if anything ever happens to me?" she asked.

Elaine then turned to Kevin, an estate lawyer, with a second request.

"I want to talk to you Monday morning," she said, "about changing my will."

ELAINE WAS beat by the time she arrived home from the dance at approximately 1:40. But she couldn't collapse just yet. She still had to drive babysitter Michelle Rotante home.

Tim, who had gotten home at around 12:20 a.m., would later say he was sound asleep when Elaine returned from dropping Michelle off. He proved, however, to be sleeping lightly enough to be awakened by a thud shortly after 2:30 a.m. Some fifteen minutes later, he was on the phone with a 911 operator, pleading for help. He told the operator he'd found his wife in the bathtub, completely submerged underwater. He'd managed to pull her out of the tub, but she wasn't breathing.

"Hurry," Tim blurted into the phone.

CHAPTER 6

IT WAS 2:55 a.m. when a call regarding an "unconscious subject" came in to the Greensboro Fire Department's Station No. 12, which is located on Pisgah Church Road, directly across the street from Yester Oaks. Because of the station's close proximity to the complex, it was only a matter of minutes before firefighters Willie Jones and Bobby Mitchell arrived at Tim and Elaine's apartment. They rushed past Randy, Sandy, and Todd, who were standing outside in front of the apartment, and then up the stairs to the second floor, where they noticed the door to the bathroom was closed.

"Greensboro Fire Department," Jones yelled. "Do you need help?"

"Hold on," Tim shouted from inside the bathroom.

Despite Tim's instruction, Jones tried, to no avail, to open the door simply by turning the knob. But by pushing on the door with one hand while the other turned the knob, he managed to open it enough to stick his head inside. Jones could see Elaine stretched across the bathroom floor, with her feet up against the door. Tim, meanwhile, was leaning over her, performing mouth-to-mouth resuscitation. Jones reached his left arm around the door and moved Elaine's feet enough so that he was able to open the door fully. He and Mitchell then entered the bathroom. Jones couldn't help but notice there was vomit everywhere—on the floor, on Elaine's body, and in the bathtub. He also saw that the bathtub contained no water and that the bathroom floor was dry.

Jones and Mitchell checked Elaine for a pulse, without success. Seeking more room to work, they carried Elaine, who wasn't breathing, out to the upstairs hallway and began attempting CPR themselves. Moments later, two paramedics from Guilford County Emergency Medical Services arrived on the scene. Once upstairs, the paramedics, with Jones's and Mitchell's help, carried Elaine down to the living room. They attached her to a heart monitor, but the read-out showed Elaine was in cardiac standstill. In other words, there was no heart activity whatsoever.

As the paramedics fought to save Elaine's life, Tim told Jones he'd been awakened by a "thump," that he'd waited a few minutes before checking it out. He also mentioned to the firefighter that he and Elaine had argued that evening about a golf vacation he was planning on taking.

"Is she going to be okay?" Tim asked Jones after the paramedics began working on Elaine.

"They're doing the best they can," Jones assured him.

While one of the paramedics started an IV and began administering a series of cardiac drugs designed to jump-start Elaine's heart, the other placed a tube down her throat to ensure an airway was clear. They also used electrical defibrillator paddles in an attempt to literally shock Elaine's heart into beating again. But Elaine failed to respond to any of their efforts, so the paramedics loaded her onto a stretcher and, with Jones's and Mitchell's help, carried her out to their parked ambulance. One of the paramedics continued working on Elaine as the ambulance sped toward Wesley Long Hospital. But the heart monitor, to which they'd kept Elaine attached, continued to show no heart activity.

By the time the ambulance pulled up to the entrance of Wesley Long's emergency room, it was roughly 3:30 a.m. and Elaine was, for all intents and purposes, dead. Even so, Wesley Long physician Vincent Cheek and Dr. Elizabeth Stewart, the physician from the family practice group that Elaine sometimes visited, continued, in the hospital's emergency room, to try to resuscitate her. They did, at one point, detect a slight pulse. But it quickly disappeared. At 4:16 a.m., with no remaining hope of reviving Elaine, she was pronounced dead.

Afterwards, Stewart spoke briefly with Tim, who was waiting outside the emergency room. Tim told the doctor that he and Elaine, who were in the process of separating, had been to a party Saturday night. He then repeated some of what he'd told firefighter Willie Jones, about hearing a noise and about waiting before knocking on the bathroom door. Tim also told Barnes how he had begun administering CPR after finding Elaine in the bathtub. He said he even tried the Heimlich maneuver because it appeared there was something stuck in her mouth or lodged in her throat. He was afraid, though, he'd done it too hard. Tim said he called 911 when he realized Elaine still wasn't breathing. He did not, however, mention, as he had to Jones, having argued with Elaine about an upcoming golf trip. Instead, he mentioned to Barnes that Elaine had been drinking at the dance that night.

IT WAS a little before 3:30 a.m., just as the ambulance carrying Elaine pulled away from Tim and Elaine's townhouse, that the first Greensboro police unit arrived on the scene. Brenda Gilmore-Vance, a patrolwoman from the department's fourth district, was the first officer to respond. Outside the apartment, she encountered firefighters Jones and Mitchell, who were just about to leave. She and Jones spoke briefly. He outlined what had happened after he and Mitchell arrived at the apartment. He also told her that in his opinion, "something didn't seem quite right."

Gilmore-Vance asked Jones to accompany her inside the apartment. Together, they walked upstairs, and Jones pointed out where Elaine had been when he and Mitchell first entered the bathroom. He described how they had carried her out to the hallway so they'd have more room to work. Jones then left, but Gilmore-Vance remained behind to give the bathroom another look. Because Jones had told her that it at least appeared that Elaine had drowned, Gilmore-Vance expected to find quite a bit of water splattered about. But the bathroom floor was dry. So, too, was the tub, she noticed, after running her hand along the inside. To Gilmore-Vance, this didn't make sense.

Gilmore-Vance conducted a cursory search of the entire apartment, checking to see whether anything else stood out. Inside the master bedroom, her eyes were drawn first to the bed. It appeared someone had, at one point, been sleeping in it. She also noticed a pair of headphones and two damp handkerchiefs lying on top of the bed. Gilmore-Vance then returned to the bathroom for a second look. By this time, a police photographer had arrived on the scene and had begun taking pictures. Shortly thereafter, Gilmore-Vance left the apartment and drove to Greensboro police headquarters.

CHAPTER 7

GREENSBORO POLICE Officer Steve Goode arrived at Wesley Long Hospital at about 3:50 a.m. Later, after emergency room physician Dr. Vincent Cheek informed him that all attempts to revive Elaine had ceased and that she had been pronounced dead, Goode spoke briefly with Dr. Elizabeth Stewart. Stewart told Goode it appeared to her that Elaine had choked on her own vomit. She said Tim had told her what had happened that night, and that every time he tried to get Elaine to start breathing again, chunks of vomit spewed out of her mouth.

Goode then approached Tim, who had been waiting outside the emergency room, and asked if he would mind coming down to Greensboro police headquarters to answer some questions. It was around 5:25 a.m. when Goode, with Officer Brenda Gilmore-Vance also present, began interviewing Tim in the conference room of the department's Criminal Investigations Division. At Goode's request, Tim described not just what transpired after he found Elaine in the bathtub, but also what had occurred at the dance that evening and how he and Elaine and the kids had spent the day of November 3. Later, in his report on Elaine's death, Goode wrote that Tim told him the following:

> I took all the kids fishing to Jaycee Park. Dave Turner and his son, Michael, accompanied us. [They] live in our same apartment complex. At approximately 6 p.m., we arrived back home. At that time, Liz Maple . . . and Elaine, my wife, were drinking wine on the back porch. I had been to the refrigerator earlier and, at that time, there was a full container of wine. When I arrived back

with the kids from fishing, this container of wine only had about two glasses left in it. Our family sat down to eat at around 6:15 or 6:20 p.m. I set the table because me and my wife have an understanding that I would help out. We had chicken and drank water and Elaine drank two glasses of wine. I gave Randy a bath about 6:45 p.m. and put Sandy in the bathroom in the master bedroom. Todd didn't want a bath. I took a bath also and then played cards with Sandy from 7:55 p.m. until about 8:15 p.m. I then went to pick up the babysitter at Regents Park Lane. Her name is Michelle Rotante. I do not know her phone number, but I do have it somewhere at home. One thing about Elaine, when I turned her over, I hit her in the chest. I didn't hit her very hard, so I hit her again. When I hit her in the chest, she went down in the water. I just couldn't get her to breathe. I want an autopsy done and I want you to know that. I want somebody to do an autopsy.

We were getting along okay, but we were under stress. I had a lot of pride and I never abused her. It happened, in my opinion, that we were just growing apart. I remember when we were on 220 where we had a business together. I was working outside when the sheriff came in . . . and told me that my kids were involved in an accident. They were rear-ended by a lady going 55 miles per hour. I couldn't believe how lucky we were. After that incident, our relationship broke down. Elaine had been going to a psychiatrist because she was hurt over her father dying. The psychiatrist said she had suppressed feelings. We went to a party tonight and left around 8:35 to 8:40 p.m. It was at St. Paul the Apostle Catholic Church on Horse Pen Creek Road. We drove two cars to get over there. I drove my truck and she drove her '85 Chevrolet Celebrity.

We talked a few times at the party, but we didn't talk much. At around 12:20 a.m., I talked to Celia outside. I talked to Celia about the fact that Elaine had gotten very upset with me and very boisterous and had used the 'F' word at me several times, throwing things at me. Elaine would sometimes even use the 'F' word in front of the kids and even called me a fucking asshole about two weeks ago.

I got home around 12:40 a.m. and paid the babysitter. The babysitter did not leave and stayed at the house because Elaine was going to take her home when she got home. I was in bed by 12:45 a.m. Up until last week, I let Elaine use our bathroom. [But] last week she [said] she wanted to use the kids' bathroom because it made her feel more independent. I had been asleep for a little while. I fell asleep with the Walkman ears on my head and I woke up with the Walkman ears still on my ears. They were hurting me and I took them off and after a couple of minutes, I heard a noise. It sounded like a shampoo bottle falling or something. I didn't think much of it at first. I had to go to the bathroom and used the master bedroom. I don't know what kind of time lapse occurred during this period of time because I wasn't looking at a watch nor a clock. I then went downstairs and got a drink of water, and then went back upstairs. The door was still closed. I knocked and got no answer. I called, "Elaine, Elaine," but got no response. I then went back to my room and pondered what to do. I went back downstairs to get a screwdriver. I went back up the stairs, went to the bathroom door and began to jiggle it with a screwdriver, trying to get the lock to pop open. When I got it open, the door . . . I looked and saw Elaine in the bathtub under water. I thought she just may have passed out or something and called to her and got no answer or response. I walked over to her and lifted her head up. At this time, Sandy came to the door and was asking what was wrong and I told her to go back to bed. I grabbed Elaine's nightgown and put it under her head and pushed on her stomach a couple of times but nothing but vomit came out of her mouth. I then started saying, "No, no, Elaine. No, Elaine." I pushed . . . on her stomach and watched the stuff come out of her mouth again.

The mat was not down. I don't know if she slipped and fell. I just don't know. It was hard to give her mouth-to-mouth because her saliva kept coming into my mouth. The fan was on in the bathroom at the time also. Elaine never used the bath mat. I don't understand that. I pushed on her stomach and got more vomit. I tried to find a place on her chest, but her chest felt soft . . . I couldn't tell her chest from her stomach. At this point, I think I tried to let the water out of the tub. I pulled her out of the tub and onto her back. I laid her over the tub with her head hanging over the water and pushed her against the tub, trying to get the stuff out of her mouth. When that didn't work, I laid her back on her back and tried to push on her stomach and again, got nothing but vomit out of her mouth. I then attempted a form of the Heimlich maneuver to try to get the water out of her. This did not work either. I called 911 after trying to get the water out of her. I ran to the bathroom where the cordless phone was. After going to retrieve it, I was still trying to give her mouth-to-mouth. The dispatcher told me to lift her head in an attempt to ventilate, but all I was getting was more stuff in my mouth. When I found her, her head was under the water and her feet were out of the water at the spigot end. Her knees were bent and she was flat on her back. Elaine has not had any health problems over the past year and she had been doing pretty well. At the time that this occurred, my three kids were all in the house. My oldest one, Randy, was in the room that was straight across from the bathroom where I found my wife. My six-year-old, Todd, was in the same bedroom as Randy. Sandy's bedroom is right beside Randy's and Todd's. [She's] seven.

At one point, Gilmore-Vance, too, asked Tim to relate what had happened after he returned home from the dance. Later, she wrote the following in her report on the incident:

He stated to me that he was downstairs listening to his music with his headphones and he thought he heard a thump. He said he kind of waited around because his wife was a very private person. She did not appreciate him just walking in on her. He said after maybe four to six minutes, he decided he better check and see about her because he didn't hear any movements. When he went to the bathroom door, the door was locked. He stated he knocked lightly to see if he could get her attention because he didn't want to wake up his children. When she didn't answer the door, he stated he went to find something to open the door with. He said he found a screwdriver that he opened the door with. When he opened the door, he saw his wife laying in the tub completely submerged. He stated to me that he walked over, lifted her head from the water. He took her gown and put it behind her head, trying to keep her head up out of the water, and he attempted to give her CPR while she was still in the tub with water. He then, at some point, let the water out of the tub. He said he attempted to lift her up, but she was much heavier than he thought she was so he got in the tub behind her and lifted her much like you would if you were giving someone the Heimlich maneuver. He said he stepped out of the tub with her, dragging her out of the tub. He said she was full of fluid so he tried to get some of the water out of her. He laid her on her back—he laid her back across the tub, face down, towards the tub, and pressed in her back trying to get the fluid out of her. At this point, she vomited. He stated he then laid her on the floor and tried to give her CPR. He then went and called E.M.S. He thought maybe all of this took about 10 to 12 minutes from the time that he realized she had fallen.

Gilmore-Vance's reason for having Tim repeat the same story he had just related to Goode was to see whether any of the details changed from one version to the next. Any discrepancies, she knew, were a clue that Tim might not be telling the truth. It turned out there were discrepancies in the two versions. The second time Tim told his story, for instance, he did not mention Sandy getting up and coming to the door.

After the interview was over, Goode and Gilmore-Vance spoke briefly outside the conference room. Goode then went back inside, thanked Tim for his cooperation, and asked him if he wanted a ride home. Tim accepted the officer's offer and, a short time later, Goode drove Tim back to his and Elaine's apartment. Goode went inside with Tim, but only to retrieve the screwdriver that Tim said he had used to try to open the lock on the hallway bathroom door.

Gilmore-Vance, in the meantime, had driven to Fire Station No. 12 to interview firefighters Willie Jones and Bobby Mitchell. Later, she would record their comments, too, in her report on Elaine's death.

"When they arrived," Gilmore-Vance wrote, recounting what Jones had told her, the children were downstairs standing at the doorway and outside on the entrance stoop. A neighbor, who was supposed to be a babysitter . . . was standing in the foyer. [Jones] and Bobby Mitchell were directed upstairs to the bathroom. When they got to the bathroom, the bathroom door was closed. When Mr. Jones attempted to open it, something was blocking it. Mr. Jones stated that he cracked the door enough to put his head inside so that he could see what was wrong, and he saw a white female victim laying on the floor with her feet against the door. [He] said Mr. Boczkowski was on top of her attempting CPR. Mr. Jones stated he reached down, lifted her legs and opened the door. Her legs were wet on the bottom side and her body was blue and cold. The bathroom was too small for them to do CPR, so Mr. Jones and Mr. Mitchell lifted her and moved her into the hallway. Jones stated the female had vomited all over the bathroom and that each time Mr. Boczkowski would press on her chest, trying to clear the airway and give her CPR, vomit was spewing out of her mouth. E.M.S. arrived and it was too close in the hallway for them to administer aid. The victim was carried downstairs to the living room where they attempted to revive her . . . Then E.M.S. transported her to Wesley Long Hospital.

Gilmore-Vance also noted several comments made by firefighter Mitchell:

Fireman Bobby Mitchell stated the body was blue and cold. When he lifted her to move her from the bathroom to the hall, he said that the body felt clammy. When they arrived, there was no water in the tub and there was no water on the floor.

Gilmore-Vance punched out for the day shortly after interviewing the firefighters. But once home Monday morning, she couldn't shake the image of the bathtub in which Elaine had allegedly drowned. It was the size of the tub, in particular, that bothered her the most. Gilmore-Vance simply couldn't envision how a woman Elaine's size could drown in that bathtub. Determined to satisfy her curiosity, Gilmore-Vance decided she would conduct an experiment in her own bathtub which, coincidentally, was the same brand and roughly the same size as the one in Tim and Elaine's upstairs hallway bathroom.

Gilmore-Vance, who at 5'3", 149 pounds, stood one inch taller and weighed two pounds less than Elaine at the time of her death, lay down in her bathtub so that her head was lying flat against the bottom of the tub. She turned the faucets and began to fill the tub with water. But because the tub was equipped with an overflow valve, it never filled with enough water so that Gilmore-Vance's head was completely submerged. The result left Gilmore-Vance in complete agreement with firefighter Willie Jones. Something wasn't right.

CHAPTER 8

IT WASN'T long before friends of Tim and Elaine's in Greensboro began receiving word of Elaine's death. Among the first to hear the news were Kevin and Marianne. It was around 6:30 a.m. when the phone rang in the couple's High Point home. A groggy Kevin lifted the headset off the receiver. At the other end of the line was Father Jim. He was calling from the church rectory.

"Something terrible has happened," the priest told Kevin. "Elaine is dead."

How could that be? Kevin thought. Only five hours earlier, he and Marianne had been standing in St. Paul's parking lot talking to Elaine. Kevin asked Father Jim what he knew. The priest said he didn't think he should talk about the details over the phone. Not surprisingly, the cleric's response raised Kevin's suspicions. But Kevin's own ideas about what might have happened to Elaine, for the time at least, had to take a back seat to a more immediate task at hand: breaking the news to Marianne, who was lying in bed beside him. There was the baby to think about, after all. Marianne was four months pregnant.

"I have some very sad news," Kevin told his wife after waking her as gently as he could. "Elaine is dead."

"She just started wailing and rocking back and forth," Kevin would later recall. "She was so upset I was worried she would have a miscarriage."

Kevin and Marianne dressed as fast as they could, then, with Kevin behind the wheel, headed to Greensboro. Kevin told Marianne he would drop her at her sister Gerri's home, which was about ten minutes from Yester Oaks, then go on to Tim and Elaine's to see what he could learn. He didn't think she should be there, he told his wife, until he had a better grasp of the situation.

It was around 7:30 a.m. when Charlie Connolly, a mutual friend of Tim and Elaine's who'd also been at the dance the night before, received a call from Tim. Elaine had died, Tim told him. Could he come over? Because his wife had already taken their car to church that morning, Charlie walked to the nearby home of Jim and Celia Borowicz, who also belonged to St. Paul's. After hearing the news, Jim offered to drive Charlie over to Yester Oaks. Charlie, who in the past had made himself available to fellow church members who had suffered a death in the family, greeted Tim with a hug upon arriving at Tim and Elaine's apartment.

Tim seemed a little out of it, Charlie would later recall. "He just kind of had this sort of blank look," he said.

Yet at the same time, Charlie said, Tim was more composed than one might expect under the circumstances.

Charlie asked Tim if there was anything he could do. But before Tim could answer, the phone started ringing, diverting Tim's attention for the next several minutes.

When Kevin Rochford finally arrived at Yester Oaks, Tim was upstairs lying down. Randy, Sandy, and Todd, meanwhile, were still next door at Liz Maple's apartment. Kevin asked Charlie and Jim, who had remained with his neighbor, if they knew what had happened to Elaine. Both said they still weren't quite sure.

A short time later, Tim awoke and came downstairs. Impassively, he told Kevin the same story he'd told the police: how he'd been awakened by a "thump," how he'd gotten no response after knocking on the bathroom door, and how he'd discovered Elaine was submerged in a bathtub full of water.

There was, however, one major discrepancy between the version of events Tim gave to the police and the one he gave to Kevin. In recounting what had happened to Officer Steve Goode, Tim had said that after jiggling the door, he had managed to "pop" the lock off the door. But when relating what had occurred to Kevin, Tim said he eventually managed to get into the bathroom by prying the hinges off of the door.

Tim's explanation of how he'd managed to get the door open didn't sit right with Kevin—so much so that Kevin went upstairs to check out the bathroom for himself. Standing in the doorway, Kevin quickly concluded that Tim had either misspoken or out-and-out lied to him. The hinges, it turned out, were on the inside of the door. There was no way Tim could have pried them off the door while standing in the hallway.

Kevin's morning became stranger still when, a short time later, Tim asked him to accompany him to the master bedroom upstairs. Once there, Tim pulled out a small metal box from which he removed two life insurance policies in Elaine's name. How long would it take, he asked Kevin, for him to file a claim and receive the pay-out? Kevin was stunned. Elaine had been dead less than ten hours. How could Tim already be wondering about cashing in on her life insurance?

Again, it was money that was Tim's main concern. "Don't you think it's a little premature to be thinking about that?" an incredulous Kevin asked Tim.

Tim looked at Kevin, but said nothing.

Later, the two men would have a second conversation that would leave Kevin even more disturbed. "Tim asked me to come out to the front stoop with him," Kevin recalled. Once outside, he said, Tim held his arms straight out with his palms up.

"Do you notice any marks?" Tim asked.

"No, I don't," Kevin responded.

"Well, the police were taking pictures of my arms," Tim said.

Kevin repeated that he didn't see any marks. But Tim, strangely enough, insisted there were bruises on his arms and offered an explanation for their presence.

"They're from a motorcycle accident," he said.

Kevin was at a total loss, not only because he couldn't

see any bruises on Tim's arms, but because, to the best of his knowledge, Tim, at the time, did not own a motorcycle.

By this point, Kevin had, for all intents and purposes, begun to discount Tim's version of events. He was convinced that something other than what Tim claimed had happened to Elaine had actually occurred. There was the implausible anecdote about taking the bathroom door off its hinges. And the early mention of the insurance policies. And Tim's bizarre insistence that there were bruises on his arms that were the result of a motorcycle accident. To Kevin, all of the above added up to the likelihood of foul play, especially when combined with earlier events. Kevin's thoughts drifted, for instance, back to the dance the night before and Elaine's stated desire to change her will.

Elaine's request didn't exactly surprise Kevin. Although he never knew Tim to be physically abusive—and Elaine had never made any claims to that effect—he knew she feared that Tim had the potential to snap. What if something had happened to make Elaine more fearful? Kevin thought. She hadn't said anything along those lines to Marianne. But what if she had written something in her journal? Convinced it might offer some answers and that it was somewhere inside the apartment—"Elaine never went anywhere without her journal," Kevin would later say—he began searching for the spiral notebook. He would find it, he figured, and turn it over to the police, but a fairly thorough search of the apartment, undertaken after Tim had gone upstairs to go back to sleep, proved fruitless. Eventually, Marianne and her sister, Gerri, who arrived at Tim and Elaine's about an hour after Kevin, began looking for the journal, too. Tim had called Marianne at her sister's house and asked her to come over and help him break the news about Elaine to Randy, Sandy, and Todd, who were about to return from Liz Maple's.

"We turned the place upside down," Kevin would later recall. "We looked in her car. We even went through the Dumpsters outside."

It was while searching through the trash that Kevin

shared his suspicions with Father Jim, who had arrived at the apartment a short time earlier and joined in the search. Kevin told the cleric he thought it was possible that Tim, after coming home from the dance, had read Elaine's journal and become angry. Kevin theorized that a jealous Tim had confronted Elaine once she returned to the apartment and that things had gotten out of hand.

Eventually, Kevin asked Tim straight out if he knew where the journal was. Tim claimed to have no idea, but Kevin was skeptical. In the end, the fact that the journal was nowhere to be found only served to further Kevin's belief that Tim was somehow to blame for Elaine's death. But what ultimately sealed this likelihood in Kevin's mind was a conversation he had with his sister-in-law, Gerri, at Tim and Elaine's apartment. While Marianne was in the living room with Tim, helping him explain to Randy, Sandy, and Todd what had happened to their mother, Gerri told Kevin about a conversation she'd had with Sandy and Todd a short time earlier. She was standing at the kitchen sink, washing dishes, she said, when she asked Sandy and Todd, who were sitting at the kitchen table, if there was anything she could do for them. According to Gerri, Sandy started talking about how her bedroom was right next to the upstairs hallway bathroom and how she'd woken up the night before to the sound of her parents arguing.

"No, Tim, no. Stop," Sandy told Gerri she'd heard her mother cry. "No, Tim, no. Stop."

Todd, Gerri said, was somewhat less forthcoming. But he, too, said he had heard "some yelling."

Gerri's recounting of what Sandy and Todd had told her left little doubt in Kevin's mind that Tim had killed Elaine. And thankfully, he thought, it appeared the police were already onto him. Why else would they have wanted to take photographs of Tim's arms that morning, bruises or no bruises?

For Kevin and others who shared his suspicions, the remainder of Sunday afternoon had an almost surreal quality to it. Throughout the afternoon, church members and neighbors stopped in and out. Chris Cheek, eventually, was among them. Chris had driven to Salisbury, NC, early Sunday morning to teach a church class. Her initial plan, after finishing the class, was to go to Charlotte to visit some friends and then to Gastonia, where she was scheduled to teach that night. But not long after she got in her car following the Salisbury class, she got what she described as "a horrible gut feeling." Convinced she needed to return home at once, Chris, instead of heading to Charlotte, drove straight to Greensboro.

"Why are you back?" Chris's husband, puzzled by his wife's presence, asked as soon as she walked in the house.

"I don't know," Chris replied. "I just needed to come home."

That was around 11 a.m. About two hours later, Charlie Connolly's wife, Mary, called with the news of Elaine's death. Chris got right into her car and drove to Tim and Elaine's.

But later that afternoon, those who had gathered at Tim and Elaine's were told their presence was no longer required. The issuer of the pronouncement? Tim's father, Buc.

Buc and Rose Boczkowski had arrived in Greensboro at about 4 p.m. and headed directly to Yester Oaks. Kevin, who had met Tim's parents a number of times, was among the first to greet them at the apartment.

"That must have been a hard drive," Kevin said, aware that the couple had just spent some eight hours in their car.

"Oh, no," Buc said, contradicting Kevin. "It was a beautiful day to drive."

"A beautiful day to drive"? Kevin thought, replaying Buc's reply in his mind. He had just driven hundreds of miles after learning his daughter-in-law, the mother of three of his grandchildren, had died unexpectedly, and he was talking about what a beautiful drive he'd had. Was he in shock? What kind of answer was that?

But whatever time Kevin was going to spend pondering his exchange with Buc, it wasn't going to be at Tim and

Elaine's. Within minutes of walking in the door, Buc cleared the apartment.

"Everybody get out," Buc ordered.

Tim, Kevin said, was standing in the living room but said nothing. The kids weren't there, having left earlier with Jim and Celia Borowicz to eat and then stop at the church.

"He practically shoved people out the door," Kevin would later recall. "Afterwards, we all stood outside wondering what had just happened."

BY THIS time, word of Elaine's death had begun to spread to Tim and Elaine's friends back in Pittsburgh. Maria Crendall heard the news from Elaine's mother.

"Maria, did you hear?" Mitzie Pegher asked her daughter's longtime friend almost matter-of-factly. "Elaine died."

The first thought that ran through Maria's mind was that she must have misheard what Mitzie said. But before she could utter a single word, Elaine's mother continued on. "That sonuvabitch," an angry Mitzie cursed. "I know he killed her."

"Oh, my God, Mitzie, what happened?" Maria asked.

Mitzie told Maria what little she knew, which was essentially what Tim had told her when he'd called from Greensboro: that Elaine had been drinking and that she'd passed out in the bathtub and drowned. Mitzie was especially irate that Tim had waited until the morning to call her and that by the time she found out about Elaine's death, Buc and Rose already were on their way to North Carolina.

"I am so sorry," said Maria, who was still finding it difficult to digest the news of Elaine's death.

Maria offered to call the rest of Elaine's friends in Pennsylvania with the news, but when she did, she kept Mitzie's accusation against Tim to herself. She'd dismissed it anyway. Maria knew that Elaine, who'd recently reconciled with Mitzie, had visited her mother about a month earlier and told her that she and Tim were breaking up. Mitzie, Maria thought, undoubtedly blamed Tim for the split. Now, overcome with grief over the death of her daughter, it made sense that she would hold her soon-to-be-ex–son-in-law accountable for that, too.

Maria and husband Mark, Tim's oldest friend, decided that Mark would go to Greensboro for Elaine's funeral while Maria stayed behind in Pennsylvania with their children. Paul and Angela Di Marco made a similar decision. Paul would go to Greensboro while Angela remained home with the kids.

Mark and Paul flew to Greensboro the night before Elaine's funeral mass, arriving just in time to attend her viewing on Tuesday night, November 6. At the funeral home, they found Tim sitting by the casket with Randy, Sandy, and Todd huddled around him.

"You could tell he had been crying," Mark would later recall. "The kids were upset, too. They were obviously grieving."

That, of course, was to be expected. But what Mark and Paul didn't expect was the reception they received from members of the St. Paul's congregation and from Father Jim.

"When they first moved down there," Mark said, "when they were still telling us how great it was, they would talk about how much they loved their new church and how they'd made so many new friends there. But at the funeral, we were literally shunned. Most of the people there wouldn't talk to us and when they did, they weren't very nice. Even the priest ignored us. And it wasn't just the people from Greensboro. We tried at one point to talk to Elaine's mother, Mitzie, who we'd known for years, and she snubbed us, too. We couldn't understand what was going on. Then we realized that we were being treated that way because we were friends of Tim's. And because everyone there was angry at Tim, they were angry at us, too."

ELAINE'S FUNERAL took place the morning of November 7 inside a jam-packed St. Paul's. Father Jim officiated, the choir sang, and, at one point, dozens of Elaine's friends from St. Paul's parish, candles in hand, lined both sides of the center aisle.

Elaine, who, *per* Tim's choice, was dressed in her Christmas outfit from the previous year, was interred in a mausoleum crypt at Westminster Gardens Cemetery in Greensboro. Tim was familiar with the crypts because that summer, he had asked Yester Oaks neighbor Liz Maple, who worked at the cemetery, for a sales presentation. Tim also had had the option of burying Elaine back in Pennsylvania. Mitzie Pegher had offered him a burial plot next to Elaine's father's and brother's, but Tim rejected the possibility out of hand. Greensboro, he insisted, would be Elaine's final resting-place.

Though the service by the crypt was brief, it boasted a most bizarre moment. At one point, Tim stepped up to Elaine's casket and actually lifted its lid. "There was an audible gasp from everyone there," Kevin remembered. "No one had ever seen anyone open a casket after it had been closed, presumably for good."

Oblivious to the mourners' reaction, Tim instead focused his attention on helping Randy, Sandy, and Todd each place a note inside their mother's casket. In doing so, he seemed very much the concerned father. Kevin, however, couldn't help but wonder whether Tim was simply acting the part of the grieving family man to elicit sympathy from the mourners.

It was also at Elaine's funeral that Tim and Buc exchanged words with Kevin in the church's foyer. "They accused me of spreading rumors that Tim was responsible for Elaine's death," Kevin would later recall. "But I was actually doing just the opposite. I was telling people to keep their suspicions to themselves because I knew Tim would jump at the first chance he could to sue somebody for slander."

As for Buc and Tim, Kevin said, "I told them, essentially, to get out of my face."

Mitzie Pegher, on the other hand, wasn't about to let the possibility that Tim might sue her to keep her from saying exactly what she pleased. She and Elaine's father had approved of Tim when he and Elaine first met. In the mid-

1970s, Pittsburgh and the surrounding area were terribly depressed. Steel mills were shutting left and right, leaving many young men Tim's age with few options work-wise. Tim, however, because he'd learned a trade and had actually started his own business, was in a position to provide for Elaine. The fact that he was Catholic and active in the church pleased the Peghers, too. It was only after her daughter had married Tim that Mitzie grew to detest him. She blamed Tim for turning Elaine against her. She held Tim responsible, too, for cutting her off from her grandchildren by moving them hundreds of miles away. Now she was blaming Tim for Elaine's death.

"He did it," insisted Mitzie, who, along with Elaine's sister, Janet Wisniewski, stayed with Kevin and Marianne Rochford while in Greensboro for Elaine's funeral. "He did it."

CHAPTER 9

SHORTLY AFTER the funeral, Elaine's case was assigned
to Ken Brady, a detective with the homicide unit of the
Greensboro Police Department's Criminal Investigations
Division. Brady, who had joined the department in 1966
and become a detective five years after that, was considered
one of the force's top investigators.

Brady, a tobacco-chewing, just-the-facts-ma'am type,
began his investigation by conferring with Officer Steve
Goode, and with Officer Brenda Gilmore-Vance, who
shared, in addition to her incident report, the results of the
test she'd performed in her own bathtub the morning of
Elaine's death. The detective also conducted a routine background check on Tim. He learned that Tim had no criminal
record. He discovered, too, that whatever domestic problems Tim and Elaine might have been experiencing, they
never resulted in the police or any other agency being called
to their apartment.

Within a matter of days, Brady stopped by the townhouse and spoke briefly with Tim. He also began interviewing friends of Tim's and Elaine's and church members
who had seen the pair at the St. Paul's dance the night of
November 3. Kevin and Marianne, who Brady would eventually interview a half a dozen times, told the detective
about some of the problems Tim and Elaine had been
having and about how they'd decided to divorce. Kevin,
too, told Brady of Elaine's desire to change her will, about
Tim's obsession with money and his eagerness to collect
on Elaine's life insurance policies, and about the conversation Gerri Minton had said she had with Sandy and Todd
the morning of Elaine's death. Although Brady never said

as much, Kevin felt from the start that it hadn't taken long
for the detective to reach the same conclusion he had: that
Tim had killed Elaine.

On November 28, some three-and-a-half weeks after
Elaine's death, Brady conducted his first in-depth interview
with Tim at Greensboro police headquarters. Although it
was only an interview, as opposed to an official interro-
gation, Tim brought along Greensboro attorney Doug Harris, the same lawyer who had represented him in the
still-pending lawsuit he had filed against the driver who had
rear-ended Elaine some fifteen months earlier. Tim told
Brady how he and Elaine had relocated to Greensboro in
1986, about their recent separation, and about how they'd
gone separately and not as a couple to the dance at St.
Paul's. Tim mentioned, too, that while Elaine did not have
any major illnesses that he knew of, she had been complaining about pain in her legs and tenderness in her breast
and had also been seeing a psychologist named Bill
Springs.

Tim told Brady he had gone to sleep in the master bedroom upstairs only to be awakened by a noise he couldn't
identify. "I got up, went to the bathroom downstairs, and
got me some ice water," he said. "She wasn't on the couch.
The babysitter was gone and I heard the fan in the bathroom. I felt that Elaine was home. I went back upstairs,
tapped on the bathroom door, and called her name. I heard
water running and it was in the tub. I got no response. I
went back to my bedroom, trying to decide what to do. I
had given CPR before to my child and I knew the situation."

At that point, Brady said, Tim started to ramble. He then
began to cry. Through his tears, Tim told the detective that
neither he nor Elaine was seeing anyone else. He also mum-
bled something that sounded to Brady like "there had been
no physical harm done." After a few minutes, Brady succeeded in steering Tim's attention back to the events of
Sunday morning. Tim described how he used a screwdriver
to pry open the lock on the door. Inside the bathroom, Tim

said, he found Elaine lying nude in the bathtub. At the same time, he heard Sandy getting up from her bed.

As Tim told Brady:

> I pulled Elaine up really waiting for her to slap me in the face. I thought she was sleeping. I told Sandy to go back to bed and shut the door. I then started CPR on her in the tub. I didn't know what to do. I hit her in the sternum twice. There was no life. I kept trying CPR. I tried to get her mouth clean of the stuff that was in her mouth. I then pulled her out of the tub and laid her head toward the door and I told Randy to call 911. He said, "Why?" I then went out and called 911. I told them that, "I need an ambulance. My wife is hurt." I told the kids to get dressed and go downstairs and show the ambulance where we were at. I don't know what they did then. It seemed like a while before anyone got there. I talked to the dispatcher and he told me to take her pulse. I gave her more mouth to mouth. I lifted her up, put her over the side of the tub, [and] pushed on her back, hoping to get her mouth clean. I let the water out of the tub right after I went into the bathroom.

Eventually, Tim mentioned to Brady that Elaine had kept a diary for several years and that he would be glad to turn it over so the detective could read it for himself. Following Doug Harris's lead, Tim then got up and left.

About two weeks later, Brady spoke briefly with Randy, Sandy, and Todd at the elementary school the three children attended. But, because he was a police officer, the detective was unsure whether Sandy and Todd would repeat the statements they'd supposedly made to Gerri Minton. A counselor at the school, Joyner Elementary, had recommended that Brady talk to all three children at once and had arranged for the trio to be brought down to a school office. With the counselor and a Greensboro police youth officer present, Brady explained to the children that he was trying to find out what had happened to their mother. He said he had heard about some things they had said and that he needed to ask them a few questions. Brady had been hoping that Sandy, in particular, would speak up. But her response to each of Brady's questions was a stony silence. It didn't take Brady long to conclude that the children weren't going to tell him whether they'd heard or seen anything that night—or anything else, for that matter—so he thanked them for coming down and sent them back to their respective classrooms.

Brady knew that a statement from Sandy in which she described hearing her parents arguing in the bathroom the morning of Elaine's death would be a key piece of evidence against Tim. But at that point, evidence was the least of Brady's concerns. No matter how much evidence he managed to uncover implicating Tim in Elaine's death, it was useless as long as the cause of death on Elaine's death certificate remained "undetermined," which is exactly what Brady explained to Randy Carroll when Carroll, one of Guilford County's assistant district attorneys, inquired about Elaine's death.

Carroll, it turned out, had heard about Elaine's case from Chris Cheek, who, at the time, was working as a guardian *ad litem*—a volunteer appointed to represent the interests of a child in a legal situation—for the North Carolina judicial district that included Greensboro. Carroll and Cheek had run into each other on the steps of the Guilford County Courthouse in Greensboro about a month after Elaine's death. Cheek mentioned to the prosecutor that a friend of hers had died under suspicious circumstances and that, to date, no one had been charged in connection with her death.

"Who's handling the case?" Carroll asked.

"Ken Brady," Cheek told him.

"If there was someone Brady could charge," Carroll assured Cheek, "he would."

Carroll told Cheek he would look into the matter. Shortly thereafter, Carroll called Brady. He learned that Brady, too, was convinced that Elaine's death was not an accident. But Brady told Carroll his hands were tied be-

64   FANNIE WEINSTEIN AND RUTH SCHUMANN

cause of Elaine's autopsy report. Under North Carolina law, he could not seek a warrant for an arrest without an official cause of death.

"Brady," Carroll would later say, "was as frustrated as everybody else."

CHAPTER 10

IN THE months following Elaine's death, Tim was well aware he was living under a cloud of suspicion. But his response, rather than trying to defend himself or set the record straight, was to cut himself—and the children—off from those he perceived as doubtful of his innocence. He stopped seeing Kevin and Marianne altogether. Kevin, in a sense, was relieved. He was convinced Tim had committed murder and was glad to have him out of his and Marianne's lives. The children were another story. Randy, Sandy, and Todd had spent so much time at Kevin and Marianne's over the past few years that it had become something of a second home for them, and Sandy, in particular, had become extremely close to Kevin and Marianne's daughter, Madison. So for the children's sake, Kevin, on several occasions, contacted Tim and asked if he and Marianne could see the children. Tim flatly refused. Kevin then asked Tim if he would at least allow the kids to get together. Again, Tim refused.

Kara Ruffin, who lived next door to Tim and Elaine with her mother, Liz Maple, said she and her mother also became *persona non grata* with Tim.

"We'd run into him outside the apartment every so often, and, just by the way he looked at us, it was clear he didn't want anything to do with us," Ruffin said.

Randy, Sandy, and Todd, too, all but disappeared, according to Ruffin. "Before Elaine died, we saw them all the time," she said. "But afterwards, they hardly ever played outside. And when we did see them, they didn't even say hello. It was like they weren't themselves anymore."

Ruffin and her mother blamed the change in the kids' dispositions on Tim. "We figured he told them not to talk to us," she said.

Tim did stay in touch with some friends from St. Paul's, most notably Jim and Celia Borowicz, who refused to believe that Tim would have hurt Elaine. "They're good, religious people," Kevin Rochford said. "I think they just couldn't fathom that a husband could kill his wife."

But for the most part, Tim focused on getting on with his life and seeing that Randy, Sandy, and Todd got on with theirs. He decided, for the time being at least, that they would remain in North Carolina.

Though they'd managed to get through Thanksgiving, thanks in part to Rose Boczkowski's decision to stay on in Greensboro after Elaine's funeral to help her son with the housekeeping and child-rearing duties, Tim was certain the upcoming holiday season would prove to be a difficult one, especially for the children. As a result, he made plans for him and the kids to spend Christmas back in Pennsylvania.

Mark and Maria Crendall were thrilled when they learned Tim would be coming to town for the holidays. After the way Mark and Paul DiMarco had been treated at Elaine's funeral, they worried how Tim would get by on his own in Greensboro. At the same time, they were puzzled by something Tim had said to them. When he phoned Mark and Maria to tell them about his upcoming visit, he also asked if they would call Paul and Angela.

"I'd like us all to get together," Tim said. "I want to tell you guys what really happened."

Mark and Maria didn't know what to make of Tim's pronouncement. What did he mean, they wondered, by "what really happened"?

Several weeks later they found out. A few nights before Christmas, Tim and the DiMarcos got together with the Crendalls at home. (Randy, Sandy, and Todd spent the night with Buc and Rose.) His four oldest friends gathered around him as Tim recounted his version of the events of the morning Elaine died. His story echoed the earlier accounts Tim had given. But what struck the group most was the matter-of-fact manner in which Tim related the tale.

"It was like he was talking about something he'd seen on the news," Maria would later say, "not something that had actually happened to him."

Eventually, Tim took out Elaine's journal—the same one Kevin and others had been unable to find—and began reading from it. He recited numerous entries, including ones in which she wrote about how unhappy she was and the very last one, the one in which Elaine described the dream she'd had about Father Jim.

Tim's friends were at a loss. Why was Tim reading Elaine's journal to them? Maria pondered whether his goal was to convince them that Elaine had taken her own life. But in Maria's mind, the entries Tim read, rather than suggesting Elaine was despondent, indicated she was very much looking forward to the future.

"Elaine had changed," Maria thought. "There was no doubt about that. But no way did she sound like someone who was thinking of ending her life."

Maria would later find herself wondering about Tim's mental state after his behavior at the gathering. After putting down Elaine's journal, Tim had pulled out a handful of Polaroids of himself in which he was wearing only his underwear. He passed them around to the group, explaining that his father had taken them not long after Elaine's death.

"Look," he insisted, "there aren't any marks on me."

Maria was dumbfounded.

"Why is he showing us these pictures?" she would later recall thinking at the time. She wondered, too, why Tim had even had Buc take them. It didn't make sense—unless he was worried the police thought he had something to do with Elaine's death. And if that was the case, why hadn't Tim said so? He had mentioned something about an investigation and about being questioned by the police, but had never given his friends the impression that he himself was a suspect.

But he was a suspect—a reality that Tim continued to

face after returning to Greensboro at the start of the new year. On January 16, at Ken Brady's request, Tim paid a second visit to Greensboro police headquarters. Again, he was accompanied by attorney Doug Harris.

Brady asked Tim to tell him again exactly what happened after he awoke early Sunday morning. As he had while being interviewed by the detective back on November 28, Tim began at one point to ramble. This time, Brady didn't take as long to break in. Instead, he cut Tim off and told him matter-of-factly that his version of events simply didn't jibe with other information he had gathered during the course of his investigation. Brady mentioned, for instance, the conversation Gerri Minton said she had had with Sandy and Todd the morning of Elaine's death—the one in which they said they'd heard their parents arguing in the bathroom. Tim claimed he was unaware of any statements the children had made. "We pray as a family daily," he said.

Unsure of the relevancy of Tim's response, Brady changed the subject and asked Tim about the status of his and Elaine's relationship. Tim told the detective that although he and Elaine had agreed to separate, he was disappointed their relationship had run its course. Brady then asked Tim about an incident Kevin and Marianne had told him about, an incident Elaine had mentioned to them. It seemed that one day, while Tim and Elaine were still living in Claysville and going through a difficult time financially, Tim delivered Elaine and the kids to his parents' home, then drove back to Claysville, turned on the gas inside the house, and left. His plan, Elaine confided to Kevin and Marianne, was to blow up the house in order to collect on his and Elaine's homeowner's policy. But when Buc caught wind of the plan after Tim returned to his parents' house, he insisted his son go back to Claysville to shut off the gas. Tim grudgingly agreed, and the house never blew.

"It was all an accident," Tim told Brady.

But before Tim said another word, Harris declared the interview over.

* * *

ABOUT A month later, Guilford County Coroner Janice
Hessling officially accepted the results of Dr. Deborah Radisch's autopsy on Elaine. This meant "undetermined"
would continue to be listed as the cause of death on
Elaine's death certificate. Hessling's decision ended any
hope Brady had of charging Tim with Elaine's murder.
Brady refused, however, to declare the case closed. Instead,
he simply set the file atop his desk and turned his attention
to his next case. He was certain, though, that at some point
in the future, he and Tim would cross paths again. And
when they did, he would be ready and waiting.

CHAPTER 11

IT WAS via word of mouth that friends of Elaine's in Greensboro learned in the spring of 1991 that Tim had decided it was time for him and the kids to move back to Pittsburgh. For those who remained convinced Tim was to blame for Elaine's death, his planned departure was a bitter pill to swallow.

"I just couldn't believe that someone so dumb could get away with killing someone like that, that they couldn't figure out how he did it," Kevin Rochford would later recall thinking at the time.

Kevin, however, did find some solace in his confidence that the law eventually would catch up with Tim. And there was also the possibility, Kevin thought, that Tim would do himself in.

"Tim being Tim, I knew he'd say something or do something and end up implicating himself," he said. "I knew he'd screw up."

WITH HIS mother's help—Rose Boczkowski had returned to Greensboro with her son and grandchildren after New Year's—Tim spent the very beginning of spring packing his and the kids' belongings and saying a few goodbyes. Some of his and Elaine's friends, Jim and Celia Borowicz in particular, had in fact stood by him over the past five months.

It was Good Friday, 1991, when the Boczkowski clan arrived back in Pittsburgh. Knowing it would be nearly impossible for Tim to re-establish himself and take care of three small children at the same time, Buc and Rose suggested to Tim that he and the kids temporarily move in with them. Tim readily agreed. Because of debts that had to be settled and back taxes that had to be paid before he was able to leave Greensboro and, because he had used the $25,000 he received from Elaine's life insurance policy to cover funeral and moving costs, Tim had little cash at his disposal. As a result, the prospect of living rent-free was an attractive one. And with his parents around, he wouldn't have to worry about finding—and paying for—childcare.

Over the next couple of months, Tim focused his energies on getting his life back in order. Work-wise, he decided that what made most sense was for him to return to the profession he knew best. So with financial assistance from Buc, he got back into the dental products business, ultimately opening a lab he named Dental Smiles, in a professional building in suburban Pittsburgh. As for the kids, as Elaine had when they first moved to Greensboro, Tim enrolled them in school and in various after-school activities. "He did what he could to make their lives as normal as possible," Maria Crendall said.

Tim would say it was for the children, too, that he had a change of heart about Elaine's final resting-place. Not long after returning to Pittsburgh, Tim called Mitzie Pegher and said he wanted to have Elaine's body moved to the plot Mitzie had originally offered him. He told her she had been right in the first place. Elaine should have been buried in Pittsburgh. At first, Mitzie said Tim could have the plot. But the intense ill will she harbored for her former son-in-law had swelled to the point where she did a little rethinking of her own. Mitzie called Tim and told him she'd had her own change of heart. She approved of his decision to have Elaine buried in Pittsburgh, she said. But as far as a cemetery plot was concerned, he would have to buy one himself. Despite Mitzie's refusal to give him the plot, Tim had Elaine's body disinterred and brought back to Pittsburgh. On June 4, 1991, Elaine was buried at St. Stanislaus Cemetery in the northern Pittsburgh suburb of Millvale, in a grave located at the top of a hill, under a twelve-foot-high statue of the Holy Family.

In Tim's mind, Elaine's burial provided him with a degree of closure he felt had been missing from his life. Tim believed, too, that enough time had passed that he could begin dating. Upon his return to Pittsburgh, Tim was anything but shy when it came to telling friends he very much hoped to meet someone new.

"I really miss Elaine," he told Mark and Maria Crendall one day. "But I really want to get married again."

Tim's pronouncement didn't surprise Maria in the least.

"Tim was the kind of person who hated being alone," she said.

And in a matter of weeks, he no longer would be.

CHAPTER 12

IN THE spring of 1991, Tim, who was about to turn 36, joined the Catholic Alumni Club of Pittsburgh. According to CAC materials, the organization is designed "to provide a friendly setting for single Catholics to meet and develop friendships with people who share their faith." In July, at a club dance at the Candlelight Lounge in Pittsburgh, he met another relatively new member—a 32-year-old insurance claims representative named Maryann Fullerton.

The day after the dance, Maryann called her longtime friend Shirley Marks.

"You'll never guess who I met last night," Maryann told her friend. "An old neighbor of yours. A guy named Tim Boczkowski."

Tim had mentioned to Maryann that he'd grown up in a house on Sprucewood Drive in Ross Township, the same street where Shirley had lived with her family. Shirley listened as Maryann gushed on about Tim, who, she said, had been recently widowed. Although she didn't say anything to Maryann at the time, Shirley was struck by the fact that Maryann was so taken with her fellow North Hills High graduate.

"I didn't really know him," said Shirley, whose mother still lived across from the Boczkowskis. "All I knew was that he had been married, and that his wife had choked to death on some kielbasa. Still, I was surprised Maryann was so excited. I didn't think he was her type."

Maryann was equally effusive about Tim when she talked to longtime friends Gay Barbiaux and Eileen Datt, after the dance. "The first words out of her mouth were, 'I met a nice man at this church function, and he has three wonderful kids,' " Gay would later recall.

"She said she was definitely going to see him again," added Eileen.

Though Tim was overweight and balding, and wasn't the best dresser—he tended to wear tacky polyester suits, shirts that were a size too small, and ties that were a couple of inches too short—Maryann was definitely attracted to him. By the end of the summer, the two were dating steadily.

"She acted like she was really interested in him," said Eileen, who met Tim for the first time when Maryann brought him to Eileen's daughter's first birthday party. "She even said to me at one point, 'You know, he could be the one.' "

MARYANN, LIKE Tim, had grown up in the North Hills. Her father, Lew Fullerton, was an AT&T salesman who'd met Maryann's mother, Pat, on the job. After marrying, Pat decided that once they started a family, she would leave her job as a long-distance operator so she could raise their children full-time.

When Maryann was born, on March 24, 1959, Pat and Lew lived in a two-story house in Aspinwall, a middle- and upper-class suburb northeast of Pittsburgh. When she was three, they moved to a three-bedroom, red brick, ranch-style home in nearby Shaler Township. By this time, Maryann had a 15-month-old brother named John.

Something of a tomboy, Maryann spent grades one through eight at St. Bonaventure Catholic School in Glenshaw. She then attended Vincentian High School in Ross Township, graduating in 1977. It was during her very first week at the parochial Vincentian that Maryann met Eileen Datt, a fellow freshman. "We just hit it off," said Eileen, who quickly became Maryann's best friend.

Maryann was an excellent student—earning mostly A's and B's—but she was as interested in the non-academic side of school. She played the xylophone for the Victors, the school's marching band, and took part in activities like the school's annual talent show. One year, her rendition of Barbra Streisand's "Evergreen," which she sang while accompanying herself on guitar, was the show's biggest hit.

Maryann also had a knack for running afoul of school authorities. "The nuns at Vincentian were pretty strict," Eileen said. "We were always getting in trouble for something—talking in class or passing notes. Also, it was much easier to play hooky if you went to public school. There, you could just check in and leave. But at Vincentian, if you didn't show up, they would call your house to see where you were."

Even so, Maryann and Eileen regularly snuck out of school by climbing through the first-floor window of an empty classroom. Once free, they'd head for a nearby mall where they'd lunch on pizza. Then there was the time when word reached the nuns at Vincentian that several students had gone swimming in their underwear in the nuns' pool. The girls were eventually caught, Maryann among them.

Because Vincentian had gone co-ed only a short time before Maryann and Eileen began attending, there were only a handful of male students—maybe three or four, according to Eileen—in the 1977 graduating class, which boasted a total of sixty students. To make up for this dearth, Vincentian scheduled activities with North Catholic High, a nearby all-boys' school. "We always used to go to dances at North Catholic," Eileen said. "We'd meet guys there, talk to them afterwards, and then maybe go out a couple of times. But it was never anything serious."

During her senior year, Maryann worked as a waitress at a Lum's in the North Hills. It was there that she met Shirley Marks, who worked as a cook, and Gay Barbiaux, a fellow waitress.

"Everybody liked Maryann," said Shirley. "She was that kind of person."

"She fit in pretty easily wherever she went," added Gay. "That's why she had so many friends."

According to Eileen, about half of Vincentian's 1977

graduating class attended college. Maryann, she said, was among those who simply were not interested. Maryann kept her waitressing job at Lum's for a short time after graduation, then began working as an assistant to Dr. John Schrenker, the Fullertons' family dentist. She left there after about a year to take a position as a claims representative for Travelers Insurance.

"She wanted to make more money and to start some kind of career," Eileen explained.

Eventually, the job at Travelers enabled Maryann, who worked in the firm's downtown Pittsburgh office, to move out of her parents' home and into her own apartment, a modest one-bedroom in Ross Township. The move gave Maryann a degree of independence she'd never had before, removing her from the watchful eye of Pat and Lew, who found it difficult to let their little girl go.

"Maryann's parents were kind of overprotective," Eileen said. "They kept track of everything she did and always waited up for her."

"Even when she was in her early twenties, her parents sometimes called her several times a day—at work and at home—to check on her," added Gay, who remained friendly with Maryann after both had left Lum's. "She didn't mind that so much. She was really close to them. But there were some things Maryann didn't tell her parents because she didn't want to upset them, like if she met a guy who wasn't Catholic."

At this point, Maryann's social life, to a great extent, revolved around the North Hills bar scene. Most Wednesday nights, she and Eileen could be found downing beer and pizza at The Spare Room. They also frequented the King's Inn, a neighborhood bar and restaurant in Ross Township. On Friday and Saturday nights, Eileen said, "we went wherever there was a good band. There was this one band, The Harvest Brothers, that we really liked. We used to follow them around."

Maryann remained friendly with Shirley and Gay. The beach in Erie, Pennsylvania, was a favorite destination of hers and Gay's. And after Gay married in 1979, Maryann went on a couple of vacations with her and her husband, Bob—once to Las Vegas, another time to Florida.

By the time Maryann and Eileen reached their mid-twenties, however, they began spending less time bar-hopping and more time at get-togethers at friends' homes. They also made regular visits to Eileen's mother's cottage in Indian Lake, about an hour-and-a-half southeast of Pittsburgh.

During these years, Maryann, a 5'4" blue-eyed, strawberry blonde who wore her hair below her shoulders, went out with a number of men, including a co-worker at Travelers who she saw on and off for about two years, and a Ross Township police officer. She spent about a year, too, with a man she had met through Eileen's future husband, Chuck. But much to her disappointment, each of these relationships ended for one reason or another.

According to Shirley Marks, Maryann, from the time they met, often talked of finding Mr. Right. "She definitely was hoping to meet someone," said Shirley, who, like fellow Lum's alum Gay, never lost touch with Maryann. "But then after a while it didn't seem to matter as much to her. She said she had her career and a lot of good friends and that was enough."

Gay Barbiaux agreed. "I know she would have liked to have met someone back then," she said, "but it wasn't her main goal in life."

Even so, Maryann remained hopeful that someday she would be a wife and mother.

According to Eileen, Maryann "loved her job" at Travelers and had been promoted several times. This enabled her eventually to upgrade apartments. Located at a Ross Township complex called the Cascades, Maryann's new apartment was both larger and more upscale than her first. "But Maryann wasn't a materialistic person in the least," Eileen said. "What she really wanted was to get married and have a family."

Around the beginning of 1990, shortly before her thirty-first birthday, Maryann began attending Mass at Nativity of the Lord Catholic Church on Pittsburgh's Upper North Side. She quickly became friendly with a number of Nativity members as well as the church's musical director, Sister Pat Baker. Maryann was introduced to Sister Pat one day by a fellow worshipper who heard her singing during Mass. "She should be a cantor," the woman told Sister Pat.

Shortly thereafter, Maryann joined the church's choir and became a cantor, a position that required her to spend Monday nights practicing with Sister Pat and the church's other cantors.

"She had beautiful range," Sister Pat said of Maryann, an alto. "It was great to work with someone who sang as well as she did. I liked her right away. She was a very warm person. She was always the one who said, 'Let's have a party.' She loved bringing people together."

Then, in May 1991, Maryann joined the Pittsburgh chapter of the Catholic Alumni Club. In July, she met Tim.

The most compelling evidence that Maryann had fallen hard for Tim was her decision to bring him to church with her just two weeks after they met. "I remember standing near the organ after Mass, waiting for her to come introduce him," Sister Pat would later recall. "Not long after that, he and the kids started coming to church every Sunday."

Tim, too, had begun mentioning Maryann to friends like Mark and Maria Crendall and Paul and Angela Di Marco. He admitted to his friends that he was a little apprehensive about introducing them to Maryann because he knew how fond they all had been of Elaine. He also thought they might be shocked by how much Maryann resembled her. But he was so taken with Maryann that before the end of the summer, he brought her to a picnic at a local park so she could meet the foursome. "We were all immediately taken with her," Maria said of Maryann.

Maria remembered, too, being struck by how close Tim and Maryann seemed even though they'd been dating for only a matter of weeks. "The way they acted," she said, "made it seem like they had known each other for a lot longer than they actually had."

Paul and Angela also liked Maryann. But they, like Mark and Maria, were struck more, initially, at least, by the speed at which Tim and Maryann's relationship progressed. The foursome, too, couldn't help but note a number of striking similarities between Maryann and Elaine. For starters, there was the strong physical resemblance. Both, too, were family-oriented and deeply religious.

Tim, Maryann, Mark, and Maria went out together a number of times over the next several months. Soon, Maryann and Maria were spending time together on their own as well. "You know how sometimes you meet someone and you just click?" Maria said. "That's how it was with me and Maryann. We just hit it off from the start."

The same was true for Maryann, and Tim's kids—Randy, Sandy and Todd. "By the time we met her," Maria said, "she'd already met the kids and according to Tim, they really liked her."

All in all, Tim's friends couldn't have been more pleased. "I remember saying to Mark one day, 'Boy, I hope they stay together,' " Maria would later recall.

Maryann's friends, too, could not have been more thrilled for her. "He seemed to make her happy," said Shirley Marks, who, not long after Tim and Maryann began dating, had them to her home in the South Hills for a spaghetti dinner. "He was very affectionate, too. Tim would sit there with his arm around Maryann's shoulder and gaze into her eyes."

But in the end, it was the way Maryann talked about Tim that ultimately led Shirley to realize how serious her friend was about her new beau. "She would talk about what a good provider and what a good father he was," she recalled.

Maryann was equally passionate, Shirley added, whenever she'd describe something she and Tim had done with Randy, Sandy, and Todd, or something that had transpired between her and the trio. Moreover, she said, if Tim wasn't around and the kids got out of hand, Maryann would step in and do whatever disciplining was required. "If they got a little too rambunctious, Maryann would say, 'Okay, let's settle down,' or if they misbehaved during a meal, she would remind them of their table manners," Shirley said. "If you didn't know any better, you would have thought she was their mother."

Sister Pat echoed Shirley. "She took to those kids so quickly, and they took to her," she said. "It was remarkable. But there had always been something very maternal about Maryann."

But Eileen Datt, for her part, wasn't quite sure what to make of Maryann's relationship with Tim. "He was really nice, but he wasn't the kind of guy she usually dated," she said. "She'd always dated decent-looking guys, and he was kind of dorky."

At the same time, Eileen conceded, Tim and Maryann had a lot in common. "Like Maryann, he was very religious," she said. "He went to church all the time. And it seemed like he was a really great dad. I thought, 'Maybe they're perfect for each other.' "

Gay, too, had mixed emotions when it came to Maryann and Tim. "The first time I met him," said Gay, recalling the day Maryann brought Tim to a "Christmas in July" party that Gay's sister threw that summer, "I couldn't help but think she could do a lot better. Maryann was so pretty and so outgoing."

Gay also couldn't help but shake the feeling that Maryann was more in love with Tim's children than she was with Tim. "She always used to talk about Tim and the kids," Gay said. "It was never just about Tim. It seemed like they never really did a lot on their own. Maryann never said anything like, 'Tim and I went dancing last night.' It was always, 'We went to the park with the kids.' But Maryann seemed so happy, so I thought, 'Well, as long as he's a good man . . .' "

TIM AND MARYANN grew closer through the fall, though their courtship was not without its bumps. Sometime before

Thanksgiving, Tim admitted to Maryann that he'd had a vasectomy after Todd was born.

"She was really upset," Eileen recalled. "She said, 'I finally meet someone, and I'm falling in love with him and he drops this on me.' "

According to Eileen, Maryann seriously considered ending her relationship with Tim. " 'Now what do I do?' " she asked her oldest friend at one point. " 'Should I dump him? What if I never meet anyone else?' She was really going back and forth for a while."

Eileen wasn't sure what to tell Maryann. The vasectomy seemed less an issue than the recent death of his wife, Eileen thought. "It seemed awful quick to me," she said, "that he would be so seriously involved with someone else." At the same time, Eileen couldn't help but think, " 'What if Tim is the one and Maryann lets him go?' I finally told her, 'If you really feel so strongly about Tim and the kids, maybe this was meant to be. Maybe you were meant to marry someone like him—a widower with three children.' "

By the time the holiday season rolled around, both Maryann's friends and her family couldn't help but wonder if they might be attending a wedding sometime down the road. Maryann herself only fueled the speculation. At Christmas, she sent a card to her aunt, Eleanor Camp, in which she wrote warmly about Tim: "I'm sure you've heard about the man I've been dating who I met through the Catholic Alumni Club. He's a widower and doing a wonderful job with his kids. I've never been so happy."

Maryann, in fact, brought Tim and the kids to her parents' house on Christmas day. Another of Maryann's aunts, Ruth Schumann, was there and would later recall being impressed when, while looking out the picture window in the Fullerton living room, she saw Tim pull up in a old brown Mercedes.

Pat, on the other hand, wasn't exactly ecstatic that her daughter was dating someone who'd been married before to a woman with whom he'd had three children. Her sister, Eleanor, shook her head when Pat told her how she felt.

She saw nothing wrong with the fact that Tim already had kids. What mattered most, she told Pat, was that Maryann was happy. Pat shrugged. Maybe Tim did deserve the benefit of the doubt.

As it turned out, the collective hunch Maryann's friends and family had about the possibility of wedding bells proved to be on target. In the spring of 1992, less than a year after they'd met, Tim asked Maryann to marry him, and she accepted. They then set a date for the following June.

"I remember when they told me and Mark," Maria Crendall would later say. "We were all out somewhere, and Maryann held out her hand and said, 'Hey, look,' and there was this ring on her finger. We were so happy for them."

Sister Pat Baker said she still remembers the day Maryann came by the church to show off her engagement ring. "I can still see her face," she said. "She was radiant."

As far as Maryann's family was concerned, by the summer of 1992, Tim already seemed like one of them. At a family reunion in late June at the Shaler Township home of Jean Zappa, one of Maryann's thirty-three first cousins, attendees would later recall being impressed by the fact that Tim didn't seem the least bit overwhelmed by Maryann's large—and tight-knit—extended clan.

Maryann had been similarly accepted by the Boczkowski family, especially Randy, Sandy, and Todd, each of whom, a month earlier, had given Maryann a Mother's Day card. "Maryann came over one day to show them to me," Gay Barbiaux said. "She was so overwhelmed that the kids had taken to her the way they did. It was like they already considered her their mom."

Tim was eager to introduce Maryann to friends back in North Carolina, too, so near the end of the summer of 1992, the two drove to Greensboro in Tim's Mercedes, where they visited with Jim and Celia Borowicz and others.

Kevin Rochford heard Tim was back in town, but never actually saw him. Marianne didn't see Tim either, but she became especially upset when she learned of his visit. To her, it seemed like Tim was flaunting the fact that he had gotten away with murder.

One person who did see Tim was Kara Ruffin, who had lived next door to Tim at Yester Oaks with her mother, Liz Maple. Kara, at the time, was waitressing at a Greensboro restaurant. Out of nowhere, Tim came up and hugged her. When she realized who it was, Kara was puzzled. After Elaine's death, Tim had stopped talking to her and her mother. He didn't even give them a chance to say goodbye to Randy, Sandy, and Todd, to whom they had grown close while Elaine was still alive. But what puzzled Kara even more was the woman who was with Tim when he came into the restaurant. "After he hugged me," she said, "I glanced away. That's when I saw Maryann. She looked just like Elaine. It was eerie."

TIM AND Maryann spent the remainder of 1992 planning their wedding and looking for their first home.

"Maryann was so excited," Shirley Marks recalled. "She'd call me every couple of days to tell me about the caterer she'd hired or the flowers she had picked out."

Tim, it appeared to Shirley, seemed content to let Maryann handle all the arrangements: "He said whatever kind of wedding she wanted to have was fine with him."

As for their future home, Tim and Maryann, after shopping around, decided to build a four-bedroom, two-story house in the new phase of a fifteen-year-old Ross Township subdivision. Maryann used most of the $30,000 she had in her 401K account as a down payment on the mortgage and on construction costs.

On March 20, 1993, just under three months before their wedding, Tim and Maryann and Randy, Sandy, and Todd moved into their brand new home at 306 Noring Court. Pat Fullerton, a devout Catholic, did not approve of her daughter's pre-marital living arrangement. The house, however, was ready for occupancy, and neither Tim nor Maryann thought it made sense for Maryann to continue paying rent on an apartment when they also had a mortgage to pay every month. But Maryann did place one caveat on the move. Because she and Tim technically would not be husband and wife for another two and a half months, she insisted they sleep in separate rooms.

Maryann loved her new house and delighted in furnishing it. Although she and Tim kept some of the furniture they already owned between them, Maryann spent a fair amount of money on new items. And all through the house she hung photos of family and friends. As Maria would later put it, "Maryann was happy. Tim was happy. The kids were happy. Things couldn't have been better."

Tim and Maryann liked their new neighbors, too, and quickly became friendly with Wes and Sue Semple, who lived next door. Their son, Wesley Jr., was the same age as Todd. "They seemed like a typical suburban American family," said Wes, who taught social studies at Shaler Area High School and who, coincidentally, had had Maryann's brother, John, as a student.

And for all intents and purposes they were. In a letter to her cousin, Kathy Dunford, Maryann described what it was like to become a mother all of a sudden, and the bond she'd already begun to feel with her stepchildren. "It is a full-time job," she wrote, referring to the task of raising three young children.

> Don't let anybody fool you. I have been working my butt off. Up at 7 a.m. every day and never get to bed before 11 p.m. Grandma B. is helping out with the kids this week as they are on Easter break. This morning, I felt like a new Mom leaving her newborn at a babysitter's for the first time. But once I got there, I was okay. I wish I had more time, but baseball practice starts this week and we have lots of running to do . . . See you at the wedding.
>
> Love,
> Maryann, Tim, Randy, Sandy & Todd.

Tim and Maryann married June 12, 1993, at the Nativity Church, worship site of Incarnation Parish. Their wedding, however, wasn't the only cause for celebration that day. June 12 was also Tim's thirty-eighth birthday. Maryann loved the idea of getting married on her husband-to-be's birthday. It would make her wedding day that much more special, she told friends. It also made it less likely, she joked, that Tim would forget their anniversary.

Maryann had asked Gay Barbiaux to be her maid of honor and Eileen Datt and Shirley Marks to be bridesmaids. All three wore long, fuchsia, off-the-shoulder dresses. Randy and Todd, both of whom wore the same gray tuxedo as Tim, served as best man and ring-bearer, respectively. Sandy, dressed in a long pink satin dress sewn by Maryann's cousin, Diane, handled flower-girl duties.

Maryann wore a long-sleeved white satin wedding dress with a long train. By all accounts, she made for a beautiful bride as her father, Lew, escorted her down the aisle. They walked not to the tune of "the Wedding March" but to a favorite hymn of Maryann's—"Christ, the Victor." Once they reached the front of the chapel, Lew lifted his daughter's veil and kissed her on the cheek. Then he shook Tim's hand and joined Pat in a front-row pew, while Maryann took her place beside her husband-to-be.

Father Almade began the ceremony with some brief welcoming remarks. "We are here at Nativity Church, a part of Incarnation Parish," he said, "and we are very happy to be here to help celebrate the marriage of Maryann and Tim."

After opening readings, Father Almade read from the Gospel according to John: "Jesus said to his disciples," he began, " 'There is no greater love than this, to lay down one's life for one's family. You are my friend if you do what I command you. I no longer speak of you as slaves, or slave does not mean what matters about you. It was not you that chose me. It was I that chose you to go forth and bear fruit. Your fruit must endure so all that you ask the Father in my name He will give you.' "

Then, Father Almade offered his homily. He began by saying how glad he was to be officiating at Tim and Maryann's wedding, adding that theirs was a "special relationship." He also said Tim and Maryann, because of their devout beliefs, were an example for other couples to follow.

After the homily, Tim and Maryann exchanged vows. Maryann also recited a special vow she had written for her new stepchildren.

"I, Maryann, accept for life, the responsibility of being a mother to Randy, Sandy, and Todd," she said, her eyes welling with tears. "I promise I will do my best to guide and nurture them, to love and respect them for all the days of my life."

She then hugged all three children. Moments later, Father Almade pronounced Tim and Maryann husband and wife.

CHAPTER 13

WHEN IT came to their honeymoon, Maryann told Tim she thought they should go away for a week at the most. She didn't want to spend any more time away from Randy, Sandy, and Todd, who, by this time, called her "Mom." At one point, she even considered including the trio in their plans. "At first, Maryann was talking about going to Niagara Falls and bringing the kids," Eileen would later recall. "I said, 'That's insane. You guys have to go by yourselves.' "

In the end, Tim and Maryann ended up spending a week at a Sandals Resort in Montego Bay, Jamaica. Upon their return, they picked up where they'd left off before the wedding. Tim went back to work at his dental lab, while Maryann concentrated on being a full-time mom to Randy, Sandy, and Todd. It was, according to Sue Semple, who stopped working when Wesley Jr. was born, a role Maryann relished.

"From the time we met, I could tell she was really excited about becoming their mother," said Sue. "She even told me once that if she and Tim ever split up, she would fight him for custody. She said, 'I didn't bear them, but I love them and I would do anything for them.' And she meant it."

Sue and Maryann talked at least once a day and enjoyed each other's company. But in Sue's mind, Tim was another story entirely. Her take on him was not unlike that of Kevin Rochford's, back in Greensboro. "He turned me off from day one," Sue would later admit unapologetically.

"He was always looking for a deal," she added, recalling one incident in particular. Not long after she and Wes installed a utility shed in their backyard, Tim came over and asked where they had gotten it. They told him the name of the store and Tim went to check it out. But after learning it cost somewhat more than he was looking to spend, Tim instead went to a lumber store and bought the wood he'd need to build an identical shed himself. Sue had no problem with Tim wanting the same shed. But she was put off when she learned that Tim, in order to obtain the discount the lumber store gave to building professionals, had told the salesman there that he was buying the wood on behalf of the builder who had built his and Maryann's house.

Sue was turned off, too, by what she saw as a controlling Tim's habit of forcing Maryann to be the family disciplinarian and then later, undermining her authority. Once, for instance, Maryann grounded Todd for a day for misbehaving. But that same night, after coming home from work, Tim took Todd out for ice cream. "Maryann called me the next day," Sue remembered. "She was so upset. She said Tim hadn't even asked her what had happened."

In the same way that Maryann confided in Sue, Tim confided in Wes. Not long after Tim had moved into the neighborhood, he told his neighbor about his life before he and Maryann met. "He said his first wife had been depressed," Wes would later recall. "He said she had been unhappy living in Greensboro and that she wanted to move back to Pittsburgh."

Tim also told Wes that Elaine was dead, but did not elaborate on how she died.

"Everything he said left me with the impression that she had committed suicide," Wes said. "He never actually said that, but he certainly implied it."

THE REST of 1993 flew by, and before Tim and Maryann and the kids knew it, Maryann's legal adoption of Randy, Todd, and Sandy was on the verge of becoming a reality.

"The final hearing is set for March 31," Maryann wrote to her aunt, Claudia Dunford, in a letter dated March 24, 1994—Maryann's thirty-fifth birthday. "Then there is a ten-

day waiting period before the final decree is filed to allow
time if anyone wants to contest. We do not anticipate a
problem there, so by April 10th, I should 'officially' be a
mom . . . We are all excited about the proceeding and are
looking forward to celebrating the solidifying of our new
family."

Maryann was eagerly anticipating the day the adoption
became final. In fact, once she had the final adoption certificate in hand, she framed it and hung it in the family
room. But she and Tim often didn't see eye to eye when it
came to the kids. As she did with Sue Semple, Maryann,
on occasion, complained to Eileen Datt about Tim's un-
willingness to put up a united front when it came to disciplining the children.

"He was always undoing everything she did," Eileen
said. "At one point, she got so fed up that she told him that
if he didn't start backing her up, she was going to put the
adoption on hold."

Whether or not Maryann would have carried through on
her threat is unclear. But, according to Eileen, putting her
foot down seemed to do the trick.

"After that," she said, "it didn't seem to be as much of
an issue."

Tim, on the other hand, would have argued that, at the
time, there was a much greater threat to his and Maryann's
marriage than their differing opinions about disciplining the
children. The problem: Maryann's drinking. And as it
turned out, Tim wasn't the only one who thought she had
a problem with alcohol.

Not long after Maryann began cantoring at Nativity
Church, Sister Pat Baker several times noticed the smell of
alcohol on Maryann's breath when Maryann arrived at
choir practice. "It wasn't like she was tipsy when she'd
come to practice or sing," Sister Pat said. "She functioned
just fine. But there was a distinct smell on her breath, and
it wasn't mouthwash."

Maryann did, from time to time, have a tendency to get
a little toasted at church social functions. "She'd get overly

friendly," the nun would later recall, "even more friendly than she normally was. She'd get glass-eyed and would hang on people. She was definitely drinking too much."

But it wasn't until two church members who were also cantors, Jackie Wainwright, and Joe Baranowski, approached Sister Pat and mentioned that they, too, felt Maryann had a problem with alcohol, that Sister Pat decided it might be time to act.

"At first, they were hesitant to say something because they weren't especially close to Maryann," Sister Pat said. "But they were really concerned so they came to me and said, 'Something's wrong.' It was then that I started to think to myself, 'If Maryann really does have a drinking problem and it goes unchecked, she could lose all the happiness she has. And what if she gets in an accident?' I remember worrying about her driving home after this one party in the fall of 1993. We tried to talk her out of it before she left, but she insisted she was okay."

It was at this point that Sister Pat approached Father Almade.

"I'm concerned about Maryann," she told the priest.

"We talked long and hard about it," Sister Pat continued. "Finally, he said, 'Maybe a group of us should sit down and say to her, "Maryann, this is what we see. We think it's a problem, and we don't want it to get so out of hand that it starts to affect your daily life. Will you consider going for an evaluation?" '"

Sister Pat agreed this was the best way to tackle the situation. The two talked some more and decided Father Almade should call Tim and ask him to come to his office. There, he, Sister Pat, and the church members who had approached Sister Pat would share their concerns with him. A short time later, Father Almade phoned Tim with the invitation. He did not, however, tell Tim what the meeting was about.

"We all sat in Father Almade's office and told Tim what we had observed," Sister Pat said. "We told him we were concerned and that we felt that if we didn't say something,

Maryann might end up getting hurt and that we couldn't live with that. He could have told us to go to hell. We knew we were risking that. But he didn't. He thanked us profusely, and then he started crying."

"I didn't think anyone else noticed," he told the group.

According to Sister Pat, Tim said he'd talked to other people before about the fact that he thought Maryann was drinking too much, but they didn't believe him. He told us she drank three or four jugs of wine a week. He even said that Todd, whose chores included bringing the family's recycling bins to the curb each week, once commented to him, 'Mom sure drinks a lot.' We told him we thought Maryann should be evaluated—we could have been wrong, after all—and offered to do whatever we could to help. At that point, Tim told us that Maryann was outside in the car.

" 'Wait here while I go get her,' " he said to the group.

About a half hour later, Tim and Maryann walked into Father Almade's office.

"I don't know what he said to her out there, but she was really nervous," Sister Pat said. "We started from the beginning, telling her the same things we had told Tim. She didn't get defensive, but she told us she didn't think she had a problem. Then she started crying. We begged her to go for an evaluation and she said she would. We all ended up crying. We hugged her and kissed her and told her we were one hundred percent behind her. She actually took it all rather well. She even, about a week later, sent all of us cards saying she knew it must have been hard for us to do what we did and thanked for caring."

Maryann kept her promise to Father Almade, Sister Pat, and the others. On March 21, 1994, she visited the Gateway Rehabilitation Center, a chemical dependency treatment center with locations throughout southwestern Pennsylvania. She told the counselor she met with that some of her friends thought she had a drinking problem and had asked her to talk to someone professionally. In the end, the counselor told Maryann he didn't think she was a substance abuser but suggested she consider some outpatient counseling to keep from becoming one. Maryann, ultimately, chose not to follow up on his recommendation.

On March 24, three days after her visit to Gateway, Maryann wrote to her Aunt Claudia. She said how excited she was about her adoption of Randy, Sandy, and Todd becoming final. She boasted, too, about how well the kids were doing in school. "All together, they had 19 'A's last report period," she wrote. "Randy is getting excited about picking his classes for junior high next year. He's growing up on me—much too quickly."

Finally, Maryann mentioned some renovations she and Tim were having done. "We started putting a deck on the back of our house," she wrote. "The decking is complete. The railing and roof should be done sometime next month. Now Tim wants a hot tub!"

The hot tub would remain a point of contention between Maryann and Tim for some months. Maryann thought was it was a waste of money, but Tim seemed obsessed with the notion of installing one. "He was so bent on getting a tub, he was driving everyone crazy," Sue Semple would later recall.

Tim also raised eyebrows during the summer of 1994 when he began telling their friends that Maryann had a drinking problem.

One of the first people Tim mentioned it to was Wes Semple. At one point during a Cub Scout retreat over Father's Day weekend, Tim told him in passing that there was something he needed to talk to Wes about "when the kids aren't around." A short time later, when Todd and Wesley Jr. and their fellow scouts were off at an activity, Tim told Wes he thought he should know that Maryann had a drinking problem, just in case one of the kids came over to Wes and Sue's one day and said something was wrong with Maryann. "He said he wanted me to have an idea of what was going on so I would know what I was dealing with if I went over to his and Maryann's house and found Maryann on the floor," Wes said.

According to Wes, Tim spoke very matter-of-factly.

There was no sense of urgency whatsoever in his voice. Wes didn't know what to make of what Tim had told him. "The most I'd ever seen her drink was two beers," he said, and that was at a neighborhood block party earlier that year. Even at backyard parties, Wes said, Maryann usually had no more than a glass or two of wine. And more than once, he'd seen her turn the wine in her hand into a quasi–wine cooler by mixing it with ginger ale.

Strangely, Tim didn't mention his continuing concern to Father Almade, Sister Pat, or the two church members who had attended the meeting in Father Almade's office. But if he had broached the subject with Sister Pat, chances are she would have questioned his sincerity, especially after the scene she witnessed at a going-away party held for her at a choir member's home in June. The celebration was thrown to wish Sister Pat good luck at her new parish, St. Scholastica, in nearby Aspinwall. Sister Pat had not seen Tim and Maryann together, outside of church, since the meeting in Father Almade's office.

"Maryann was drinking, and I remember being taken aback by that," Sister Pat said. "But I was really taken aback when I saw Tim serving her drinks. I saw him bring her two large glasses of wine."

Over the course of the summer, Tim mentioned Maryann's drinking to Wes several more times. "Every once in a while, he'd make a comment sort of in passing," Wes said. "Once, I was out in our backyard and he came over and said Maryann was drinking so much that Todd knew Maryann's preferred brands of beer and wine.

"I didn't know what to make of it," Wes said. "I kept looking at Maryann for signs of what he was saying, but I never saw any. She never slurred her words. I never saw her stumble or stagger around, none of the things you'd expect to see if someone was drinking a lot."

Wes later learned he wasn't the first person to whom Tim had expressed concern about Maryann's drinking. The previous Christmas, Maryann had asked her parents to baby-sit while she and Tim attended a church dance.

Pat and Lew were expecting to see Maryann when she and Tim came by after the dance to pick up the kids, but to their surprise, Tim was by himself when they opened their front door.

"Where's Maryann?" Pat asked.

"She's in the car," Tim said. "Drunk."

"What?" Pat exclaimed. "Bring her in here."

Tim went out to the car, then returned to Pat and Lew's with Maryann in tow. Maryann, it turned out, was drunk. Pat was angry, but also concerned. She insisted Maryann stay with her and Lew that night.

As SOON as construction on the wooden deck behind the house was completed in the summer of 1994, Tim insisted the installation of a hot tub follow immediately. "It was all he talked about," Sue Semple remembered. "He kind of drove everyone crazy."

Maryann simply felt they could find a better way to spend the $1,000-plus it would cost to buy the tub and have it installed. "I keep telling Tim we don't need it," Maryann told Maria Crendall on the phone one day. "But he keeps insisting."

Maria would later say it was obvious the tub had become a serious point of contention between Tim and Maryann. "Whenever she mentioned it," Maria said, "I could hear this edge in her voice."

Eileen Datt said it was obvious to her, too, that Maryann hated the idea of the tub. "It's just another toy he has to have," she said Maryann told her one day over the phone. During that same conversation, Eileen, who knew about Tim's history of heart problems from Maryann, told Maryann she had heard that people with bad hearts weren't supposed to use hot tubs. Maryann said Tim had checked with his doctor and that the doctor had given the go-ahead.

In the end, Tim won out and by the end of the summer, he and Maryann not only had a new deck but a new hot tub to go with it.

Tim was so thrilled with his pricey acquisition that he

insisted on showing it off to anyone who came by the house. When he did so, according to Maria, Maryann made herself scarce. She would later recall Tim demonstrating all the tub's bells and whistles when she and Mark stopped by to visit one day. "We were out on the deck with Tim," she said, "but Maryann never came out of the house. She still thought it was a big waste of money."

As it turned out, the hot tub ended up costing Tim more than its sale price plus installation. In exchange for her agreeing to let him buy the tub, Tim agreed to join a group of Maryann's girlfriends and their husbands on a Caribbean cruise that October. Tim was as thrilled about the cruise as Maryann was about the hot tub. But if that's what it took for Maryann to give in on the tub—and for Tim to get what he wanted—it was a price he was willing to pay.

CHAPTER 14

IN THE spring of 1993, Maryann began working part-time for a Pittsburgh lawyer named Bob Eddins, researching insurance claims related to cases he was handling. But her family remained her first priority. She always made sure she was home in the afternoon when the kids returned from school, or available to shuttle them around to their various after-school activities. "She poured her heart and soul into taking care of those kids," said Maria Crendall.

Tim and Maryann, meanwhile, settled into what appeared to be a comfortable life together. Like most husbands and wives, they had their share of issues. Tim, for instance, sometimes balked at the notion of Randy, Sandy, and Todd spending time with Maryann's parents. Maryann didn't understand why. Since she had legally adopted the kids, Pat and Lew were their grandparents. Why shouldn't they get to know them?

Early on, Maryann questioned, too, why the kids never saw Elaine's mother or any other members of Elaine's family. But the more Tim told her about what life with Elaine had been like, the more she understood the estrangement. According to Eileen Datt, it was about a month after she and Tim began dating that Maryann explained to her what had happened to Tim's first wife. She said Tim had told her that Elaine was an alcoholic. He said they had been at a party and that Elaine had gotten drunk and that when they came home, she went to take a bath and either choked on her own vomit or drowned. The coroner, he said, had never been able to determine an exact cause of death. Maryann also asked Eileen never to ask Tim about Elaine because he didn't like to talk about the past.

Maryann shared some of what Tim said about Elaine with Gay Barbiaux, too. According to Gay, Tim told Maryann that Elaine "used to lock the kids in their rooms all day and just sit around and drink."

Tim had told Maryann more than once that Elaine had neglected the children, and what transpired the day Maryann and Tim took the kids to visit Elaine's grave only supported what Tim had said. Maryann told friends that the kids showed absolutely no emotion as they stood by their mother's grave. She concluded, as a result, that what Tim had told her must have been true and she never suggested bringing the kids to the cemetery again.

What Tim did not tell Maryann was that Mitzie Pegher very much wanted to see her grandchildren. But she could never bring herself to ask Tim directly. One day, however, Tim Wisniewski, the husband of Elaine's sister, Janet, called his former brother-in-law, told him how much Mitzie missed Randy, Sandy, and Todd, and asked if there was any way she could see them. Tim told him he would think about it. A short time later, Tim called back and said he was willing to let Mitzie see the kids—on three conditions. She would have to come to the lake at North Park in Elaine's hometown of Wexford, the meeting had to take place on a Sunday afternoon, and he had to be present throughout.

"Well, that's not going to happen," a resentful Mitzie said after Tim Wisniewski relayed Tim's offer. Mitzie, it seemed, wanted the children to come to her home. Tim didn't care. If his kids were going to see their grandmother, he would be the one to decide where and when.

The Peghers doubted they would ever hear from Tim after that. But shortly after Janet's husband relayed Mitzie's response to Tim, Mitzie received a registered letter from Tim stating that he wanted it on the record that Mitzie had refused his offer to let her visit her grandchildren.

Mitzie Pegher died in April 1994 without ever seeing Randy, Sandy, and Todd again. When Maryann learned of her death, she thought it was only right that the kids attend her funeral. But Tim was adamantly opposed. Tim and Maryann, in the end, agreed to let the kids decide for themselves whether or not they wanted to go. When they said no, Maryann dropped the subject.

BUC AND ROSE Boczkowski were another source of tension between Tim and Maryann. According to Sue Semple, Maryann was unhappy that Tim had given Buc and Rose a key to their house. Tim said he did it so Buc, who sometimes helped with handyman's work around the house, could come and go when he needed. But Maryann simply didn't feel comfortable with that. She also didn't like the way Buc sometimes talked to his son during his and Rose's frequent visits. For example, if Tim offered to help clear the table, Buc would berate him. "He would say things like, 'That's a woman's job,' or 'I'm going to get you your own apron with your name on it.' "

Buc and Rose, in fact, were one reason Maryann began to have qualms about going on the October cruise. Tim's parents had agreed to watch the kids while Tim and Maryann were away. But Maryann felt that they, like Tim, tended to be much more lenient than she was. "What if she lets them eat chocolate bars or cold pizza for breakfast?" Maryann remarked to her neighbor Sue shortly before the week-long Norwegian Cruise Lines cruise was scheduled to set sail.

But Maryann managed to set her concerns aside, and, on October 14, she and Tim and several other couples they knew, including Eileen Datt and her husband, Chuck, and Gay Barbiaux and her husband, Bob, flew to San Juan. There, they boarded the ship that would take them to a number of Caribbean islands, including St. Lucia, St. Kitts, St. Thomas, and St. John.

On several occasions during the cruise, Tim mentioned Maryann's "drinking problem" to their friends. While in St. Lucia, Tim told Chuck he sometimes found Maryann passed out on the couch with beer bottles scattered across the floor. Afterwards, Chuck told Eileen what Tim had said.

Eileen, who by this point had been friends with Maryann for some twenty years, knew Maryann didn't have to drink very much before she started feeling the effects of alcohol.

"It would hit her all of a sudden," Eileen said. "She'd be fine one minute, then it would hit her. But I never saw her falling-down drunk. I never thought she was an alcoholic."

But Eileen didn't think Maryann, on the cruise at least, was drinking any more than the rest of the group. She, too, found it strange that Tim, at least once a day, would go to one of the ship's bars to get a drink for Maryann. "If he thinks his wife has a drinking problem," she thought, "why does he keep getting her drinks?" Chuck, who had never liked Tim to begin with, dismissed what Tim had said about Maryann outright. "She wasn't drinking any more than anyone else," he said.

At another point during the cruise, Tim pulled Bob Barbiaux aside and told him essentially the same thing he had told Chuck Datt. He also said that Sandy would get up in the morning and count how many beers Maryann had drunk the previous night. Bob had heard Tim spin this tale before. One night during the 1992 holiday season, Tim and Maryann and the kids had stopped by Gay and Bob's house. They had been making the rounds of friends' homes— "They'd made at least five or six stops," Gay would later estimate—and Maryann had reached the point where she was slightly tipsy. She even stumbled a bit after bumping into the living room coffee table. "It was right in the middle of the room, and she tripped over it," Gay would later recall.

Tim responded by angrily rushing the kids out to the car, which was parked out front.

"Let me help Maryann out to the car," Bob offered after Tim came back up to the house. It was at this point that Tim made a comment to Bob about how much Maryann had been drinking that night.

The next day, Gay called Maryann to see if everything was okay and if Tim was still mad.

"Oh, don't worry about him," said Maryann, who recalled the incident in its entirety.

Tim had also made a comment to Bob about Maryann's drinking the weekend he and Wes Semple went on the Father's Day Cub Scout retreat. The first night Tim and Todd were gone, Maryann brought Randy and Sandy over to Gay and Bob's house. Not long after they arrived, Tim called from the retreat. "If Maryann drinks too much, please let her stay at your house," Tim had said.

When Tim broached the subject on the cruise, it was the third time he'd discussed it with Bob. When Bob told Gay what Tim had said, she was as perplexed as Eileen had been. "Why would he say that?" a disbelieving Gay remarked.

Over the course of the cruise, Tim never said anything to Eileen or Gay directly about Maryann's drinking. But both would later recall how Tim, after the group had disembarked, stopped to ask everyone how much their bill for incidentals was. His and Maryann's, he remarked out loud, was $353, and most of it, he claimed, was Maryann's drink tab.

Maryann, not surprisingly, defended herself. "That whole bill is not my bar tab," she protested. "We bought T-shirts and photos, too. And you had that massage. That was $100 and that had to be charged. They wouldn't take cash."

Back in Pittsburgh after the cruise, Maryann returned her attention to another lifelong dream: having a child of her own.

"Maryann wanted a baby," Eileen said, "more than anything in the world."

But because Tim had undergone a vasectomy—he once told Maryann that he could not have it reversed because his heart might not withstand the reversal procedure—Maryann had no choice but to be artificially inseminated.

"No way," Tim said when Maryann first broached the idea. Then, over the summer and almost out of the blue, Tim changed his mind. He said he would agree to let Maryann be inseminated as long as he could pick the sperm donor. Thrilled, Maryann began taking some pre-insemination tests. Now, back from the cruise, she began anticipating her next appointment, scheduled for November 7.

Eileen, meanwhile, couldn't get Tim's suggestion that Maryann had a drinking problem out of her head. Maybe he was right. After all, Maryann had been ticketed twice for drunk driving during what Eileen referred to as her and Maryann's "bar-hopping" days ten years ago. The first time was early one morning, after Maryann and Eileen had spent the night partying.

"We were at this bar, listening to a band," Eileen said. "We left there at around two, then went out to eat, so I'm sure it was late. Maryann dropped me off and was on her way home. She was going around a bend and she actually went off the road. She was fine, but her car was pretty much totaled."

Eileen would later argue that Maryann seemed okay to drive. "If she would have been all over the road," she said, "I would have made her stop."

Within a year or so of that incident, Maryann was ticketed for a second time. And, because it was the second time, her driver's license was suspended.

"She'd gone out to dinner with the girls from work," Eileen recalled. "Again, she was on her way home, and a policeman saw her roll through a red light.

"We were young and immature and didn't think anything could hurt us," Eileen admitted.

If Maryann was drinking as much as Tim said she was, how could she still be taking care of the kids, running a household, and working part-time? Eileen wondered. "Where would she find the time to drink that much?" she asked herself.

At the same time, why would Tim say Maryann was drinking so much if it wasn't true?

As Eileen would later say, "When I really thought about it, I had no reason to doubt him."

On Friday, October 28, Maryann called Eileen at work. Eileen listened to see whether Maryann sounded drunk. If she did, she would know Tim was telling the truth.

"I couldn't be totally sure, but it sounded like she had been drinking," Eileen said. "I could also tell she was upset about something, but that wasn't new. She hadn't seemed herself for a while. She would be really short with people. That wasn't like her at all. I'd say, 'You need to chill out. What's wrong?' Then she'd start complaining about Tim. That actually happened on the cruise the first night. Maryann and I were sitting out on the deck, splitting a beer. It had been obvious to me that she hadn't been enjoying herself so far, so I said, 'You need to relax.' Then, at one point, she said, 'You think Tim's so wonderful, but he's not.' I didn't ask her what she meant by that. We were just chatting and we started talking about something else."

By the time the conversation ended, Eileen was convinced that maybe Maryann's drinking was out of control. Next, Eileen called Gay. It turned out Gay had begun to feel similarly herself. So the next day, on Saturday, October 29, Eileen phoned Maryann and confronted her.

"Gay and I think you have a drinking problem," Eileen told her best friend.

"Well, I don't," Maryann snapped, "and it upsets me that you guys would even think that."

Unconvinced, two days later, on Halloween, Eileen called Tim at work.

"Chuck told me what you said to him on the cruise," she said, "and Gay and I have been talking, and we're really concerned, too."

"I'm so glad you called," Tim told Eileen. "Maryann is out of control, and I can't handle it on my own anymore. But I've got too much on my plate right now. Randy had an altercation at school. Let me get back to you."

That same day, though, Tim began calling other friends of Maryann's. He told them he was planning a November 9 "intervention" to confront Maryann about her drinking. Shirley Marks was among those Tim phoned.

"Shirl, Maryann's having a problem with her drinking," he told his wife's longtime friend. "She's drinking two cases of beer and a couple of jugs of wine a week." He then told her about the intervention and asked if she could come.

It had never dawned on Shirley before that Maryann might be drinking too much. But she had noticed that Maryann, over the past few months, had seemed somewhat more stressed out than usual. "She seemed a little more tense, a little more edgy," Shirley said. "We'd be on the phone, and she'd start talking really fast and listing all the things she had to do. She sounded overwhelmed."

Shirley told Tim she would be there.

"He sounded like he was really concerned," she said. "He also made it sound like he had talked to a professional and that they had suggested the intervention. I figured if that's what they told him to do, then that's what we should do."

Then, before they hung up, almost as an afterthought, Shirley asked Tim if he was going to tell Maryann's parents about the intervention. He said he was, but not until the day it was scheduled to take place because it was essential that Maryann not find out what he was planning.

The next day, on Tuesday, November 1, Tim called Eileen to tell her about the intervention. "Maryann's drinking ninety beers and five gallons of wine a week," he said.

Tim asked Eileen to call some of Maryann's friends and anyone else Eileen thought should be present. He also asked her to phone Gay because he had doubts as to whether she'd be willing to participate. Tim knew Maryann had told Gay about the meeting at Father Almade's office and about her subsequent appointment at Gateway.

"She was more embarrassed than anything," Gay would later recall, "and I got the feeling that she went to that appointment at Gateway just so Tim and the others would feel okay that she was okay."

"She was a social drinker," she said of Maryann. "At the end of a long day, she would have a couple of glasses of wine to unwind. She didn't seem out of control."

Gay, too, said she and husband Bob thought it was strange that Tim had been willing to marry Maryann if he thought she had a drinking problem, especially in light of what they'd been told about Elaine. "He had told us his first wife was an alcoholic," Gay said. "If that was true, why would he marry someone he thought had a drinking problem and put himself and his kids through the same thing they'd gone through with her? I thought it was kind of odd. I also couldn't figure out how she'd find the time to drink so much. She was always doing something—running the kids around, cleaning the house . . ."

At the end of their November conversation, Eileen told Tim she'd participate in the intervention and agreed to make the calls he'd requested. Before hanging up, though, she asked Tim a straight question. "Don't you think it would be a good idea to get someone professional involved in this?" she asked. "Do we really know what we're doing? I don't want it to seem like we're attacking her."

Tim told Eileen that he had contacted someone, but that he didn't think it was necessary that they be there. "And they want $1,000 just to show up," he added.

Later that day, Eileen phoned Gay. Gay didn't know what to do. Ever since they'd returned from the cruise, she'd been watching for signs that Maryann was drinking too much, but hadn't seen any.

"I just don't think she has a problem," Gay told Eileen.

"Well, you should call Tim and tell him that."

Gay did just that.

"I really don't think Maryann has a problem," she told her friend's husband.

Tim swore that she did, telling Gay that Maryann was drinking a case of beer a night, plus wine. And the night before, he said, she was up drinking until 3 a.m.

"How can I help?" Gay asked, suddenly alarmed by what Tim had told her.

"Come to the intervention."

Albeit with some reluctance, Gay said she'd be there.

"If this is really what you think needs to be done," she said, "I'll be there—for support."

As he had with Shirley, Tim asked both Eileen and Gay not to say anything to Maryann about the intervention. "If she finds out, she won't come," he warned them. The pair agreed not to mention it. But when Gay spoke with Maryann after her initial conversation with Tim, she did ask Maryann about her drinking habits.

"I tend to speak my mind," Gay said, "and I just came right out and said, 'Maryann, do you think you're drinking too much? Are things getting out of hands?' "

"I'm fine," Maryann insisted. "I don't know why you all think something's wrong."

Maryann and Gay talked briefly before Gay cut the conversation short.

"I just kept thinking, 'How are we going to do this to Maryann?' " she said. "We're just going to have her come into this room and then we're all going to gang up on her?"

On November 2, Gay had her second conversation with Tim about the intervention. He called to say that it was still on, but that instead of holding it at the church, it was going to be at his parents' house.

Gay told Tim she would be there. Bob Barbiaux had agreed to be present, too, even though he had serious reservations. "I didn't want to go," Bob would later say. "I didn't think Maryann had a problem, but Gay was going so I felt I should, too."

Around the same time, Tim called Eileen to tell her of the location change for the intervention. He also told her that he had changed his mind about the artificial insemination and that he planned to tell Maryann at the intervention that he didn't want to go through with it.

Eileen was speechless. "That was all Maryann talked about," she said. "She wanted a baby so bad."

Immediately, Eileen began to have second thoughts about the intervention. "I had such mixed feelings," she said. "I wanted to help, but I felt really uneasy about the whole thing. Then when he said he was going to tell her in front of everyone that he wasn't going to go through with the artificial insemination ... But if Tim was right about how much Maryann was drinking, we had to get her to stop."

During the same call, Tim told Eileen that Maryann was upset that she hadn't called her since the weekend. "I was avoiding her," Eileen would later concede, "but only because I felt I was betraying her by taking part in the intervention."

Gay had avoided phoning Maryann, too. "I was sick to my stomach about the whole thing," she said. "I was afraid, too, that I would say something about the intervention by accident."

Eileen, however, did call Maryann towards the end of the week, and the two friends talked for about a half-hour.

"I appreciate you being concerned," Maryann told Eileen, referring to Eileen's mention of her drinking during their last conversation. "But I really don't have a problem."

CHAPTER 15

As THE week of November 7 approached, Maryann became more and more excited about the pre–artificial insemination tests she was scheduled to undergo, unaware that Tim had reconsidered the procedure. But there were problems on the homefront, too. There was the incident with Randy at school, the altercation. Maryann thought he might benefit from counseling, but Tim wouldn't hear of it. Todd, meanwhile, had been experiencing some physical problems. At one point, a doctor recommended that Todd visit a psychologist. Again, Tim absolutely refused. But Maryann felt so strongly about getting help for Todd that she had decided that over the coming weekend, she would try to change Tim's mind.

Maryann spent the morning of Sunday, November 6, at church. On her way home, she stopped at the grocery store to pick up a few things. Later, she chatted with her mother about a wedding she and Tim and the kids had gone to the night before, describing gleefully how Sandy had tossed her shoes off and taken to the dance floor in just her socks. After dinner, Maryann sat down at the dining room table and began sorting through and paying bills. At around 9: 15, Eileen called, and the two friends gabbed for about an hour. Maryann, at one point, told Eileen about the trouble Randy had gotten into.

"Everyone says I'm too strict," she said. "But see what happens? You have to be tough sometimes."

Maryann also talked about the second-grade Catholic Christian Doctrine class she was teaching at church. "She told me how she'd been sitting on the floor in a circle with all the kids and how they were listening to her so intently,"

Eileen would later recall. "It made her so happy."

The pair said goodbye at about 10:15 p.m. But five minutes later, Eileen called back. During their earlier conversation, Maryann had had a question for Eileen's mother, and Eileen was calling back with the answer.

It was Tim, though, who answered the phone this time. According to Eileen, he sounded like his usual, cheerful self. "Well, I guess you girls want to talk some more," he said before handing the phone to Maryann, who then spoke to Eileen for twenty minutes or so.

Tim, at the time, was in the family room, where he'd settled in at 9 p.m.—after putting the kids to sleep—to watch the killer-nanny flick *The Hand that Rocks the Cradle*.

A little after 11 p.m., after the movie was over, Tim suggested to Maryann that they take a soak in the hot tub.

According to Tim, Maryann, after leaving the bills she'd been working on stacked neatly on the dining room table, changed into her bathing suit. She then exited the house through the sliding glass kitchen door that opened on to the deck and made her way to the roughly eight-by-eight-foot tub. But before slipping into the tub to escape the chilly air—the temperature was in the mid-forties that night, and there was a slight wind—she called to Tim, who was still in the house, and asked him to bring out some wine. Tim grabbed a bottle of white zinfandel from the refrigerator, poured one glass for himself and another for Maryann, and then joined her in the warm, bubbling water. Tim would later say that after an hour or so, he got out, returned to the house, toweled off, and went upstairs to take a shower. Eventually, he came back downstairs to the kitchen. Almost reflexively, he peered out the window above the sink, expecting to find Maryann still relaxing in the tub. But it took only an instant for Tim to realize something was wrong. Terribly wrong. Unable to see Maryann, he ran out to the deck, where, to his horror, he discovered her floating in the tub on her side. He rushed back inside the house and made three phone calls: one to next-door neighbors Wes and Sue Semple, one to his parents, and one to 911.

When the phone on Wes Semple's nightstand rang, it was precisely 12:48 a.m. Though sound asleep, Wes was certain of the time. The numbers on his digital alarm clock were three inches tall, and the clock itself sat less than a foot away from the bed.

"Wes, I need your help," Tim pleaded. "I need your help. I need your help."

"I'm coming," Semple told Tim. "I'm hanging up the phone, and I'm coming."

"Which one is it?" a startled Sue Semple asked, thinking something had happened to one of her elderly parents.

"Neither," Wes said as he jumped out of bed. "It's Tim next door."

Wes threw on some clothes, flew downstairs, raced out the front door and walked hurriedly over to his driveway. From there, he could see the light on Tim and Maryann's back deck was on. Wes scurried across his lawn, opened the fence gate that separated his house from Tim and Maryann's, and climbed the steps leading to the deck. Immediately, he could see Maryann, sitting in the tub in an upright position. But she wasn't moving or making even the slightest sound. It was then that Wes noticed Tim. He had just emerged from the sliding kitchen door that led out to the deck. He was wearing a pair of jeans, and his arms were wrapped around a corrugated cardboard box. Tim dropped the box and asked Wes to help him lift Maryann out of the water. But because of the tub's position, they were unable to do so. At that point, Tim reached into the box and pulled out a breathing device designed to aid with CPR. Once a volunteer fireman, he tilted Maryann's head back and began attempting to breathe life back into his wife. Wes watched intently but felt instinctively that it was too late.

"I'll always remember Maryann's face that night," Wes said. "She had the most angelic look, like she was at peace."

IT WAS 12:52 a.m. when Ross Township Police Officer David Sysca heard a call over his squad car radio regarding a "possible female passed out in hot tub of residence." Sysca, who was on routine patrol only a few minutes from Tim and Maryann's house, headed immediately to Noring Court. Because he also monitored the Emergency Medical Services channel on the radio, Sysca knew too, that by the time he arrived at Tim and Maryann's, there was a chance the woman would be in cardiac arrest. So after parking in front of the house, he raced to the back of his car, opened the trunk, and grabbed his CPR kit. At that very moment, a second Ross Township policeman, Officer Thomas Hess, pulled up to the house. The two officers hurried to the front door. Sysca rang the doorbell. There was no answer, but moments later, they heard someone calling from the side yard.

"Can you come to the back?" Wes Semple yelled. "We need help."

Sysca and Hess ran around to the side of the house, then followed Wes into the backyard and onto the deck. Sysca would later recall looking to his left and seeing Tim attempting to place a mask over Maryann's mouth. She was sitting upright in the hot tub, but was clearly unconscious.

"Help me save her," Tim pleaded with Sysca and Hess.

Working together, Sysca, Hess, Tim, and Wes lifted Maryann out of the tub and laid her gently on the deck. Tim then resumed affixing the mask, the kind rescue personnel typically use to avoid contracting diseases while performing CPR, over Maryann's mouth while Sysca began performing chest compressions. Within a matter of minutes, Scott Long, a volunteer paramedic with Ross/West View Emergency Medical Services, arrived on the scene. Long was home when he received a call on his pager about an "unresponsive female in a hot tub." After the page came in, Long jumped in his truck and raced to Tim and Maryann's. As soon as he pulled up to the house, he saw Ross Township Police Officer William Barrett, who had arrived on the scene shortly after Sysca and Hess, standing in the side yard. Barrett directed Long to the deck, where he found David Sysca and Tim still attempting to perform CPR on Maryann.

"What's going on?" Long asked Sysca.

Sysca told him they had just lifted Maryann out of the tub.

"Who's that?" Long asked next, nodding toward Tim.

"That's the husband," Sysca replied. Sysca then told Long that he didn't think Tim was managing to get any air into Maryann's lungs.

Long looked over at Tim and realized Sysca was right. Tim had put the CPR mask on upside down. As a result, the tube that attaches to the mask, and into which the person performing CPR is supposed to blow air, was actually in Maryann's mouth.

Long told Tim he would take over. He then knelt down beside Maryann, flipped the mask over, and began blowing into the tube. Long stopped at several points to see if he could detect a pulse. He never could, and at no point when he was present did Maryann ever breathe on her own. Although he didn't say so at the time, Long knew not only that Maryann was dead, but also that she probably had been dead for some time. The signs were all there: her eyes were fixed and dilated and her nail beds were purple, an indication that she had been without oxygen for some time. Also her body was cold to the touch.

Still, Long continued to work to revive Maryann and was doing so when fellow Ross/West View volunteer paramedic Stacy Tamburo arrived on the scene at a minute or so past 1 a.m. She was met at the front door by Officer Hess, who directed Tamburo to the kitchen.

"She's out there," Tim, motioning toward the deck, told Tamburo. "And I think she's very sick."

Immediately, Tamburo started an IV so she could administer a battery of cardiac drugs that might result in jump-starting Maryann's heart. Long and Tamburo then inserted a tube into Maryann's trachea so there would be a clear passageway to her lungs should she throw up.

Wes Semple, as he watched the paramedics work on Maryann, couldn't help but be struck by Tim's demeanor. "He seemed concerned," Wes said of Tim, who was standing on the deck, "but not overly distraught, considering what was going on. I would have thought somebody in that situation would be more emotional."

At one point while she was working on Maryann, Tamburo looked up and saw an older gentleman standing beside her. It was Tim's father, Buc, who had arrived at the house along with Tim's mother, Rose, shortly after Tamburo had.

"Is she dead?" he asked.

"We're doing everything we can to revive her," Tamburo told him. "But at this point, she has no pulse and she's not breathing."

Back in the kitchen, where Long had asked Tim to wait while he and Tamburo worked on Maryann, Tim had a conversation with his mother.

"What happened?" Rose asked her son.

"We had an argument," Tim replied.

"About what?"

"You know, her drinking. It's always her drinking. She had about thirteen or fourteen beers, and we argued. But then we went out to the hot tub, and we made up. Everything was okay and I went in the house, but when I came out, I found her under the water."

Tim looked over to Officer Barrett, who was also standing in the kitchen and who had obviously overheard Tim and Rose's conversation.

"I wish Gary Waters was here," Tim said. "I don't want none of this coming back on me."

Gary Waters, Barrett knew, was a detective with the Ross Township Police Department.

Eventually, Tim went back out onto the deck, where he was approached by Stacy Tamburo who was trying to find out what she could about Maryann's medical history and what she'd been doing that day.

Tim began by telling Tamburo that Maryann had had "a very bad cold" and that she was taking a prescription decongestant. He also told Tamburo that he and Maryann were in the hot tub "celebrating an upcoming event." Tim said that at 11:15 p.m., he got out of the tub and went back inside the house. A short time later, he said, Maryann got out of the tub and joined him in the house. According to Tim, not long after that, they both went back out into the tub. At approximately 12:15 a.m., Tim said, he got out and went to take a shower. Then, sometime between 12:30 and 12:45, he came back outside. It was at this point that he discovered Maryann still in the tub, but unconscious. Tim also told Tamburo that Maryann had drunk fourteen beers, but never said anything, as he had to his mother, about he and Maryann having argued.

By this time—1:04 a.m., to be exact—two more paramedics, Carmen Hart and Jim Weslager, who'd driven to Tim and Maryann's from the Ross/West View E.M.S. headquarters in one of the squad's ambulances, were out on the deck. The rescue crew decided at this point their best bet would be to try to jump-start Maryann's heart using electric defibrillator paddles. The paramedics moved Maryann away from the tub and nearer to the house, to an area that was dryer and better lit. But the paddles, too, failed, and the paramedics realized there was nothing left for them to do but transport Maryann to the hospital as quickly as possible.

Hart found Tim in the kitchen and told him she and her fellow paramedics were going to transport Maryann to nearby Passavant Hospital.

"No," Tim told a startled Hart, "I want you to take her to Allegheny General."

"Passavant is closer," Hart said.

"No," Tim repeated. "I want her to go to Allegheny."

"Just let us take her to Passavant," Hart said, trying to reason with Tim. "Then, once she's stable, you can have her transferred to any hospital you want."

Tim continued to insist that Maryann be taken to Allegheny General, which was some five minutes farther away than Passavant. Realizing she wasn't about to change Tim's mind, Hart went back out on the deck and repeated the conversation she'd had with Tim to her fellow paramedics.

"We're going to Passavant," Jim Weslager insisted.

"No, if he wants us to take her to Allegheny, let's just take her to Allegheny," Stacy Tamburo interjected.

That decided, the paramedics loaded Maryann onto a stretcher and carried her out to the ambulance. Hart then climbed behind the wheel while Long, Tamburo, and Weslager jumped in the back so they could continue to treat Maryann on the way to the hospital. Tim was given the option of riding up front next to Hart, but declined, opting instead to drive with his mother. Buc, meanwhile, declared he would remain at the house with the kids.

As soon as the ambulance pulled into Allegheny General, Maryann was rushed inside the emergency room. But as the police and paramedics already knew, there was little that could be done. At 1:40 p.m., Maryann was pronounced dead. A short time later, Father Chuck Christen, one of two Catholic priests on duty that morning, administered the Sacrament of the Sick, prayed the Vigil of the Deceased, and anointed her with holy oil.

Stacy Tamburo, who had remained in the emergency room where the physician on duty had struggled to revive Maryann, finally left after learning the doctor had pronounced Maryann dead. In the hallway outside the emergency room, she walked past Tim and Rose. Although they'd already been informed that Maryann was dead and were on their way to view her body one final time, the paramedic couldn't help but be struck by the fact that they didn't seem to be the least bit upset—Tim, especially so.

Said Tamburo, "He showed absolutely no emotion."

When she finally returned home Monday morning, Tamburo told her husband about the call. She told him about having noticed a number of bruises on Maryann's chest. She also described how Maryann's stomach had been so distended that, until being told otherwise, she thought Maryann might be pregnant, and how that distension suggested Maryann had been dead for some time before the call. Finally, she told him that Tim simply didn't seem as distraught as one might expect him to be under the circumstances.

"There's something wrong," Tamburo said. "That woman did not drown."

CHAPTER 16

AFTER TIM and his mother left for the hospital, Officers Hess and Barrett found themselves back inside the house talking with Wes Semple and Buc.

"There are three children upstairs sleeping," Wes noted at one point, "and they have no idea what's going on."

"That's a shame," Barrett said. "They have no idea their mother may be dead."

"Oh," Wes said, "she's their stepmother." He then went on to explain to Barrett that Tim had been married previously.

"Do you know how we can get ahold of her?" Barrett asked, referring to Tim's ex-wife, the mother of the trio of children asleep upstairs.

"She's dead," Wes replied. "She died when they were living in North Carolina."

Barrett turned to Buc and asked him how his former daughter-in-law had died.

"I don't want to talk about it," Buc said matter-of-factly.

"Why?" a curious Barrett wanted to know.

"I just don't," Buc insisted.

"We'll find out what happened," Hess said.

"She died under similar circumstances," Buc revealed begrudgingly. "She drowned in the bathtub."

CHAPTER 17

GARY WATERS, a veteran of sixteen years of service with the Ross Township Police Department, was the first detective to arrive on the scene. Officer William Barrett, upon calling Ross Township headquarters to request a detective be sent, reported that Tim had commented, "I wish Gary Waters was here." The Ross Township police dispatcher, as a result, contacted Waters at his home at about 1:40 a.m. Waters was told that a 35-year-old woman had passed out in a hot tub and had been taken to Allegheny General Hospital. He was also told that one of the uniformed officers at the scene had overheard the woman's husband mentioning Waters to his mother.

"Boczkowski," Waters said, repeating the husband's last name aloud.

The detective realized the name did ring a bell. Growing up, a family by that name belonged to the same church as the Waters family—St. Sebastian's in Ross Township. He was pretty sure, too, that he'd gone to school with one of the Boczkowski sons. But that had been some thirty years ago. He wouldn't necessarily recognize his former schoolmate if he were standing next to him. Above all else, Waters had no idea why he would be mentioning him by name to his mother as his wife lay dying on the deck behind their home.

Before leaving his house, Waters called Officer Barrett for an update.

"What do you have up there?" he asked.

Barrett essentially repeated what the police dispatcher had told the detective, including the fact that Tim had mentioned Waters's name to his mother. He added, too, that he and Officer Sysca had overheard Tim saying, "I hope they don't try to pin this on me."

"Also," Barrett said, "I think you should know that we learned here that four years ago, in North Carolina, the husband's first wife died under similar circumstances."

It was roughly 2 a.m. when Waters arrived at the scene. Ross Township Police Officers Barrett, Hess, and Sysca were still there. So were Buc Boczkowski and the kids, who were upstairs asleep. Tim and his mother, Rose, however, had yet to return from Allegheny General. Waters talked briefly with the officers, including Barrett, who told him exactly what he'd overheard Tim saying.

"I wish Gary Waters was here," the officer said. "I don't want none of this coming back on me."

Waters considered Tim's comment, but again it made no sense. The mystery would be solved soon enough, though, once Tim returned from the hospital. In the meantime, after learning that there were three children sleeping upstairs, Waters went to check on them. He quietly opened the door to Randy and Todd's bedroom and shined his flashlight inside. Both appeared to be sound asleep. Waters closed the door and moved on to Sandy's room. She, too, he found, upon peeking inside, was clearly asleep.

Because Tim had told the responding officers that Maryann had drunk fifteen cans of beer on Sunday, Waters next began looking for evidence of alcohol consumption.

First, though, he asked Buc's permission.

"Do you mind if we look around?" he asked Tim's father.

"Check everything you want," Buc offered. "You've got full cooperation here."

Waters walked out to the deck and over to the hot tub. When he looked inside, he saw a number of items floating around, including a pair of eyeglasses, an elastic hair tie, a piece of white plastic, and a white handkerchief.

The detective then walked back into the kitchen, which, he noted, was nearly spotless, something you wouldn't necessarily expect to find in a household with three small children. Waters opened the refrigerator. Inside was one unopened 12-ounce can of Stroh's Light and a half-full gallon bottle of white zinfandel.

Waters walked downstairs to the basement where he found the box for a case of Stroh's Light with twelve empty cans inside. The cans, however, were completely dry, suggesting to Waters that they had been drunk some time ago. He eventually made his way out to the garage, where he found another box for a case of Stroh's Light. This one contained twenty-four empty cans, but like those in the basement, they were completely dry.

Suspecting he might have a homicide on this hands, Waters decided to call the Allegheny County Police Department, which has countywide jurisdiction, for investigative assistance. In fact, the forty-man Ross Township department, whenever it had a suspicious death on its hands, almost always contacted ACPD for help.

Waters was still in the basement, near the stairs leading up to the kitchen, when, at about 3 a.m., Tim and Rose returned. They entered the basement through the garage and Tim, upon reaching the place where Waters was standing, looked at the detective, then looked away. He then began climbing the stairs leading to the kitchen. Rose followed behind her son, and Waters behind Rose. Neither Tim nor Rose said a word the entire time.

Once upstairs, the first thing Tim did was go over to Buc and hug him.

"I'm going to need you, Dad," he told his father.

At that point, Waters introduced himself.

"Gary, you've changed," Tim said. "You look different." He then added, without missing a beat, "You know about Maryann's drinking problem. You used to date her."

Waters wasn't exactly sure what Tim was talking about.

"What was her maiden name?" the detective asked.

"Fullerton," Tim told him.

Immediately, Waters realized who Tim was talking about. Twelve years earlier, in the fall of 1982, he and Maryann had dated for about four months. Waters, how-

ever, did not remember Maryann having a drinking problem
at the time.

"I want to thank you for not helping her when she got
arrested for drunk driving and she asked you to get her out
of it," Tim said. "I want to thank you for that."

Waters did recall learning that Maryann was ticketed for
DUI some time after they'd stopped seeing each other. But
at no point did she ask him for help. "What is this guy
talking about?" he thought.

Waters asked Tim to tell him what had happened that
night.

Tim explained that at around 11:10 p.m., he invited
Maryann to join him for a soak in the hot tub.

"Go ahead," he said she told him. "I'll join you in a
little while."

Tim said he got in the tub and that Maryann joined him
about fifteen minutes later.

"I'd like a glass of wine," Tim said Maryann stated once
they were already in the tub.

Tim didn't say how he responded to Maryann's request.
He did, however, mention to Waters that Maryann had already consumed between thirteen and fifteen beers that evening. Tim told Waters that after a brief soak, both he and
Maryann got out of the tub, returned to the kitchen, and
poured each other a glass of wine. They then went back
out to the tub, where Maryann proceeded to drink not only
her glass but a good part of Tim's, too.

"I'm not much of a drinker," Tim made a point of noting
to Waters.

Tim said that at about 12:30 a.m., he informed Maryann
he was going to get out of the tub.

"I'm going to stay in for a while," Maryann replied.

Tim said he went into the house, changed out of his
bathing suit, and put on a pair of jeans. At about 12:50
a.m., he said, he glanced out the kitchen window, expecting
to see Maryann still in the tub, but he couldn't see her head,
which didn't make sense. Concerned, Tim dashed out to
the tub where he found Maryann lying on her right side,

unconscious. At no point did he mention, as he had to his mother, that he and Maryann had been arguing that night. He also didn't say anything about them celebrating an upcoming event, as he had to paramedic Stacy Tamburo.

"I want to go upstairs and lay down," Tim said before Waters could get out another question.

Waters, in deference to the fact that Tim had just lost his wife, didn't object. But before Tim went upstairs, he made mental notes of what he thought might very well be key physical evidence, namely a scratch mark on the front of Tim's neck and what appeared to be a fresh "nick" on his left thumb.

At about 3:20 a.m., Allegheny County Police Department Detectives James Cvetic and Kevin McCarthy simultaneously pulled up to Tim and Maryann's house. Both were on call Sunday night and had been contacted at their respective homes by ACPD dispatch shortly before 2:30 a.m. Waters met them outside and briefed them on what he'd found out so far, including the fact that one of the uniformed officers had overheard Tim telling his mother how he "wished" Waters were on the scene. Tim's comment about Waters aroused Cvetic's suspicions.

"Somebody you love may be dead and you're talking about who you hope is sent to investigate what happened?" Cvetic, then a twenty-one-year veteran with the ACPD, would later say. "That's not normal."

At the same time, the detective felt it was important that he give Tim "the benefit of the doubt. After all, everyone grieves differently."

But Cvetic already had questions, too. "From the start, I thought it was peculiar that he had two young wives die," the detective said. "What are the odds of that happening?"

Minutes later, Waters led Cvetic and McCarthy inside the house. McCarthy headed out to the deck to retrieve the items Waters had seen floating in the tub. The white piece of plastic, it turned out, was a piece of the tub's thermometer, which somehow had been broken. Cvetic, after learning that Tim had excused himself to go upstairs, told

Waters he thought the two of them should go up and question him yet again.

The detectives found Tim asleep in the master bedroom. Cvetic, though, would later say he felt instinctively that Tim was only pretending to be asleep. "I've been around a lot of people who've just lost somebody they love," he said, "but I'd never been on a case where the victim has just been pronounced dead, the police are still on the scene, and the victim's spouse decides to take a nap."

"I thought he was faking it," Cvetic would later note matter-of-factly. Even so, he chose, at that point, not to make an issue of it.

After jostling Tim from his slumber, Cvetic and Waters asked Tim to repeat what had supposed happened one more time, so Cvetic could hear it for himself. Cvetic first, though, offered Tim his condolences.

The detective would later say he found Tim remarkably composed under the circumstances, noting that Tim "didn't seem like someone who had just woken up."

"I was not seeing the person I should have been seeing," Cvetic added. "Most people, in that situation lose the color in their face, they're teary-eyed, their hands shake. He wasn't acting like someone who had just lost someone they loved."

Cvetic and Waters asked Tim to repeat what had happened after he asked Maryann to join him in the tub. Tim did, but his answers—and the manner in which he spoke—didn't sit right with Cvetic. "He would wait a few seconds before saying anything," Cvetic said. "It was like he had to figure out what he was going to say. He was also so exact about his times that it seemed too calculated."

Meanwhile, while standing in the bedroom talking to Tim, Cvetic noticed, as Waters had, the scratch mark on Tim's neck, a mark Cvetic would later describe as "very visible." Thinking that where there's smoke, there's fire, Cvetic then asked Tim to remove his sweatshirt. When he did, Cvetic and Waters saw that Tim had scratch marks on the right side of his upper back and on his right and left sides.

"How did you get those scratches?" Cvetic asked.

"I don't know," Tim said matter-of-factly.

"That wasn't the right answer," Cvetic would later say. The detective, however, opted against pushing Tim on this point. "In a situation like that, you have to give the person the benefit of the doubt," he said.

Shortly after 4 a.m., Cvetic asked Tim if he would be willing to accompany him and Waters to Ross Township police headquarters to answer a few more questions. This way, he said, they wouldn't have to worry about waking the children. Tim readily obliged and, strangely enough, once outside, walked directly to one of the Ross Township patrol cars and got in the back seat without any prodding.

This behavior also raised a red flag for Cvetic. Simply put, Tim was being too cooperative. "When you're being interviewed by the police and you're innocent, you're going to cooperate—but only to a certain point," Cvetic said. "After a while, you're going to start to get defensive."

It was about 4:30 a.m. by the time Cvetic and Waters began interviewing Tim down at Ross Township police headquarters. Cvetic apologetically asked Tim if he would mind telling them one more time exactly what had happened the night before. Tim complied, offering the detectives essentially the same version of events he had shared with them back at the house—with one exception. A number of times, Cvetic interrupted Tim, asking him if he would repeat the times each event had taken place so he would be sure he had it straight. Tim again complied, but his answers were so exact that once again, they sounded overly calculated.

Cvetic then asked Tim for a second time how he'd gotten the scratch marks on his upper back and his sides.

"I don't know," Tim told the detectives.

Moments later, Tim amended his answer. He explained that he and Maryann had gone on a Caribbean cruise several weeks earlier and that he had gotten badly sunburned. Because his back still itched from the sunburn, he had asked Maryann, while they were in the hot tub together

Sunday night, to give him a "scratch massage." Both Cvetic and Waters, however, found Tim to be more pale in appearance than sunburned.

Cvetic and Waters then asked Tim to tell them about his relationship with Maryann—when they'd met, how they'd met, when they'd gotten married. Tim answered the detectives, but was most adamant about one point in particular: the fact that Maryann had a drinking problem. Tim told them, too, about the intervention that was planned for Wednesday. This struck Cvetic as especially odd.

"Why were you drinking wine with your wife in the hot tub if you thought she had a drinking problem and were going to do an intervention?" he asked.

Tim had no reply. Instead, he just stared ahead and said nothing.

Tim's comments about Maryann's so-called "drinking problem" didn't sit right with Cvetic. "Right away," Cvetic would later say, "he was telling everybody who would listen that his wife was a problem drinker. That's just not what you'd expect someone to be saying hours after she's died. It's the same thing when some kid dies of a drug overdose. Right after, no one says he was a drug addict or talks about how horrible that is. They're going to be crying and saying what a good kid he was."

Cvetic and Waters realized they had hit upon a sore spot when they asked Tim to tell them about Elaine, about their marriage and how she'd died.

"I don't really want to talk about that," Tim said.

Eventually, Tim did allow that the coroner had never been able to determine the exact cause of Elaine's death, but noted that she did have what he characterized as "psychological problems" and that she sometimes got depressed about "things in the past."

"What kinds of things?" Cvetic asked.

Rather than answering, Tim simply stared ahead and said nothing. He never mentioned that he and Elaine, for all intents and purposes, had separated and that they were planning to divorce at the time of her death. Cvetic asked Tim a few more innocuous questions about Elaine. But the very mention of her name, Cvetic would later note, seemed to make Tim "nervous." As a result, Cvetic steered the conversation in another direction. What he didn't want was for Tim to refuse to talk altogether.

Next, Cvetic hit Tim with a question that caught him somewhat off-guard.

"Would you be willing to take a polygraph test?" the detective asked.

"Sure," Tim replied. "I'll do it if I can take it right here."

Cvetic would later say he was certain Tim thought he was outsmarting the detectives by agreeing to take the test, but only right then and there at the Ross Township station. "I think he knew we wouldn't have one right there," Cvetic said. "But I knew we could get one pretty quickly from the state police."

Cvetic then informed Tim of his good fortune. "It's your lucky day," the detective told Tim. "Someone's coming over with one right now."

Tim, Cvetic said, was literally stunned. "He looked like a deer caught in the headlights," the detective would later say.

While waiting for a state trooper to arrive with the polygraph machine, Cvetic made mostly small talk with Tim. "I wanted to make him feel as comfortable as possible," he said, "so I asked him about the ice cream business he said he'd had in Greensboro, about his miniature golf course, about his house, about how he kept his lawn so green . . ."

Cvetic also arranged for some breakfast from a local diner to be delivered for Tim.

At about 8:15 a.m., Pennsylvania State Trooper Richard Ealing arrived with the polygraph machine in hand. After being briefed by Cvetic and Waters, he entered the interview room where Tim was sitting alone. After introducing himself, Ealing advised Tim of his rights. He also made it clear to Tim that he was not under arrest and that he was free to leave at any time he wanted.

"Did you drown your wife?" Ealing asked Tim right off the bat.

"Her name was Maryann," Tim insisted.

"Well, I know that," Ealing replied. "But is there anything wrong with calling her 'your wife'?"

"Nothing, I guess," Tim shrugged.

"Well, okay," Ealing said. "And for the purposes of this interview, I mean your wife that died last night."

"Okay," Tim replied, nodding his head.

After hooking Tim up to the polygraph machine, Ealing asked Tim a series of innocuous yes and no questions, such as "Is your name Timothy Boczkowski?" in order to be able to determine whether Tim's future answers were truthful or not. At one point, Ealing asked Tim the following four questions:

- Are you attempting to withhold any information concerning this investigation?
- Did you drown your wife?
- Did you get into a physical argument with your wife last night?
- Were you in or near the hot tub when your wife died?

Tim answered "no" to each of the questions, but the reading on the machine indicated that each of Tim's answers was deceptive in nature.

"I know you caused the death of your wife," the trooper insisted to Tim.

Tim slowly nodded his head up and down. Ealing would later note that Tim, at this point, seemed neither surprised nor agitated.

The state trooper then posed a possible scenario. "Maybe the two of you had a physical confrontation," Ealing suggested to Tim. "Maybe she assaulted you and while you were defending yourself, things got out of hand."

For a second time, Tim slowly nodded his head up and down.

A short time later, Ealing went out into the hallway

where Cvetic and Waters stood waiting and told them that Tim had failed the polygraph. The trooper and two detectives then returned to the interview room to share the results with Tim.

"You failed the test, Tim," Cvetic said.

Tim, reacting with more emotion than he had demonstrated all morning, angrily attempted to rip the band that measured his responses off of his arm.

"We know you're responsible for your wife's death," Cvetic told Tim.

Tim quietly bowed his head.

"I thought at that point he was going to confess and tell us exactly what he'd done," Cvetic said.

"Were you responsible for your wife's death?" the officers asked.

Tim, his head still bowed, nodded yes.

"Do you know how she died?"

For a second time, Tim nodded his head up and down.

"Do you want to talk to us about that?"

Yet again, Tim nodded yes.

At that point, Tim finally spoke. "I'll tell you what happened," he said, looking up at the officers, "after I talk to my attorney."

By uttering the magic word—"attorney"—Tim brought the questioning to a halt. As Cvetic would later say, "At that point, we had no choice but to discontinue the interview."

Tim's attorney, it turned out, was James Herb, a respected Pittsburgh lawyer who also happened to be the brother of Ross Township Police Sergeant John Herb.

"Do you want us to get in touch with him?" Cvetic asked.

Tim said he did.

Cvetic left the room, found John Herb, who was working that morning, briefed him, then asked if he would contact his brother on Tim's behalf.

It was roughly 10 a.m. when James Herb arrived—not at Ross Township police headquarters, but at Allegheny

County Police Department headquarters in downtown Pittsburgh. At about 5:30 a.m. a Ross Township police crime lab photographer took photos of the scratches on Tim's body. Later, Tim insisted he wanted the scratches examined, too. Happy to oblige, Cvetic offered to bring Tim to see Dr. Leon Rozin, Allegheny County's chief forensic pathologist, at ACPD headquarters.

Herb and Tim talked alone for about forty-five minutes before they were joined by Cvetic and Waters.

"So, Tim, are you ready to tell us what happened?" Cvetic asked.

To no one's surprise, it was Herb—not Tim—who responded to the detective's query. "Tim has nothing to say at this point," Herb said, answering on behalf of his client.

Minutes later, Herb and Tim left ACPD headquarters.

For the time being, at least, Tim was a free man.

CHAPTER 18

NOT LONG after Tim departed Allegheny County Police Department headquarters, ACPD Detective Kevin McCarthy arrived at the Allegheny County Coroner's Office to observe Maryann's autopsy, which was performed by chief forensic pathologist Dr. Leon Rozin. McCarthy took notes on anything that seemed relevant to the investigation into Maryann's death. He noticed, for instance, a significant number of small black-and-blue marks all over the left side of Maryann's body, on her arms, underneath her jaw line, and at the top of her chest. There were also a number of large and small black-and-blue marks on the left side of her back and on the backs of her legs. McCarthy had been a police officer for twenty-one years, but even the greenest of rookies would have concluded, as McCarthy did, that Maryann had fought for her life.

Later that morning, McCarthy shared his findings with ACPD Detective Jim Cvetic. He also told his colleague about the conversation he'd had with a Greensboro, NC, police detective named Ken Brady. Looking to learn more about Elaine's death, McCarthy had called the Greensboro police and been told he needed to talk to Brady, the detective who had handled the investigation into Elaine's death.

"Is that so?" Brady said upon learning that Tim's second wife had died earlier that morning under suspicious circumstances.

Brady had never stopped believing that Tim had gotten away with murder and, over the past four years, had kept a vow he'd made to himself to keep his file on Elaine's death atop his desk until he came up with enough evidence to have Tim arrested. The detective never let Tim believe that he had given up. Every December, Brady sent Tim a Christmas card with the inscription, "I haven't forgotten you."

CHAPTER 19

BY EARLY Monday morning, word of Maryann's death had begun to reach members of her large, extended family. Her aunt, Ruth Schumann, heard the news from her husband, George, who met her at the downtown Pittsburgh courthouse where she'd reported for jury duty that morning.

"Ruth," he said. "Maryann is dead."

"Maryann who?" she asked.

"Your niece, Maryann."

"My God," Ruth moaned. "Maryann. No. Not Maryann. Maryann?"

Once outside, Ruth stopped cold on the street. "He killed her," she blurted out.

"Ruth, I know you're upset," George said, trying to calm his near-hysterical wife. "But Tim didn't kill Maryann. She drowned in their hot tub."

"No," Ruth insisted. "He killed her, just like he killed his first wife."

George didn't know what to think. Ruth had always been somewhat lukewarm about her niece's choice for a husband. That much he knew. But that was hardly reason enough to accuse him of killing Maryann—and his previous wife, the mother of his children.

A short time later, Ruth and George arrived at Pat and Lew's. Pat answered the door, grabbed Ruth, and gave her a long hug.

"Can you believe this?" she asked her younger sister. "Isn't this something? Our Maryann is dead." She spoke as if she were talking about someone she barely knew. Ruth was stunned. "It really hasn't hit her yet," she thought. Inside, she found two more of her sisters, Maggie Fischerkeller and Donna Okarszewski. Their faces were red and swollen. It was obvious they had been crying for hours. Lew was sitting at the dinner table crying. He stood to greet his sister-in-law and her husband, but was barely able to bring himself to his feet. They hugged, and he immediately sat back down. Pat, by this time, was pacing back and forth from one end of the room to the next.

"Well, now we've experienced the worst thing that could happen to us, huh, Lew?" she said, after coming to a sudden stop behind her husband's chair. Pat's voice sounded the same as when she'd greeted Ruth and George at the door. "Nothing worse than this could ever happen to us now," she added. "We've had it all."

Ruth moved to comfort her sister but stopped dead in her tracks when Pat suddenly turned around to ask her a question.

"Did you know Maryann had a drinking problem?"

"What are you talking about?" Ruth responded incredulously. "Maryann didn't have a drinking problem."

"That's what Rose told me when I called Maryann and Tim's house this morning."

"Who is Rose?" Ruth demanded.

"Rose is Tim's mother," Donna interjected.

EVEN AS a young girl growing up in the Pittsburgh suburb of Millvale, Pat Fullerton, the third of ten children, always stood apart from her siblings. She was always more reserved, more serious. The product of a parochial education, she would have made an excellent nun, those close to her say. She disapproved of gossip and tended to give people the benefit of the doubt. In fact, she so wanted to believe in the goodness of people that when she did hear something negative about someone, she assumed there must have been some justification for that person's behavior. Her siblings say Pat didn't change much after she married and started a family of her own, and that her very nature sometimes put her at odds with her only daughter. Like Pat, Maryann was hardworking and religious, and sensitive to her mother's feelings. But as she grew older, Maryann became more and more her own person, and in doing so, sometimes made decisions her mother didn't always approve of.

As THE morning of November 4 wore on, the gathering at Pat and Lew's grew. The telephone rang constantly family, friends, members of Maryann's church—the calls came one after another, with one exception. The police had yet to call back, as one detective had promised, with more details about what had happened. But it wasn't long before information began to emerge from an entirely different source.

"It's on the news," someone shouted from the family room, moments after a local noon broadcast went on the air.

"Timothy Boczkowski found the body of his wife, Maryann, 35, in the hot tub on the deck behind their home on Noring Court in Ross Township," said the reporter, who could be seen standing in front of Tim and Maryann's house. "She was pronounced dead at Allegheny General Hospital at 1:40 a.m. Police said Boczkowski's first wife was found in a bathtub in their home in Greensboro, North Carolina, exactly four years and four days ago. They said authorities never determined whether her death was accidental."

"Well, isn't that a coincidence," Ruth huffed, her voice dripping with sarcasm.

"I thought she choked?" someone else chimed in.

"I thought she died of a heart attack," yet another party noted.

"Would all of you please stop this!" Lew demanded, throwing his hands in the air as he jumped from his chair. "I can't take this anymore! Let's just wait until we hear from the detective."

In an attempt to diffuse some of the tension suddenly in the air, George calmly asked Pat and Lew what they knew about Tim's first wife's death.

"I'll tell you what Tim told us," Lew said. "Before he and Maryann got married, he said he wanted to tell us about his first wife's death, and he said he was only going to talk about it that one time. So we sat right there, in the living room, and he said that she had drowned in the bathtub. He said the police questioned him, and that they came to the conclusion that it was an accident."

Just then, the phone rang. At the other end of the line was Allegheny County Homicide Detective James Cvetic. Since George was an attorney, Pat and Lew asked him to take the call. After a few minutes, George asked Lew to pick up the extension in the bedroom.

Cvetic told the men the police were treating Maryann's death as suspicious and that they were awaiting the results of her autopsy. He said they had questioned Tim for several hours and that he had failed a lie-detector test. He also mentioned the matter of a $100,000 insurance policy on Maryann's life, of which Tim was the beneficiary. Finally, he urged Lew not to have any contact with Tim, who was no longer with the police. He then repeated the same information to Pat after she took the phone from her husband.

"Oh, the poor guy," an empathetic Pat sighed after George had filled everyone in on what Cvetic had said. "Why did the police keep him there so long?"

"Patty!" an exasperated Ruth nearly shouted at her sister. "He killed her. That's why he's been at the police station."

"Don't say that," Pat fired back. "Don't even think that. He loved her. Why would he kill her?"

Pat simply couldn't believe that Tim—or anyone—was capable of as heinous a crime as drowning someone. And if he was, what did that say about her Maryann? That she couldn't tell the difference between a loving husband and a killer?

Realizing there was no way—for the moment—that she was going to convince her sister of Tim's involvement in Maryann's death, a frustrated Ruth simply gave up.

George fielded one condolence call after another. Then, at about 1 p.m., a call came that startled even the normally unflappable attorney. It was Tim wanting to talk to Pat. Pat rushed into her bedroom. Ruth and her other sisters followed behind. Pat cried throughout the conversation, which lasted only a few minutes.

"He said he was okay and that the kids were okay," she tearfully told her sisters. "But when I asked him what had happened, he said that he was calling from his attorney's office and that he had advised him not to talk about it. Then he asked me if I would help with the funeral arrangements. He said he would send the clothes he wanted Maryann laid out in to the funeral home tomorrow."

Earlier that day, after Tim had returned home from his interview with the police, he had had a brief meeting with Wes Semple. Again, Wes couldn't help but think Tim "was not as upset as I would have thought he would be."

That night, at around 7 p.m., Eileen Datt finally reached Tim at home.

"My God, Tim," she said. "What happened?"

"I can't talk about it," Tim replied matter-of-factly.

"Were you in the hot tub with Maryann?"

"I can't talk about it."

"Was she drinking?"

"It will all come out in the autopsy."

Eileen was flabbergasted. Her best friend had just died, and her husband was refusing to answer any of her questions.

"I'm very tired," Tim told Eileen. "I was with the police all night and all morning. They wouldn't let me go home or have anything to drink. I'm going to bed. Call Lew and Pat. They're making the funeral arrangements."

With that last tidbit of information, Tim hung up.

CHAPTER 20

EARLY TUESDAY morning, George took Pat and Lew to Devlin Funeral Home in Ross Township to make the arrangements for Maryann's funeral. Much to their surprise, they were met there by Tim's father, Buc.

"You know, I've been reading up on hot tubs, and I read where you shouldn't be drinking and going into one," he said to Pat and Lew.

Maryann's parents looked at the man and said nothing.

By the time Pat, Lew, and George returned from the funeral home, Ruth and other family members had gathered at the house. Ruth, in particular, was finding it harder and harder to keep her feelings about Tim to herself.

"You think my Maryann married a loser?" Pat yelled at Ruth during one especially heated exchange. She still couldn't conceive of the possibility.

"No," Ruth said, correcting her sister. "I think your Maryann married a murderer."

Ruth quickly realized, though, that rather than swaying her sister's opinion she was only making her more defensive. And it wasn't only Tim they argued about. Now there was also this question of whether or not Maryann had a drinking problem. Ruth maintained that she didn't. Pat, however, remained convinced that she did, especially after talking to Eileen Datt, who told them that not only did she know Maryann had a problem, she also knew about the intervention Tim was planning for November 9.

SHORTLY BEFORE 6 p.m. on Wednesday, November 9, George drove Pat, Lew, and Maryann's brother, John, to the funeral home for the family's first viewing. Tim and his mother arrived at roughly the same time. Buc came later with Randy, Sandy, and Todd in tow. Although the police felt strongly that Maryann's family should have no contact with Tim, going as far as to suggest separate viewings for the Fullerton and Boczkowski families, Pat and Lew embraced their son-in-law upon his arrival.

At Tim's request, Maryann was laid out, just as Elaine had been, in her Christmas outfit from the previous year: a white rayon pants suit she had worn for a photo with her new family.

Pat and Lew spent most of that night sitting by their daughter's casket. "I loved that little girl," Lew said more than once as he gazed at his lifeless daughter. Pat simply cried and cried.

Tim, on the other hand, struck a number of mourners as a little too cool and calm under the circumstances. "He just didn't seem that sad," Angela Di Marco noted.

When Shirley Marks arrived at the funeral home the first night of visitation, she instinctively headed towards Tim to console him. The last time they'd spoken was the week before Maryann's death. But what Shirley thought would be a comforting moment for both of them turned out to be a literally chilling one. "When I put my arms out to give him a hug, I got the weirdest sensation," she said. "He was cold, like ice."

Tim only faintly returned the gesture. As Shirley would later recall, "He just kind of barely hugged me with his fingertips."

Mark and Maria Crendall, meanwhile, got a similar response—not from Tim but from members of the Fullerton family and from friends of Maryann's who knew them only as old friends of Tim's. For Mark, it was déjà vu. He, after all, had gotten the same reception once before—at Elaine's funeral.

"People were looking at us like they had daggers in their eyes," Maria said. "By this time, word had gotten around about Elaine and how she had died. Because we had known Tim when he was married to Elaine, it was like they were holding us at fault, too. It was guilt by association."

Maria would later recall that she and Mark didn't get an especially warm reception from Tim either. "He pretty much just thanked us for coming," she said.

Maria would later say that she, more than Mark, found it hard to believe it was pure coincidence that both Elaine and Maryann died the way they did. Other disturbing thoughts kept running through her mind as well. After Elaine's brother Jimmy had died, she recalled, Tim talked about Jimmy's death and the fact that he thought he had been killed, incessantly. "Isn't it something," Tim would say, "they've never caught anyone?" At the same time, Maria said she and Mark felt, for the time being at least, that they had to believe Tim's version of events. It was too horrifying, she said, to think anything else might be true.

But not everyone was willing to give Tim the benefit of the doubt. Eileen had become increasingly suspicious of Tim. She learned from the police, for instance, that he had admitted pouring Maryann a glass of wine to drink in the hot tub. "But just a couple of days before that," she said, "he told me he was never going to serve alcohol to Maryann again."

Eileen, too, couldn't shake Tim's claim that after getting out of the tub Sunday night while Maryann remained behind, he went upstairs and took a shower. Eileen knew for a fact that Tim never took showers. A travel agent, she had booked Tim and Maryann's honeymoon and recalled Tim asking her to make sure there was a bathtub in their hotel room. "I don't take showers," Tim told Eileen. "I take baths."

Tim made the same request, Eileen recalled, when she booked the October cruise.

Then there were the newspaper and television reports Eileen had seen that contradicted what Maryann said Tim had told her about Elaine's death—namely that she'd been drinking and had drowned in the bathtub.

"I couldn't even look at him at the viewing," Eileen would later say. "At one point, he came up to me, kissed me on the cheek, and said kind of casually, 'How are you doing?' It didn't seem like he was torn up at all."

But what ultimately convinced Eileen that Tim had played a role in Maryann's death was something she spotted at the viewing.

"I happened to be standing behind Tim, near Maryann's casket," she would later recall. "I was saying a prayer, and after I finished, I looked up and saw he had scratch marks all over the back of his neck. I would have said something to him right then and there, but I knew Pat and Lew didn't want any trouble."

As details of Tim's version of what happened Sunday night spread, others also began doubting whether he was telling the truth.

Gay Barbiaux, who hadn't talked to Tim since the week before, couldn't stop thinking how it didn't make any sense that Tim and Maryann had gone in the tub so late Sunday night. For starters, Maryann had been battling bronchitis since the cruise.

"When she was sick, she took care of herself," she said. "That was why I didn't think she'd go in the tub so late at night."

She also remembered something Tim had said one night before Tim and Maryann got married, when she and Bob were out for dinner with them. "He turned to her at one point and said, 'Maryann, you're going to have to tell your friends and family not to call past ten o'clock because I've got to go to sleep early,' " Gay recalled.

Gay said Tim's comment stood out in her mind because she remembered thinking at the time, "Maryann's a pretty independent person. I don't know how she's going to handle that."

MARIA CRENDALL found it perplexing that Tim had gone down to the basement to retrieve the CPR mask when he not only knew how to perform CPR without one, but had saved his son's life doing so. According to Maria, Tim and Elaine were still living in Claysville when the incident had occurred. One day, she said, while Tim was out cutting the grass, Elaine ran outside and told Tim that Randy, who was still a baby, had stopped breathing. Tim, who had been a volunteer fireman before they married, performed CPR on Randy and successfully restored his breathing.

There was buzz, too, about whether Tim and Maryann were getting along as well as Tim claimed. Most of Maryann's friends knew she and Tim did not sleep in the same room. Tim slept in the master bedroom, and she slept in the guest bedroom, Maryann said, because he snored and she ground her teeth. Moreover, after returning home from the October cruise, Maryann mentioned to a couple of people that she and Tim did not have sex while they were away. She said it was because the walls of their cabin were so thin that they worried people would hear them. Now, friends were starting to wonder if that was just an excuse, if it wasn't something more than that.

Over the next two-and-a-half days, family and friends poured into the funeral home.

"The tension was so thick you could cut it with a knife," Eileen said. "We all eventually felt that he had killed Maryann, but we couldn't say anything about it."

Even Pat, who was anything but convinced Tim was guilty, found it difficult at times to keep her anger in check. "Where were you and the children today?" an irritated Pat couldn't help but ask Tim when he arrived at the funeral home Thursday night.

"I thought it was best that they went to school," Tim replied, "and I wanted to be there when they got home."

At around 9:30 Friday morning, Pat and Lew viewed Maryann's body one last time. Pat was sobbing so hard she seemed on the verge of choking. Lew, tears streaming down his cheeks, bade his final farewell.

"Good-bye, little girl," he whispered to his only daughter.

Maryann's funeral Mass was celebrated Friday, November 11, at the Nativity Church worship site at Incarnation Parish, the very same church where she and Tim had uttered their wedding vows some seventeen months earlier. The hearse carrying Maryann's casket arrived at about 10:45 a.m., followed by a black limousine carrying Pat and Lew, Tim, and the kids. Some family members had tried to convince Pat and Lew not to ride with Tim, to take a separate car. But they would hear none of it.

At 11 a.m. hundreds of mourners who'd been milling about outside began to take their seats in the church. The funeral home director then motioned for the eight pallbearers and twenty honorary pall bearers—all first cousins of Maryann's—to take their places beside the casket, which had been brought inside the church's vestibule.

Father Almade officiated at the Mass. Tim and the kids sat in the front pew on the left side of the church. Buc and Rose Boczkowski sat behind them. Pat and Lew and Maryann's various aunts and uncles sat in row three. Maryann's cousins, friends, co-workers, and neighbors filled rows on both sides. Among those who didn't attend was Bob Eddins, Maryann's part-time employer. He was simply too broken-hearted to make it, in part because of a note Maryann had attached to the last report she had typed for him: "Looking forward to having you and your wife over for dinner," it read. "But you'll have to bring your bathing suits so we can go into the hot tub."

Tim, by most accounts, showed little emotion through most of the service. Wes and Sue Semple, yet again, found themselves puzzled by his apparent apathy. "That's what struck us the most," Wes said. "His lack of emotion."

Shirley Marks found Tim's behavior equally befuddling. "He didn't shed a single tear," she would later recall. "He also did his best to avoid us—me, Eileen and Chuck, Gay and Bob. He wouldn't look at us and he wouldn't talk to us."

"He looked sad, and he kept his head hung," Maria Crendall said, "but I never saw any real outpouring of grief."

Maryann's funeral Mass lasted about seventy-five minutes. Afterwards, mourners followed the hearse carrying her casket to St. Anthony's Cemetery in Millvale, where she was to be buried following a brief service in a cemetery chapel, alongside other Fullerton family members, including her maternal grandparents.

Outside Nativity Church, before the funeral procession departed, Ruth Schumann took her sister Pat's arm.

"Pat, don't ride with him," she said, nodding toward Tim. "Come with us."

"No, that's okay," a deflated Pat sighed. Tim, after all, had been her only daughter's husband. "You go on ahead."

The floral arrangements—mostly yellow roses, Maryann's favorite—that had been on display during her funeral were transported to St. Anthony's and, as each mourner entered the chapel, he or she removed one. Once the service, led again by Father Almade, was over, mourners walked toward Maryann's casket to say their final goodbyes and to lay their yellow roses on top of it. But when Tim began to move toward the casket, Claudia Dunford, one of Maryann's aunt's, couldn't help herself. "Don't you ever touch that casket again," she barked at her late niece's husband.

CHAPTER 21

FRIDAY, NOVEMBER 11, the day of Maryann's funeral, came and went without the Fullertons receiving the one phone call they were anticipating most. The police had promised Pat and Lew that they would let them know as soon as they had the coroner's report on Maryann's autopsy in hand. But no one had called yet. In the five days since Maryann's death, her parents had learned more about Tim and the circumstances surrounding Elaine's death from local newspaper and TV reports than they had from the police. On Tuesday, November 8, for instance, the *Pittsburgh Post-Gazette* carried a lengthy article about Maryann's death. The newspaper reported that the police in Greensboro had considered Elaine's death suspicious, but no charges were filed because the coroner who performed her autopsy was unable to determine an exact cause of death. The *North Hills News Record*, meanwhile, reported that Greensboro police were re-opening their investigation into Elaine's death.

It wasn't only print and broadcast reports about Maryann's death, though, that led some of Maryann's relatives to become more convinced of Tim's guilt. At around 10 a.m. on Saturday, November 12, Lew Fullerton contacted his brother-in-law, George, about a phone call he'd received only moments earlier.

"George, some woman just called here," Lew said. "Her name was Pat Martino. She said she was sorry to be calling, but that she felt she didn't have a choice. She said Maryann's death wasn't an accident. She said Tim had killed her just like he'd killed Elaine. She said all kinds of other stuff, too, but I told her I couldn't deal with it now. I said I'd have you call her."

"I'll take care of it," George said as he jotted down Martino's name and phone number. "You just try to relax."

Tim also called Pat and Lew that morning. "I'm still going to have Todd's birthday party tomorrow," he told his in-laws. "Maryann planned it, and I think she'd want us to go ahead and have it."

"We're just not up to it," an apologetic Pat told Tim.

"I understand completely," Tim replied. "Remember, we love you."

Later, Pat and her sister, Ruth, would argue about the call.

"Pat, don't you see what he's trying to do?" Ruth said. "He's trying to figure out whether you think he killed Maryann. Don't talk to him again."

"You don't know what happened," Pat shot back. "Were you there? You don't know how he treated her. He loved her."

"Do you really think Maryann would have married him if she'd known the truth about his first wife?"

"All I know," Pat said, "is that Maryann is dead."

The following day, the birthday party Maryann had planned for Todd took place as scheduled. Besides Tim, Buc, Rose, and Tim's sister, Joan, the only other adults present were neighbors Wes and Sue Semple.

"Tim had said he wanted to have the party because he wanted there to be some semblance of normalcy for the kids," said Wes, adding that he could understand that sentiment.

At the same time, he found it disconcerting that Tim would want to have any kind of party only two days after burying his wife.

As far as his feelings about Tim's guilt or innocence, Wes, at that point, was at something of a loss. "I didn't know what to think," he said. But, he added, considering what he'd read in the newspaper and seen on television, he couldn't help but feel "something was not right."

Sue Semple, for her part, simply didn't want to attend the party. "I felt uneasy just being in the house at that point," she said.

She'd also had a somewhat strange encounter with Tim Sunday morning.

"I had just gotten home," she said. "Tim was out on the deck, and when he saw me, he came over to our garage. I didn't know what to say to him, so I finally said, 'Oh, Tim,' and I threw my arms around him and started crying. He said, 'I know Maryann thought a lot of you.' But then he went off on some tangent. He said he hoped he didn't have problems settling Maryann's estate. He said he'd been executor of Elaine's will and that her family didn't want him to have her golf clubs and didn't want him to have this or that. I just passed it off as the kind of thing Tim would say."

Later that day, Sue said, Tim called "to see if we were coming to Todd's party. I felt bad so I said we were. I thought we should try to make it as happy an occasion as we could for Todd."

ON MONDAY morning, November 14, Pat Fullerton's sister, Ruth Schumann, decided to call Pat Martino, the woman who had called Lew Fullerton three days earlier.

"Tim killed Elaine," Martino said matter-of-factly, "and I'm sure he killed your niece."

Martino, it turned out, had grown up next door to Elaine in Wexford, and the two had remained friends over the years. She told Ruth she was so certain she was right about Tim that after spotting Tim and Maryann's engagement announcement in the *North Hills News*, she came very close to calling Maryann and telling her exactly what she thought.

"But it seemed pointless," Martino said, explaining why she never placed the call. "I figured if she was marrying Tim, she must be in love with him. She had no idea who I was. Why would she have believed anything I said?"

Martino said, moreover, that Elaine's mother, Mitzie, had actually tried to warn Maryann about Tim. Mitzie was so convinced that Tim had killed Elaine that after reading in a local newspaper that Tim and Maryann had closed on their house, she had written Maryann a letter telling her exactly what she thought of Tim and what she suspected had transpired the morning Elaine died. But she accidentally sent the missive to the wrong address, and the letter was returned Martino said. Mitzie took that as a sign that perhaps it was better that she keep her opinions to herself, and she never attempted to contact Maryann again.

By this time, the Allegheny County Police Department detectives investigating Maryann's death were convinced that Tim was a double murderer. ACPD Detectives Jim Cvetic and Kevin McCarthy had spent the past week building a case against Tim, a case not just for murder but for first-degree murder.

"It was a matter of putting all the pieces together," Cvetic would later say of the investigation.

From interviews with friends of Maryann and Tim— Eileen and Chuck Datt, Gay and Bob Barbiaux, Maria and Mark Crendall, Sue and Wes Semple—they learned not only about the intervention Tim had planned for November 9, but about how he'd spent more than a year trying to convince people that Maryann had a drinking problem.

The detectives also talked to people who didn't know Maryann, but who could offer revealing information, such as the salesman who sold Tim the hot tub. As Cvetic would later recall, "He said it was the fastest sale he ever made."

Finally, they learned more about the $100,000 life insurance policy in Maryann's name that they'd first heard about the day of Maryann's death. Maryann, at Tim's urging, had used the $5,000 her parents had given them as a wedding gift to buy the policy after Tim told her he was unable to obtain life insurance because of his heart problem.

"You're getting older," he told Maryann, who was 34 and in perfect health at the time. "Anything could happen."

In Cvetic's mind, the insurance policy was evidence of premeditation on Tim's part. "If you've just gotten married, and somebody gives you $5,000, buying life insurance is going to be the furthest thing from your mind," he said. "You might bankroll some of it, but you're going to use the rest to buy new furniture or as a down payment on a car. Who's going to spend it on insurance?"

Over the course of the week, Cvetic and McCarthy also exchanged numerous phone calls with Greensboro Police Detective Ken Brady. Brady offered to send the detectives a copy of his entire file on Elaine's death. Cvetic and McCarthy, in turn, sent Brady copies of witness statements and other documents and records relating to their investigation into Maryann's death.

The final piece of the puzzle fell into place on Monday, November 14, when the detectives learned the results of Allegheny County Coroner's Office pathologist Dr. Leon Rozin's autopsy on Maryann. According to Rozin, none of the evidence indicated that Maryann had drowned. The cause of death, he said, was asphyxiation due to blunt force trauma to the neck. Simply put, she was strangled.

Later that day, Cvetic and Ross Township Detective Gary Waters swore out a probable-cause affidavit in which they described the events of the early morning hours of November 7. They also enumerated some of the evidence they believed was indicative of Tim's guilt, including:

- His statement, "I hope they don't try to put this on me";
- His insistence that Maryann be taken to Allegheny General Hospital even though North Hills Passavant Hospital was closer;
- The fresh scratch marks Cvetic and Waters observed on Tim while interviewing him;
- His submitting to, and then failing, a lie-detector test.

At 7:30 a.m. on Tuesday, November 15, police from both Ross Township and Allegheny County's homicide division converged on Tim and Maryann's house. They knocked on the front door and when Tim opened it, Cvetic told him he was under arrest for the murder of Maryann

Boczkowski. According to Cvetic, Tim surrendered without incident.

"I think he just saw us as a nuisance," Cvetic would later say. "He thought he was going to be in charge. He thought he was smarter than us, than the prosecutor—everybody."

Tim was arraigned at the Allegheny County Courthouse, charged with criminal homicide, and ordered held without bail at the Allegheny County Jail pending a bail hearing set for Thursday, November 17. A coroner's hearing was set for 11 a.m. Tuesday, November 29.

Pat and Lew Fullerton declined comment when contacted by reporters. But Buc Boczkowski spoke out in his son's defense. "I honestly believe he didn't do this," he told the *North Hills News Record*. "This whole thing is blown way out of proportion. We have a good son, and we believe in him."

The night of Tim's arrest, Ross Township Police Detective Gary Waters stopped by Pat and Lew Fullerton's house to offer his condolences. Pat's sister, Ruth, and her husband, George, were there, too.

"Gary, do you really think he did it?" Pat wanted to know.

"Yes," he said without a moment's hesitation. "There is no doubt in my mind."

"Maybe she fell trying to get out?" countered Pat, who, out loud at least, was still refusing to even consider the possibility that Tim might have played a role in Maryann's death.

"I don't know if he killed her in the tub or not," Waters said. "But there was definitely a struggle in that tub."

At Tim's November 17 bail hearing, Common Pleas Judge David Cercone set his bail at $1 million cash. The prosecution cash argued that such a high sum was appropriate because Elaine's death remained under review in North Carolina. Tim's attorney, James Herb, argued that, while it was true that Elaine's death was under review, authorities had yet to file any charges. Cercone ultimately refused Herb's request to lower Tim's bail, but did make one concession to the defense. He would reconsider his decision, he said, if authorities in North Carolina failed to charge Tim with Elaine's death.

Meanwhile, in Greensboro, Detective Ken Brady was doing everything in his power to see that Tim was charged. Shortly after learning of Maryann's death, Brady attempted to contact Dr. Deborah Radisch, the associate North Carolina medical examiner who had performed Elaine's autopsy. But Radisch was no longer with the North Carolina Medical Examiner's office, so Brady, instead, approached Dr. John Butts, the state's chief medical examiner. He told Butts about the initial investigation into Elaine's death and about the latest developments in the case: about how Tim's second wife had just died under similar circumstances.

At Brady's request, Butts agreed to review the initial autopsy findings. He familiarized himself with the case by reading Brady's file on Elaine's death. He also reviewed Radisch's autopsy report and examined the original photographs taken at the autopsy. As he received more information from Allegheny County authorities about their investigation of the case, Brady forwarded it to Butts, including statements given to police by Randy, Sandy, and Todd the week following Maryann's death. As Detective James Cvetic would later explain, "We needed to find out what they knew."

According to Cvetic, all three children claimed not to have heard or seen anything the morning of Maryann's death, but both Sandy and Todd said they had heard their father and Elaine, their biological mother, arguing in the bathroom the morning of her death.

"They were nervous and it was an awkward situation," Allegheny County Police Sergeant Dave Schwab told the Greensboro *News & Record* following the children's interview. "[But they] were raised in a church environment. They certainly understand right from wrong."

The passage of time was a factor, too, Schwab said, in the children's ability to relate what had happened the morning Elaine died. "There's four years' difference now in their ages," he said, "so it's easier to speak with them."

As HE waited with great anticipation for the results of Butts's review, Brady began re-contacting witnesses he'd interviewed following Elaine's, among them Kevin Rochford.

"He screwed up," Brady told Rochford. "He did it again. We're going to get him now." Brady then shared some of what he knew with Kevin about what had transpired in Pittsburgh.

"My faith in Tim's stupidity hadn't been misplaced," Kevin would later say, recalling his initial reaction to the news of Maryann's death. "I knew he would do something dumb, and he did."

Two weeks after Tim's arrest, Butts filed a supplemental report on Elaine's death with the North Carolina Department of Health. In it, he made clear that the children's statements played a key role in his ultimate findings.

"During the investigation of Maryann [Boczkowski]'s death," he wrote, "further statements were taken from witnesses who were present in the residence at the time of the death of the first wife. These statements indicate that the story offered by Mr. Boczkowski regarding the probable cause of his wife's death could not be true. These accounts indicate that Mary Elaine Boczkowski was alive in the bathroom at the same time that her husband was also in the bathroom."

Butts concluded his report with his opinion as to the cause of Elaine's death, citing, in particular, the three parallel lines going across her mid-section that Dr. Radisch observed while performing Elaine's autopsy.

"Given the evidence of chest compression and the form of the imprint of the shower track on the lower chest and upper abdomen of Ms. Boczkowski, it is my opinion that her death was the result of asphyxia due to chest compression. The additional bruising present on the body was, in all probability, incurred during an accompanying struggle.

Tim Boczkowski at the Allegheny County Courthouse in Pittsburgh, PA, during the 1999 trial for the murder of his wife, Maryann Boczkowski.

Tim and Elaine Boczkowski on their wedding day: August 11, 1979.

Tim and Elaine, Halloween, 1980.

Tim and Elaine with son Randy, 2¹/₂, and daughter, Sandy, 6 weeks, in October 1983.

Tim and Elaine's apartment in Greensboro, North Carolina.

Maryann Fullerton with friend Shirley Marks' son, Adam, September 1991. COURTESY SHIRLEY MARKS

Maryann Fullerton *(left)* with aunt Ruth Schumann *(center)* and future husband Tim Boczkowski *(right)* in October 1992. COURTESY CLAUDIA DUNFORD

Tim and Maryann Boczkowski at their June 1993 wedding. COURTESY ELEANOR CAMP

Maryann Boczkowski and father Lew Fullerton at her wedding to Tim Boczkowski. COURTESY ELEANOR CAMP

Todd and Sandy Boczkowski at Tim and Maryann's wedding. COURTESY ELEANOR CAMP

The view from the back yard of Tim and Maryann's Ross Township, PA, home. The hot tub is located behind the cross-hatched fence. RUTH SCHUMANN

The hot tub in which Maryann Boczkowski was murdered by her husband Tim. RUTH SCHUMANN

Burial site of Elaine Boczkowski, St. Stanislaus Cemetery, Millvale, PA
RUTH SCHUMANN

Burial site of Maryann Fullerton Boczkowski, St. Anthony's Cemetery,
Millvale, PA. RUTH SCHUMANN

Tim Boczkowski at the Allegheny County Courthouse in Pittsburgh, PA, during the 1999 trial for the murder of his wife, Maryann Boczkowski.
PITTSBURGH TRIBUNE-REVIEW

Tim and Elaine Boczkowski on their wedding day: August 11, 1979.

Tim and Elaine, Halloween, 1980.

Tim and Elaine
with son Randy,
2 1/2, and daughter,
Sandy, 6 weeks, in
October 1983.

Tim and Elaine's apartment in Greensboro, North Carolina.

Maryann Fullerton with friend Shirley Marks' son, Adam, September 1991. COURTESY SHIRLEY MARKS

Maryann Fullerton *(left)* with aunt Ruth Schumann *(center)* and future husband Tim Boczkowski *(right)* in October 1992. COURTESY CLAUDIA DUNFORD

Tim and Maryann
Boczkowski at their June
1993 wedding. COURTESY
ELEANOR CAMP

Maryann Boczkowski and father Lew Fullerton at her wedding to Tim Boczkowski. COURTESY ELEANOR CAMP

Todd and Sandy Boczkowski at Tim and Maryann's wedding. COURTESY ELEANOR CAMP

The view from the back yard of Tim and Maryann's Ross Township, PA, home. The hot tub is located behind the cross-hatched fence. RUTH SCHUMANN

The hot tub in which Maryann Boczkowski was murdered by her husband Tim. RUTH SCHUMANN

Burial site of Elaine Boczkowski, St. Stanislaus Cemetery, Millvale, PA.
RUTH SCHUMANN

Burial site of Maryann Fullerton Boczkowski, St. Anthony's Cemetery,
Millvale, PA. RUTH SCHUMANN

The manner of death will be concomitantly changed from undetermined to homicide."

Concurrently with his supplemental report, Butts filed an amended death certificate for Elaine. Fifteen minutes later, Ken Brady had a warrant issued for Tim's arrest.

CHAPTER 22

PAT AND Lew Fullerton typically spent Thanksgiving in Pittsburgh, usually at the home of one of Pat's sisters. But in 1994, it was only after much cajoling that they agreed to celebrate the holiday at Pat's niece Jean Zappa's house. Since Maryann's funeral, her parents had hardly left their home. Church services and occasional trips to the grocery store were the extent of their forays into the outside world. They feared running into anyone they knew. They couldn't bear the thought of anyone bringing up Maryann's death, even if only to extend their condolences. Thus, it came as little surprise to those who'd spent time with the Fullertons since they'd lost their daughter that they chose not to attend the November 29 coroner's inquest into her death. However, close to two dozen family members and friends did turn out for the proceeding. People who had known Elaine Boczkowski were there, too, as were Tim's parents, Buc and Rose, his brother, Ron, and his sister, Joan, who had taken Randy, Sandy, and Todd into her home after Tim's arrest.

Shortly after 11 a.m., Tim, handcuffed and looking somewhat shell-shocked, was brought into the room and led to the defendant's table, where his handcuffs were removed and where his lawyer, James Herb, sat waiting.

Allegheny County Deputy District Attorney Chris Conrad called Dr. Leon Rozin, chief forensic pathologist for the Allegheny County Coroner's Office as his first witness. Rozin described in detail fifty-three different bruises that he believed Maryann suffered just prior to her death. These included severe contusions on her neck and in her throat and marks on her head and chest. The pathologist said he also detected hemorrhages in Maryann's right eye. This type of injury, he explained, is indicative of asphyxiation.

Rozin, at the same time, testified to a fact that lent some credibility to Tim's version of events. According to Rozin, Maryann, at the time of her death, had a blood-alcohol level of 0.22, more than twice the legal driving limit in Pennsylvania. But he dismissed the possibility that Maryann was so drunk that she drowned. He maintained, in fact, that because her lungs were not wet, drowning was not a possible cause of death. Rozin's final conclusion: That Maryann was asphyxiated, or suffocated, as a result of blunt force trauma to the neck.

James Herb, during his cross-examination of Rozin, focused on Maryann's inebriated state, suggesting that it had contributed to her death. He also asked the pathologist whether it was possible that Maryann's bruises were a result of efforts to revive her after she was found floating in the hot tub. Rozin, refusing to veer from his earlier testimony, dismissed both possibilities outright.

As his second witness, Conrad called Ross Township Police Detective Gary Waters. Waters explained how he'd been summoned to the scene after a uniformed officer heard Tim comment to his mother that he "wished" Waters were there. He described his initial conversation with Tim the morning of November 7, and how he observed what he believed was a scratch mark on Tim's neck, and a fresh "nick" on Tim's left thumb. Waters also testified that he spotted additional scratch marks on Tim's back and sides, and about Tim's contention that he'd asked Maryann to give him a "scratch massage" while they were in the hot tub—after maintaining at first that he didn't know how he'd obtained the scratches. Finally, Waters summarized the interview he and Allegheny County Police Detective Jim Cvetic conducted with Tim at Ross Township police headquarters; shared how Tim had failed a lie-detector test; and told how Tim had offered to tell the officers what really transpired the morning of Maryann's death *before* he asked to see an attorney.

Herb, as he had while cross-examining pathologist Rozin, attempted to get Waters to concede that the police officers and the paramedics who attempted to revive Maryann could have injured her in the process. Herb also downplayed Waters's claim that Tim nodded in agreement after the detective told Tim he believed he was responsible for Maryann's death. "A nod of the head? A blink of the eye?" Herb huffed. "That's supposed to be an admission?"

Herb's arguments were not altogether unconvincing, but they weren't enough to prevent Allegheny County Deputy Coroner Arthur Gilkes Jr., who presided over the two-and-a-half-hour proceeding, from ordering Tim to stand trial. He cited the scratch marks on Tim's body, the hemorrhages Rozin found in Maryann's right eye, and the fact that Tim was the only person in close proximity to Maryann the morning of her death, then declared, "There is no question in my mind that this was a homicide."

Afterwards, family and friends of Maryann who had attended the hearing remained behind in the gallery to discuss Gilkes's decision. Although they were well aware it was only the first step in what was likely to be a long, drawn-out process, they were pleased with the result. Some even cried. Then, as they began to gather their belongings, Deputy District Attorney Conrad asked for their attention. He had some news, he told the group. The authorities in Greensboro, Conrad said, after re-examining the results of Elaine Boczkowski's autopsy and considering new evidence they'd obtained since Maryann's death, had decided to charge Tim with her murder. Allegheny County police had received a copy of the warrant, he added, and would be arresting Tim on the North Carolina charge. The crowd gathered around the prosecutor spontaneously broke into a round of applause. They had been convinced, after learning the facts surrounding Elaine's death, that four years earlier, Tim had gotten away with murder. The law, they felt, was finally catching up with him.

Later that afternoon, several of Pat Fullerton's sisters stopped by to see her and Lew. Knowing that Pat's son,

John, attended the hearing, and had already informed his parents of the outcome, the women assumed Pat would finally see the light. Much to their dismay, Pat still could not bring herself to believe her son-in-law was responsible for her daughter's death.

"How do they know it was Tim?" she asked her sisters angrily. "They could be wrong. Why would he kill her?"

Pat's sisters all began yelling back at her at once. "How could it have been an accident?" they said, almost as if they were demanding an explanation from her. "What is the matter with you?"

Lew cut the argument short before it went any further.

"Enough," he said, his declaration clearly aimed at both his wife and her sisters. "This has got to stop."

CHAPTER 23

To no one's surprise, the ill will that prevailed between the Fullertons and Tim Boczkowski's parents in the days and weeks following Maryann's death did not lessen as time went on. The stress of the situation sometimes led to ugly encounters, such as one involving the teen-aged daughter of Maryann's cousin, Judy Cignarowicz, and Tim's parents after the coroner's inquest. While waiting tables at the Eat 'n Park in Ross Township, Amy Cignarowicz noticed Buc and Rose sitting in one of the restaurant's booths. That day, a local newspaper had reported what Randy, Sandy, and Todd Boczkowski told Pennsylvania authorities that had led North Carolina authorities to their ultimate decision to charge Tim with Elaine's death.

Although they weren't in her section, Amy boldly approached the couple's table. "How'd you like the paper today?" she quipped.

"Who are you?" Buc replied.

"Maryann was my cousin."

"Were you at the inquest?"

"Yes."

"Then you heard about Maryann's blood-alcohol level," Buc said. "She was a drunk."

"I also heard that she didn't have any water in her lungs," Amy replied.

"Ask her friends," Buc insisted. "They'll tell you she was a drunk."

"Well, I've known her all my life," countered Amy, who by this time was on the verge of tears, "and I never saw her drunk."

Amy then turned and ran to the back of the restaurant.

Buc and Rose, meanwhile, stood up and headed for the door, swearing they'd never patronize that Eat 'n Park again.

The two families even fought over Maryann's belongings. At one point, Pat and Lew went over to Tim and Maryann's to retrieve some of Maryann's things. They located a few items in particular that they'd hoped to find—an aquamarine birthstone ring Lew had bought a teen-aged Maryann, some of Maryann's sheet music, framed prints Maryann had bought while vacationing, and two sets of Fullerton family silverware. Pat also took Maryann's prayer cards and prayer book, which she found in her night table, and some of her hair combs and ribbons, which she later divided among Maryann's cousins. But the bitterness between the Fullerton and Boczkowski families remained. Maryann's relatives, in fact, would later come to believe that the real reason the Boczkowskis were willing to let them take anything from Maryann and Tim's house at all is because they were about to put it up for sale and were trying to empty it.

As the spring of 1995 approached, many of Maryann's friends and relatives were still struggling with the void her death left in their lives. So they decided to mark her birthday as they did every year—with a festive get-together.

On March 24, 1995—Maryann's thirty-sixth birthday—some seventy-five of her friends and relatives convened at the suburban Millvale home of Maryann's cousin, Judy Cignarowicz, where they celebrated Maryann's birthday with a Mass and dinner. Father Manuel Gelido, a Catholic priest and friend of Maryann's, officiated. The two had met in the early 1990s, after Maryann performed at a Nativity church event celebrating the cleric's birthday. Every ensuing year, Maryann had sung "Happy Birthday" to Father Manny, as he was known, on his birthday.

"I miss Maryann's voice," he conceded.

It wasn't altogether absent, though, thanks to Maryann's cousins, Jean Zappa and Joan Zalewski. At one point during the party, the twin sisters played a cassette tape-recording of Maryann singing a selection of church hymns. Many of those in attendance agreed it almost seemed, for a time at least, like Maryann was in their midst.

A short time after the celebration, after the ground that had been hardened by the harsh Pittsburgh winter began to soften, a flat tombstone engraved with the image of the Virgin Mary was installed at the site of Maryann's grave. Several of Pat Fullerton's sisters had suggested to Pat that she leave Maryann's married name off the stone. But Pat, still uncertain of Tim's guilt or innocence, refused, insisting that the stone read:

MARYANN FULLERTON BOCZKOWSKI
3/24/59–11/7/94

CHAPTER 24

Tim's trial for Maryann's murder was scheduled to begin in early October 1995, a little less than a year after her death. But in the end, legal wrangling by both the prosecution and the defense resulted in a significant delay.

The morning of September 25, 1995, Tim was delivered to the Allegheny County Courthouse for a pre-trial hearing. As he took his seat at the defense table, he turned to the gallery and smiled at his parents and his sister, Joan. As he often did when he appeared in court, he also gave them a thumbs-up and blew them a kiss.

The main point of contention between the prosecution and the defense was whether or not the prosecution would be allowed to present evidence relating to Elaine's death. Allegheny County Deputy District Attorney Chris Conrad contended that prohibiting its admission would unfairly hinder his attempt to prove that Tim had murdered Maryann.

"The likelihood that any man in this courthouse today would have had a wife die accidentally in a tub is very remote," Conrad argued. "But this man," he noted, pointing at Tim, "would like us to believe he had two wives die by accident in a tub."

Tim's attorney, James Herb, complained that allowing jurors to hear details about Elaine's death would "muddy up the waters" and make it difficult for them to keep the facts of the two cases straight.

After listening to both sides, Allegheny County Common Pleas Court Judge David Cercone ruled that he would allow Conrad to introduce evidence about Elaine's death, but only if the defense argued that Maryann's death was an accident.

Cercone also, at Herb's request, told spectators they would not be allowed to wear buttons bearing Maryann's photo inside the courtroom. He was referring to some fifty buttons that one of Maryann's cousins, Kathy Dunford, had made for the occasion. That day, more than twenty of Maryann's relatives and friends had donned the buttons, pinning them directly over their hearts. More than a few, too, showed up dressed completely in black.

Because emotions were running high, the climate was as tense outside the courtroom as it was inside. At one point, a small group of Maryann's relatives got into a shouting match with Tim's father, Buc, while he was being interviewed.

"We know he is innocent," Buc told a reporter.

"He brutally murdered two women," Maryann's aunt, Ruth Schumann, shouted at her late niece's father-in-law.

JURY SELECTION was slated to begin on October 2. But the proceedings came to a sudden halt when Conrad appealed Cercone's ruling to the state Superior Court. Still, the case continued to make headlines. James Herb told reporters that the Fullerton family's assertion that Tim, in killing Maryann, had tried to get away with murder for a second time was "preposterous" and promised to prove Tim's innocence in court.

It would turn out to be some time, however, before Herb had the chance to prove anything in court. The state Superior Court eventually agreed to consider Conrad's appeal, putting Tim's Pittsburgh trial on indefinite hold. The delay, however, provided the Guilford County, NC, District Attorney's Office with the opening it needed to proceed with Tim's trial for his first wife's murder, and on November 1, three days short of the five-year anniversary of Elaine's death, Tim was extradited to Greensboro.

CHAPTER 25

Upon his arrival in North Carolina, Tim was taken to the Guilford County Jail where he was held without bond. At a December 11, 1995, pre-trial hearing, Tim was represented by Doug Harris, a Greensboro attorney who often handled personal injury cases. Guilford County Assistant District Attorney Randy Carroll, a veteran prosecutor with some thirty capital cases under his belt, held forth for the state.

Carroll, the son of a diesel truck driver and a homemaker, was born in 1952 in Asheville, North Carolina, and raised in Charlotte. The first member of his family to attend college, he earned his law degree from Wake Forest University in 1978, and afterwards, took a job as a public defender in Guilford County. Four years later, he joined the Guilford County District Attorney's Office as an assistant district attorney, a position he continues to hold today. Carroll is known for his passionate opening and closing arguments and as an attorney who isn't afraid to shed a tear or two while addressing jurors. He says the empathy he feels for victims' families derives from his having experienced a similarly acute loss: his first wife's death in 1988 from cancer.

At issue during the December 11 hearing before Guilford County Superior Court Judge James Davis was the prosecution's desire to seek the death penalty against Tim.

Carroll, in arguing the state's case, noted that under North Carolina law, in order for a defendant to be sentenced to death, the prosecution must prove that at least one of eleven aggravating circumstances applies to his or her case. The aggravating circumstance Carroll chose to argue in

Tim's case was pecuniary gain. To this end, he contended that Tim's motive for killing Elaine was so he could collect on the $25,000 life insurance policy in her name.

Doug Harris took exception to Carroll's argument. "This is not one of those cases where a great big life insurance policy was taken out," Harris contended. "It was your ordinary insurance policy that most families have, and it seems to me it wasn't used for any pecuniary gain." He pointed out that Tim, in fact, profited little from Elaine's death. The money he received from Elaine's insurance, he noted, was used to pay for her funeral and to cover Tim's and the kids' moving expenses.

Davis was unmoved by Harris's argument that it was hardly worth taking someone's life for $25,000. "To some people, $500 is an incredible amount of money," the judge noted. "It's all relative."

After considering the arguments presented by both sides, Davis ruled that the prosecution could seek the death penalty against Tim. Not surprisingly, Carroll wasted little time before confirming that the state of North Carolina would do so should Tim be convicted of Elaine's murder.

Two weeks after learning that Tim, if convicted, would face the death penalty, Maryann's family celebrated their second Christmas without her. On Christmas Day, they met at a rented hall. At one point during the gathering, some of Maryann's younger cousins dimmed the lights and played a song that reminded them of Maryann—the Mariah Carey–Boyz II Men collaboration, "One Sweet Day"— while holding lit candles. Afterwards, several of them read brief tributes to Maryann that they'd written themselves. Two months later, just before what would have been Maryann's thirty-seventh birthday, her family placed a seven-day votive candle atop her grave. To this day, once a week, one of Maryann's cousins removes the burnt candle from the glass-and-brass candleholder in which it sits and replaces it with a new one.

*   *   *

TIM'S TRIAL for Elaine's murder began the morning of October 21, 1996, in Courtroom 4-C of the Guilford County Courthouse in Greensboro, with Superior Court Judge Catherine Eagles presiding. Tim now had two lawyers. In addition to Doug Harris, he was being represented by Fred Lind of the Guilford County Public Defender's Office. Lind had joined Tim's defense team as a result of a North Carolina statute that allows a defendant charged with a capital crime to request that the court appoint a second lawyer to aid in his or her defense.

Buc and Rose Boczkowski were in the courtroom, as were Tim's sister, Joan Spirk, and his brother, Ron. His sister, Pat, would arrive later in the proceedings. Buc preferred to sit by himself most of the time, one or two rows behind his wife and children. On the days they attended, friends of Tim's, such as St. Paul's parishioners Jim and Celia Borowicz, sat near Buc.

Randy Carroll, despite having been transferred from the Guilford County District Attorney's Greensboro office to its office in nearby High Point, remained in charge of the prosecution. "I was probably as motivated to try this case as I've ever been to try any case," said Carroll who, on any given day of the trial, could turn around and find some twenty friends and relatives of Elaine's and Maryann's sitting in the gallery behind him. "The fact that those kids lost their natural mother *and* the mother who adopted them . . ." he added, his voice trailing off. "My heart just went out to them."

Carroll, over the previous year, had become as well versed in the facts surrounding Maryann's death as he was in those surrounding Elaine's. In fact, in late August, he had traveled to Pittsburgh to meet with, among others, Detective Jim Cvetic, who would later join Carroll at the prosecutor's table during the trial. At one point during Carroll's Pennsylvania trip, he and Cvetic met with a group of people with an interest in both cases, including Maryann's parents, Pat and Lew Fullerton, and Elaine's sister, Janet Wisniewski, and her husband, Tim. Eileen Datt and Gay

Barbiaux and their husbands were there as well. Carroll briefed those gathered on how he planned to approach the North Carolina trial. He explained that he would be introducing evidence about both Elaine's and Maryann's deaths, in that order.

"Do you really think he did it?" Pat asked Carroll.

"Yes, I do," he replied softly.

Pat started to cry.

"Maybe you're wrong."

At this point, Cvetic stepped in.

"Mrs. Fullerton," he said, "in my twenty-three years as a detective, I've never been more sure of anything than I am that Tim murdered Maryann. We even have a witness, someone who was in jail with Tim, who is going to testify that Tim told him he did it."

"How can you believe a convict?" Pat asked through her tears. "Maybe he's lying."

Janet then asked Carroll whether he planned to call Randy, Sandy, or Todd as witnesses. At this point, the children were living with Tim's parents, Buc and Rose.

He did, he said.

THE PREVIOUS night, Carroll, Cvetic, and ACPD Detective Kevin McCarthy had gone to Buc and Rose's Ross Township home, armed with court orders authorizing Carroll to interview the children. It was their statements, after all, that had helped convince North Carolina authorities that Tim had killed Elaine.

Only Rose and Sandy were home when the trio arrived at roughly 5:30 p.m. A short time later, Buc returned with Randy and Todd in tow.

"Buc went crazy," Cvetic would later recall. "He yelled for Rose to call Tim's attorney, James Herb, and then started calling us Nazis."

"It was totally uncalled for," Carroll said. "We hadn't done anything intimidating or unethical. We went out of our way to do everything the right way."

At about 6:15 p.m., Cvetic, McCarthy, and Carroll departed with the children for the ACPD's Pittsburgh head-quarters. But once downtown, the children refused to repeat what they'd told investigators when they were interviewed the week after Maryann's death. "They weren't very talk-ative," Carroll would later recall. "In fact, they were actu-ally pretty withdrawn."

At one point, Carroll tried to remind the children what they'd said. "Didn't you tell Detective Cvetic that you heard your mother scream and saw your dad holding her over the side of the tub?" he asked.

"He made us say that," Randy replied.

"They were nice kids, they were smart kids, and they were honest kids." Cvetic would later say. "But I think there were some things they just refused to believe. Who wants to think their father killed their mother and their step-mother?"

When the detectives returned the children to Rose and Buc's home at roughly 8:40 p.m., Buc launched another verbal assault, calling the officers "Nazis, Gestapo, sneaks, and liars."

The children's refusal to talk to Carroll would lead the prosecutor, down the road, to reassess whether to call them to testify against their father. But it did little to dim Carroll's view of his case as a whole. He remained convinced Tim was guilty and was confident he could prove it in court.

ON OCTOBER 23, after an eight-woman, four-man jury was seated, Carroll began his opening argument. He told the panel how Tim and Elaine had moved from Pittsburgh to Greensboro in the mid-1980s, eventually settling in an apartment in the city's Yester Oaks townhouse complex.

"Elaine Boczkowski," Carroll said, "died in the bath-room in the upstairs of that apartment in the early morning hours of November 4, 1990." Afterwards, Carroll told the jurors, "the defendant made a statement in which he said that she had been drinking heavily earlier that night. He said he heard what sounded like something falling in the bathroom and that she apparently fell, hit her head, and drowned."

"You'll hear evidence from various witnesses the defendant [said] that to," Carroll said. But, he added, "you will hear from various witnesses [to whom] the defendant gave conflicting statements. To some people he said they had an argument. To others, there was no argument. But the common theme in all of his statements, to the police as well as civilian witnesses, was that she fell in the tub after drinking heavily, hit her head and drowned. But the medical examiner will testify that there was no alcohol in her blood, and the first witnesses on the scene will say there was little to no water in the bathtub or anywhere in the bathroom."

But what the medical examiner couldn't determine back in 1990, Carroll explained, was the exact cause of Elaine's death. As a result, the police were unable to charge Tim with murder, or any other crime for that matter.

Carroll then described how Tim moved back to Pittsburgh, how he met and married Maryann, and how on November 7, 1990, four years to the day that he buried Elaine, Maryann was found dead in the hot tub behind their house.

Carroll explained how Greensboro Police Detective Ken Brady, armed with this new information, went to North Carolina's chief medical examiner and asked him to review the original report on Elaine's autopsy. He also provided the medical examiner with the statements Tim and Elaine's three children made to Pennsylvania investigators about having heard their parents arguing in the bathroom the morning of Elaine's death. About a week later, the medical examiner amended the cause of death on Elaine's death certificate from "undetermined" to "asphyxiation due to chest compression." Fifteen minutes after that, Brady obtained a warrant for Tim's arrest.

Finally, Carroll told the jurors about some of the witnesses he planned to call, including Tim and Elaine's three children and a witness who heard Tim himself admit that he had killed both Elaine and Maryann.

Carroll would later say that as he delivered his opening

argument, he couldn't help but notice Tim's lack of emotion. "It was like he was an inanimate object," he said. "He didn't even look around the courtroom. He just sort of stared straight ahead."

DOUG HARRIS, in his opening statement, attempted to paint a picture of Tim as "a normal family man."

"He had three children who were happily in school in Greensboro," Harris said. "He had a wife. He had a job. He had a home. Mr. Boczkowski was living a normal life, having never been involved in any crime ever in his life, ladies and gentlemen."

"There was some strife going on in the marriage," Harris conceded, "and by strife, I mean merely that they had had a talk. They were going to separate. They had agreed what to do and how to do it. The evidence will show that there was never, never, any violence in the marriage. Not any. The evidence will show that there was never, never any adultery or any misconduct of that sort in the marriage. The evidence will show that Mr. and Mrs. Boczkowski were normal, church-going people."

Harris told the jurors that they would be hearing from an expert witness who was going to testify that Elaine died as a result of a "dry drowning," which sometimes happens "when the body is suddenly and unexpectedly thrust [into] water. The esophagus closes so that you cannot get air. If you are immediately plucked out of the water, you live. If you stay under the water, you die the old-fashioned way."

Tim and Elaine's daughter, Sandy, Harris said, would be testifying, too—about what transpired in the upstairs bathroom in Tim and Elaine's Yester Oaks townhouse the morning of November 4, 1990.

"She heard the water running late at night. She heard the water running and running and running and then she heard some kind of strange thump. She went to the bedroom, not to the bathroom, to see who was [there]. Her father was asleep in the bedroom with his earphones on. You will hear from her mouth that she awoke her father and went with [him] to the bathroom door. [And] you will hear that Mr. Boczkowski had to get a screwdriver to get in the door."

Harris's point here was clear. If Tim had to get a screwdriver to open the bathroom door from the outside, there was no way, as the prosecution contended, that he could have been inside strangling his wife.

CHAPTER 26

CHARLIE CONNOLLY, a member of St. Paul the Apostle Parish who attended the church's Polish dance the night of November 3, was among the witnesses Carroll called to testify on the trial's first day. Carroll used their testimony to establish both that Elaine seemed to be in a good mood that night and the fact that she did not appear drunk to fellow partygoers. Connolly, a case worker for a ministry for the disadvantaged, testified that he and Elaine, whom he had seen dancing a polka with another church member at one point, spoke briefly while cleaning up after the dance. Connolly testified that Elaine mentioned a recent job interview that she felt had gone well, and how "she kind of felt like she was getting her life together . . . She felt for the first time in her life she had some choices."

Connolly added, too, that he could not recall seeing Elaine drink at the dance and that in no way did she seem impaired at the time she left. Connolly, in fact, noted that he and his wife saw Tim and Elaine regularly at church functions and on various social occasions, and that he had never considered her to be more than a social drinker. A glass of wine was her usual limit.

To suggest to the jury that the settlement Tim and Elaine were expecting to receive from Elaine's 1989 car accident was very much on Tim's mind the night of Elaine's death, Carroll asked Connolly about a conversation he'd had with Tim several weeks prior. Connolly testified that Tim had called him one day out of the blue and asked him to dinner. The two men met at a Shoney's restaurant, and, at one point during the meal, Connolly said, Tim mentioned he had a lawsuit pending against the driver who'd rear-ended Elaine.

Shortly thereafter, Carroll called Chris Cheek, a close friend of Elaine's. Cheek was one of the St. Paul the Apostle members sitting in the church library with Father Jim Weisner the night Tim came by and insisted to the priest that they had to talk about what Tim called "this situation," meaning the priest's relationship with Elaine. Cheek testified that about a month earlier, Elaine had come to her in tears, distraught over the fact that Tim had gone through her journal. According to Cheek, Elaine told her Tim had read some entries she had written about the priest and "was trying to make something very ugly of it."

"She was extremely upset," Cheek testified. "In fact, she sat and cried for about thirty minutes."

Elaine, too, Cheek said, "made reference to something that happened in the bedroom [after Tim] had read her journal. She did not talk in detail about it. There was something about being back against the bed."

Cheek also testified about a conversation she and Elaine once had about Elaine and Tim's dire financial straits. She said Elaine had told her things had gotten so tight that she was worried about not having enough money to buy food.

"How am I going to feed my kids?" Elaine wondered to Cheek.

It was this very conversation, Cheek explained to Carroll, which led her to become involved in the disposition of Elaine's estate. Cheek testified that a month or two before the first anniversary of Elaine's death, she learned not only that Tim was in town but that he was driving a Mercedes. This infuriated her. A determined Cheek said she took it upon herself to look into the matter of Elaine's will. She went down to the county courthouse and obtained a copy. It was, she said, a standard will, with Tim named as the beneficiary. But when she flipped to the page with the witnesses' signatures, she noticed that Tim had signed his name as a witness. Having worked as a paralegal, Cheek was somewhat familiar with estate law in North Carolina and knew that there, it is illegal for someone to witness a will in which they are named as a beneficiary. Cheek testified that she then filed a petition—which was granted—for a guardian *ad litem* to be appointed to protect Randy, Sandy, and Todd's interests.

Kevin Rochford followed Creek to the witness stand, and Carroll hit him immediately with a series of questions intended to suggest that financial gain—his alone—could have been the reason behind Tim's killing Elaine. He testified that sometime after Elaine's car accident, Tim asked him what he characterized as "probably the strangest question I've ever had since I started practicing law . . .

"He wanted to sue [the woman who had rear-ended Elaine]," Rochford testified, "because he thought he should be compensated because his wife wanted too much sex . . . He didn't like that . . . He said that after the accident, she changed; that, apparently, she was trying to rekindle their marriage. She was worried it had been dying out, that she could have been killed, that her kids could have been killed, and she wanted to give it one last shot, rekindle it."

Kevin glanced over to the jury box. He noticed several jurors chuckling. "It was obvious they couldn't believe he had asked me about suing that woman."

Tim had approached Rochford for legal advice on another occasion as well. Rochford said it wasn't long after a burglar had broken into King Kones that Tim told him he "wanted to find out who did it so that he could sue that person for intentional infliction of emotional distress and get some money out of it."

Rochford testified that after Elaine told him, about two months before her death, that she wanted to leave Tim, he referred her to Lee Cecil, a partner in his firm and a specialist in domestic law. "She said that she needed to get away, she needed to get on with her life, and would someone in my firm . . . help her out at a reduced cost?" he said.

Elaine told Rochford she was so strapped for cash that while she managed to keep up the premium payments on a $25,000 life insurance policy in her name, she'd been forced to let a $10,000 policy lapse. Elaine indicated to Rochford, too, that she was upset that Tim had signed a listing agreement to sell their business for less than its value without her knowledge.

Eventually, Carroll questioned Rochford about the polka dance. Rochford testified that Elaine had confided in him that because it was the first church function she and Tim would both be at since they'd agreed to separate, she was a little apprehensive about going. She told him, too, that she and Tim argued that day about Tim having bought himself some new clothes they could ill afford to wear to the dance that night. But later in the evening, Elaine admitted that she had been wrong to worry and that "she was having a great time."

Rochford testified that he saw Tim at the dance, too.

"How are you doing?" he asked Tim after bumping into him in the church foyer.

Tim said he was "doing okay," that "he was having a good time," and that "he was looking forward to meeting another woman sometime soon . . . somebody a little taller with a little smaller boobs."

Finally, Rochford testified that he, his wife Marianne, and Elaine were the last people to leave St. Paul the Apostle that night. The trio chatted in the parking lot for some twenty minutes before finally parting ways. Neither he nor Marianne would see Elaine alive again.

Moments later, Judge Eagles recessed the proceedings until 9:15 the next morning.

CHAPTER 27

THURSDAY MORNING'S testimony began with Kevin Rochford returning to the witness stand.

Carroll scored a point for the prosecution right off the bat when he asked Rochford to recall a question Elaine had asked him while he, his wife, Marianne, and Elaine were talking in the parking lot following the dance.

"She asked me to talk with her on Monday morning because she wanted to make a new will," Rochford testified. "She wanted to make sure that her husband wouldn't get anything if something happened to her."

Rochford then recalled Tim's version of events, following Elaine's return from the dance, exposing inconsistencies in Tim's various accounts of Elaine's death. Rochford testified that Tim had told him that after he knocked on the bathroom door and Elaine failed to answer, he went to get a screwdriver. Tim said he tried initially to pry the door open with the screwdriver, but when that didn't work, he "tried to work on the hinges." But when Rochford went upstairs to check out the bathroom door, he testified, he didn't see any scratch or pry marks.

"I didn't notice any marks of any significance whatsoever, certainly nothing that would [make it] look like it had been pried open in an emergency situation," he said.

Rochford, moreover, noted that the door's hinges were inside the bathroom and that the door was still attached to the hinges.

"With the bathroom door being closed and locked, would it have been possible to take the door off the hinges?" Carroll asked.

"I don't see how," Rochford said. "That's what got me concerned."

Rochford then testified about the two unsettling conversations he had with Tim the day of Elaine's death: the one in which Tim had asked Kevin how soon he could collect on Elaine's life insurance policy, and the one during which he showed Kevin what he claimed were bruises he had suffered in a motorcycle accident—bruises Kevin couldn't see.

Carroll concluded his questioning of Rochford with what seemed to be a pre-emptive strike against what he presumed would be the defense's argument that Tim never really believed Elaine's relationship with Father Jim was more than platonic.

Had Tim ever talked to him about Elaine's relationship with Father Weisner? he asked.

He had, Rochford said. "He was threatened by that relationship," Rochford continued. "He had, apparently, read [Elaine's] journal and was threatened."

Tim, Rochford testified, had also made a comment to him about yet another relationship he thought Elaine was having. "The Sunday before her death," Rochford said, "after the church service, he came up to me out in the foyer and he said, 'Do you know my wife was out until five o'clock in the morning last night? What do you think about that?' "

"What was your response?" asked Carroll.

"I didn't respond. My firm was representing her in a domestic action, so I was not about to respond."

Harris, during his cross-examination of Rochford, tried to further the defense's contention that Tim and Elaine's separation was proving to be a relatively amicable one. "Didn't she say to you the night of her death that she didn't care whether she got child support or not, [that] it didn't matter to her?" he asked Rochford. "Did she say that to you?"

"Yes, she did."

"And didn't she say to you that they had agreed the children would live with her?"

"Yes, but she was very worried that he was going to fight for custody."

"Well, they had agreed the children were going to live with her [and] she had agreed she didn't want child support, so there was no apparent fight, was there . . . Indeed, there seemed to be every likelihood she would be free of him. She was happy. Everything was going great that night, true?"

"That night," Rochford agreed. "But up until that time, she was very afraid."

"Well, in point of fact, she never said all that stuff about being afraid, did she?"

"She certainly said it in my office with my partner and I."

Harris ignored Rochford's response and, switching gears, instead asked Rochford to turn his attention to the night of the dance. His intention was to raise the possibility that Elaine was so tired that she very well could have fallen asleep in the bathtub the morning she died.

"She had had a long day, had she not?" Harris asked.

"Yes. She said she was tired."

"She helped you take down all the tables and chairs?"

"It was important for her to have the sanctuary clean for church."

"Yes, of course," Harris said, "and all of you were helping?"

"Absolutely."

"So . . . you can personally attest that she was doing a lot of physical labor and she was tired?"

"She was tired."

To discredit the state's argument that Elaine might have been having an affair and that anger or jealousy on Tim's part could have a played a role in her death, Harris touched on Rochford's earlier testimony about the comment Tim had made to him about Elaine having stayed out until 5 o'clock one morning.

"I'm asking if, as far as you knew, there was any adultery going on. There wasn't, was there?"

"Yes," Rochford responded, catching Harris off guard. "As far as I knew, there was."

"There was?" a surprised Harris responded.

"Yes," Rochford testified. "After Tim talked to me, I went to Elaine and said, 'Elaine, what's going on? We're representing you in a domestic action. Don't make our lives more difficult.' " He said he also warned her, "There's a lot of mean people out there," to which she responded, "I'm fine. They're nice people. I'm okay.' "

"And from that," Harris wanted to know, "you took that she was committing adultery?"

"That's what I inferred. That she was out until five o'clock in the morning with somebody."

The verbal sparring match between Harris and Rochford continued until Harris was satisified that he'd made his point: that Rochford's conclusion that Elaine was having an affair was just that—his own conclusion. There was no hard evidence proving or even suggesting that was the case.

Finally, Harris asked Rochford what he knew about Tim and Elaine's money problems. He knew establishing that Tim and Elaine were in dire financial straits would go a long way toward demonstrating Tim had little to gain monetarily from Elaine's death, and eliminating money as a possible motive.

"There's nothing extraordinary about a $25,000 policy, is there?"

"No."

"And Elaine Boczkowski's estate wasn't all that big either, so you knew they didn't have much?"

"That's correct," Rochford conceded.

Carroll, during redirect, tried to make the point that as far as Rochford knew, Tim was unaware that under North Carolina law, the beneficiary of a will cannot witness that will as well.

"Did Mr. Boczkowski ever tell you that he knew that

there was a problem with the will, and he wouldn't receive anything under it?" Carroll asked.

"He never discussed the will," Rochford responded.

Carroll then asked Rochford about his testimony that Elaine told him and Lee Cecil that she was afraid of Tim. Harris had shut the door on that subject by ignoring Rochford's statement to that effect. But Carroll re-opened it and, in doing so, opened a can of worms that left the defense squirming.

"You mentioned that you were present with your partner, Lee Cecil, when Elaine Boczkowski expressed some concerns for her safety?" Carroll asked.

"Yes, I was," Rochford replied.

"Mr. Harris didn't ask you about that," Carroll reminded Rochford. "Tell the jury about that."

"When I introduced her to my partner, Lee Cecil, I sat in just as a friend. She talked about her situation. Lee asked if she was at all fearful. She said she was very fearful. She explained that when her husband was under financial strain, he tended to be very destructive."

"Tended to be what?" Carroll asked, well aware of the dramatic impact Rochford's repeating his answer would have on the jury.

"Destructive. Violent."

Harris objected. He knew where Carroll was headed.

"Overruled," Eagles declared.

"During the course of that conversation," Carroll continued, "did she indicate whether or not she was afraid of him, as a result of that?"

"Yes. Based upon past history, she was afraid of what he might do."

"And what past history was that?"

Harris objected again. "I'd like to be heard out of the presence of the jury," he then asked Eagles.

After Eagles excused the jury, Harris, knowing Carroll was going to ask Rochford about the incident with the gas back in Claysville, voiced his objection to Rochford being allowed to testify about it. Eagles said she would rule on

Harris' objection after hearing Rochford's testimony, and asked Carroll to proceed.

"Exactly what [did she say] was the basis for those concerns?" Carroll asked with the jury still out of the courtroom.

Rochford explained that Elaine had told him that in the past, Tim, whenever he was facing financial problems, tended to act erratically. He also testified that during her initial meeting with Lee Cecil, Elaine related a story she had shared with Rochford before. He said she described how one Sunday morning, when she and Tim were still living in Pennsylvania, Tim told her to gather the children because they were all going to spend the day at Tim's parents' house. Elaine said that after dropping her and the kids at his parents', Tim went back to their home in Claysville and turned on the gas. His goal, she said, was to blow up the house so he could collect on their homeowner's insurance policy. But after returning to his parents' house and telling his father what he had done, Buc insisted they return to the house to turn off the gas and prevent any explosion.

Harris contended that Rochford should not be allowed to testify about the incident for three reasons: First, it wasn't even "remotely" related to Elaine's alleged murder. Second, the police had never investigated the incident. And third, Tim was never charged with any crime. Thus, he insisted, there was no verifiable proof that the incident even occurred. Carroll argued that Harris opened the door to Rochford's testimony when he asked Rochford whether Elaine had any concerns about her safety. He also noted that he planned to call Lee Cecil as a witness later in the trial and that Cecil would corroborate Rochford's testimony.

After considering both lawyers' arguments, Judge Eagles decided to allow Rochford to testify about the incident.

"In light of the fact that the defense has asked numerous questions of several witnesses already about the lack of fear [and] lack of violence in the relationship," she stated, explaining her decision, "I believe I'll overrule the objection."

Once the jury returned to the courtroom, Carroll again asked Rochford about the incident. He then revisited the question of whether or not Elaine was having an affair. Although in North Carolina, the prosecution is not required to prove motive, Carroll knew the possibility that Elaine was being unfaithful would raise the question of motive in jurors' minds.

"Were you aware as to whether or not Timothy Boczkowski had had a vasectomy?" Carroll asked Rochford.

"I was aware that he had had a vasectomy," Rochford responded. "Yes."

"And at some point after Elaine's death, were you aware of birth control pills being found in her pocketbook?"

"She had birth control pills. Yes."

"How did you learn about that?"

"They were in her purse."

"Did you see them for yourself?"

"My wife did. My wife found them."

Under re-cross, Harris zeroed in on Rochford's testimony that Elaine had told him that Tim could be destructive and violent when under financial strain.

"You made some reference to potentially violent acts." he said. "The truth is that you, yourself, don't know of any acts of domestic violence involving Tim and Elaine Boczkowski, do you?"

"No, sir, I don't."

Harris then queried Rochford about the fact that there was no mention of the gas incident in Elaine's diary.

"Would it surprise you to learn that there's not any mention whatsoever of this Pennsylvania incident in that diary? Not a scrap. Would that surprise you?"

"No, it wouldn't surprise me."

"Would it surprise you to learn there's not a scrap of mention in her personal diary, in which she supposedly [wrote] everything, of any kind of fear of her husband? Would that surprise you?"

"No, that wouldn't surprise me," Rochford replied.

Harris thanked Rochford and sat down at the defense

table. Clearly, he was satisfied he'd made his point. A few minutes later, Eagles called for a fifteen-minute recess. Rochford had been on the stand for ninety long minutes that morning, and all parties, the judge appeared to sense, could use a break.

CHAPTER 28

FOLLOWING THE recess, Harris, in anticipation of Carroll calling attorney Lee Cecil as his next witness, renewed his objection to testimony about the gas incident. Carroll promised Eagles he would not dwell on the subject. Again, Eagles overruled Harris's objection.

Once on the witness stand, Cecil testified that he met with Elaine at least three times, the last time being on October 18. He last spoke with her by phone, he said, on October 31. When Carroll asked him about any fears Elaine may have had for her safety, Cecil recalled a conversation he'd had with her about a separation agreement he was in the process of drafting.

"When I mentioned it to her, she said, 'I don't want to talk to him about the agreement. He's going to go ballistic.' She was concerned how he would react when he realized he would have to pay . . . child support or that he would have to divide [their] property with her."

"Did you or Mr. Rochford ask her the basis for that concern?" Carroll asked.

"We did," Cecil replied.

"Now before we get to that, did she relate at any time that he had physically abused her?"

"I don't recall any specific instances of physical violence," Cecil said. "I recall her telling me that when they would discuss the financial aspects of their divorce, that he would become irrational."

"Do you recall the example that she gave you and Mr. Rochford when you asked about her concerns?"

Cecil related how Elaine had talked about Tim's unsuccessful attempt to blow up the couple's Pennsylvania home.

During his cross-examination of Cecil, Harris forced the attorney to admit that he did not have any independent knowledge of the gas incident, that he only knew about it because Elaine had mentioned it to him. Harris, however, was unable to prove that Elaine had made up the story, or that Rochford and Cecil were perjuring themselves.

The next witness to take the stand was Greensboro firefighter Willie Jones, who, with fellow fireman Bobby Mitchell, had carried Elaine out of the bathroom and into the hallway.

After Jones described how he and Mitchell attempted to resuscitate Elaine, Carroll asked the firefighter if he had talked to Tim that morning.

"He told me that he and his wife had been in an argument, and that she was upset with him about a trip he was about to take with somebody else," Jones responded. "Some golf trip."

Jones also testified that Tim told him that he'd heard a "thump" but that "he didn't check it out [for] a few minutes because he didn't think it was anything."

It was while cross-examining Jones that Harris began laying the groundwork for the defense's argument that Elaine could have suffered some of the bruises on her body at the hands of rescue personnel or during her autopsy.

"I heard you say that you and your partner lifted her out and took her into the hallway," Harris noted. "Because of the tight conditions and her body weight . . . would it have been difficult for you to move her out by yourself, in your view?"

"Moving a dead body, or a body that's dead weight?" Jones replied. "Yes, sir, it's kind of difficult for one person."

But Carroll, during his re-direct, took Jones back to his description of how Elaine's feet were up against the door when he first looked into the bathroom.

"You said her head was at the door and her feet were at the tub?" Carroll asked the firefighter.

"Yes, sir," Jones said. "But if I was to step inside that

bathtub," Jones explained, "I would have more than likely had [the person] by the upper extremities than the lower extremities coming out . . . That would have meant that [their] head would have been at the door and not at the tub."

Carroll's intention here was clear. The fact that Elaine's head was up against the tub while her feet were at the door suggested that Tim never actually pulled Elaine out of the tub, a direct contradiction of what Tim claimed to have done.

However, Harris, during his re-cross of Jones, suggested that one possible reason Tim had placed Elaine's head against the tub and her feet against the door was to ensure that her head did not get hit should someone open the door.

"Anybody opening the door would have hit Ms. Boczkowski's head, just as you hit her feet when you tried to open the door when you came in, true?" Harris asked the firefighter.

"Yes," Jones conceded.

It was roughly 12:30 p.m. when Judge Eagles excused the jury for lunch. At that point, Harris said he had an issue to raise.

"If Your Honor please," he began, "I notice a number of . . . people in the courtroom wearing little ribbons commemorating Maryann Boczkowski. I don't object to the sentiment, but I do think that it might be inappropriate to be [wearing them] inside the courtroom and I would ask that [they] be instructed not to wear that sort of thing while the trial is going on in front of the jury."

The ribbons Harris was referring to were actually small purple "victim" ribbons that were attached to buttons bearing Maryann's photo. Before court resumed Thursday morning, four of Maryann Boczkowski's aunts who had driven from Pittsburgh to Greensboro for the trial met with Randy Carroll in his office. Each had on one of the buttons. They were the same ones they'd been ordered to remove during the coroner's inquest in Pittsburgh.

"Will it be okay if we wear them here?" one asked the prosecutor.

Carroll said he had no problem with the display, but suspected Judge Eagles very well might. His intuition proved correct.

"Well," Eagles said, "out of an abundance of caution, I think I will ask people in the courtroom to remove any photographs that they might be wearing of anybody involved in the case when we come back from lunch."

CHAPTER 29

FOLLOWING SOME brief testimony by one of the first paramedics to arrive at Tim and Elaine's apartment, Carroll called Greensboro Police Officer Brenda Gilmore-Vance to the stand.

Gilmore-Vance, in response to Carroll's asking her to describe the scene she encountered upon entering Tim and Elaine's apartment, testified that firefighter Willie Jones accompanied her inside the townhouse, then directed her to the upstairs hallway bathroom. Once there, she went inside for a closer look.

"It being a drowning," the policewoman said, "I expected to find a lot of water splattered on the floor . . . and I [didn't]."

Even the vomit she noticed inside the bathtub was a "dry clump," she testified.

Gilmore-Vance went on to explain that she was so surprised to find the bathroom so dry that she went and checked the bathroom off of the master bedroom, thinking that maybe she had somehow misunderstood Jones. But that bathroom, too, she said, was completely dry.

"Officer, have you at any time yourself attempted to submerge yourself in a tub of water?" Carroll asked next.

Before Gilmore-Vance could utter a word, Harris objected and asked again to be heard out of the presence of the jury. Harris knew Carroll was about to ask Gilmore-Vance about an experiment Greensboro Police Detective Ken Brady conducted with her help after learning of Maryann's death. The purpose of the exercise was to demonstrate that it was essentially impossible for someone of Elaine's

size to be totally submerged in the bathtub in Tim and
Elaine's upstairs hallway bathroom.

"Your Honor, what you're about to hear is one of the
strangest, most unscientific tests I've ever heard in my life,"
Harris argued.

Judge Eagles said she wanted to hear Gilmore-Vance'
testimony before ruling on Harris's objection.

"Would you describe what occurred for Her Honor
please?" Carroll asked the policewoman.

"I dressed in leotards and a T-shirt as a minimum of
clothing, got in the tub and filled water in it until it started
to cover my head. The water came up to the side of my
face, up to my cheek bones, and by the time it got to that
level, it was enough water that my head floated up. The
only way I could keep my head down for the water to be
[over] my head was to hold it down, and the water started
going out the overflow valve before it was ever enough to
cover me."

Gilmore-Vance testified, too, that she performed the
same test in her own bathroom after her shift ended the day
Elaine died.

"I had a tub the same size," she testified, "and, at that
time, I weighed, basically, the same that the victim
weighed, 150 pounds."

During her experiment, too, Gilmore-Vance said, "the
water started running out before it actually covered my
face."

Harris, while cross-examining the policewoman, fired
off a series of questions about a number of physical differ-
ences between her and Elaine, and some circumstantial var-
iants. His goal in doing so was to convince Eagles that both
of the experiments held little scientific value.

Eagles pondered both sides' arguments.

"I'll overrule the objection," Eagles declared. "You can
bring the jury back in."

By this point, however, Dr. Elizabeth Barnes, one of the
doctors who treated Elaine in the Wesley Long emergency
room the morning of her death—at the time, she went by

er maiden name, Stewart—had arrived at the courthouse. Carroll asked for permission, which Eagles granted, to call Barnes to the witness stand before recalling Gilmore-Vance. Barnes, who, at the time of Elaine's death, also worked in the family practice group that Elaine sometimes visited, described being called to Wesley Long the morning of November 4 by Dr. Vincent Cheek, the emergency room physician on duty. Barnes testified that she and Cheek redoubled the efforts of the paramedics who had tried to resuscitate Elaine. At one point, she said, they did detect a pulse. "But it was a 'temporary response,' " Barnes explained. "We never had her breathing again or had her heart going again on its own."

Carroll asked the doctor to recollect the conversation she had with Tim outside the emergency room that morning. His intention was to show how Tim, from the start, offered conflicting versions of what had transpired the night of the dance and the morning of Elaine's death.

Barnes testified that at no point did Tim mention to her, as he had to firefighter Willie Jones, that he and Elaine had argued Saturday night. He did, however, stress to Barnes that Elaine had been drinking at the dance Saturday night, something he never brought up with Jones.

Then, in an attempt to support Rochford's testimony that Elaine had begun seeing someone after she and Tim separated, Carroll asked Barnes why Elaine had visited another physician at Barnes's practice on Thursday, November 1. Barnes referred to Elaine's patient file.

Barnes, reading from the file, testified, "She and her husband have separated and although she has no serious relationships in her life, the potential exists in the near future and she wishes not to be caught without a form of birth control available to her."

Fred Lind questioned Barnes for the defense. He completely ignored the issue of the birth control pills and instead, focused on possible ways Elaine could have suffered the bruises observed on her body during her autopsy, including one on the top of her head.

"Doctor Barnes," Lind began, "if Elaine Boczkowski had hit her head on the side of the bathtub, that could account for the bruises on the head, could it not?"

"It's difficult for me to imagine a fall that would involve the top of the head hitting the edge of a shower or bath."

"How about any resuscitative efforts? There's been testimony that when the [firefighters] came in, she was lying down . . . next to the bathtub . . . in a small area. Certainly, if the head were [to be] pushed back in a resuscitative effort, that could cause a bruise on top of the head, couldn't it?"

"In the course of normal resuscitation, bruises around the face might make sense, because you put a mask [there] to breathe for someone. But bruises on the top of the head would not be part of the normal resuscitation effort."

Lind continued this line of questioning for several minutes, but at no point did Barnes give any ground.

"How about if somebody passed out, slipped, and hit their head in the bathtub? That certainly could cause a bruise, couldn't it?" he asked.

"Certainly, but it's the location of the bruises," Barnes insisted. "Most people don't fall on top of their head."

Carroll, after Lind pronounced that he had no further questions for Barnes, stood up and posed only a single query. "In your medical opinion, would the bruises be more consistent with a struggle in which Timothy Boczkowski had her pinned over the edge of the tub—"

Before he could finish, Harris objected.

"Overruled," Eagles declared.

"—choking her to death while she was flailing around hitting her head?"

"That would seem to be more likely," Barnes agreed.

"Move to strike," Lind requested.

"Denied," Eagles declared.

UPON RECALLING Gilmore-Vance, Carroll picked up where he'd left off: by asking the policewoman to describe the experiment she conducted in her own bathtub the same day Elaine died.

"And having observed the tub in the apartment and your own tub," Carroll asked, once the officer had finished, "are they approximately the same size?"

"As far as I could tell."

"Okay, and—"

"Objection," Harris snickered.

"Overruled."

"I object to him sitting over there laughing," Carroll said to Eagles.

"Ladies and gentlemen, it will be up to you to evaluate the testimony," Eagles told the jury. "And I'll ask all counsel," she added, "to keep their own opinions to themselves."

CHAPTER 30

FRIDAY MORNING, early in his cross-examination of Gilmore-Vance, Harris asked the policewoman about what he referred to as the "little experiment" she had conducted in her own bathtub the morning of November 4. He fired a series of questions in rapid succession. His goal: to convince the jury that both bathtub experiments were completely unscientific.

Harris also questioned the patrolwoman about her search of Tim and Elaine's apartment.

"You looked around the bathroom real carefully?" he asked.

"Yes."

"Did you note that the sliding glass doors were not off the track?"

"No, they were not off the track."

"Did you note that such items as her glasses were on the sink?"

"Yes."

"Various toiletries were on the sink?"

"Yes."

"They had not been disturbed. They had not been thrown around?"

"No, they had not."

"So far as the sink, there were no signs of struggle in that bathroom, were there?"

"As far as the sink . . . The only things I saw out of place were a gown that was on the floor, near the tub, and her underwear, which was on the floor, near the toilet."

"And [those] were both dirty, weren't they?"

"Yes, they were clothes that she had been wearing, it appeared."

"Those looked like they might have been knocked down [accidentally] somewhere along the [line]?"

"Right."

"Everything else was in its proper place?"

"Yes, everything else was in place. The rest of her clothes were folded and hanging across a rack."

"You also went and looked around the rest of the apartment pretty thoroughly?"

"Yes."

"And you didn't see any signs of struggle anywhere else in the apartment? Did you look in the other bedroom or the hallway? Was there any sign of struggle anywhere?"

"No."

Harris succeeded in making his point. If there had been a struggle in the bathroom or anywhere else in the apartment the morning of Elaine's death, it did not appear to have been an especially violent one.

Carroll, as his next witness, called Dr. Deborah Radisch. It was Radisch, then associate chief medical examiner for the state of North Carolina, who performed Elaine's autopsy. Radisch described in detail a number of external injuries she observed on Elaine's body during the autopsy, beginning with the three indented parallel lines that she found going across Elaine's mid-section. The top one measured eleven inches in length, the middle one, ten, and the bottom one, nine. Radisch also testified that she observed roundish areas of bruising on the inside of both of Elaine's upper right and left arm; a "rather indistinct area of bruising" on the right side of Elaine's body; and an "area of an abrasion, where the skin had been scraped off, sort of running in a diagonal fashion" on the right side of Elaine's upper back.

Radisch testified that she would not attribute any of these injuries to any of the resuscitative efforts undertaken to save Elaine's life. She also noted that Elaine's blood had tested negative for a number of drugs, including alcohol, and that she found no evidence of heart disease or any other problems with her heart or cardiovascular system that could have contributed to her death. As far as internal injuries, Radisch testified that she found five "very recent bruises" on Elaine's scalp, a round bruise on the top of her head, two smaller bruises on the right front side of her head, a slight bruise over her left ear and a bruise on the back of her head.

"Doctor, would the five bruises that you described for the jury be consistent with resuscitative efforts?" Carroll asked.

"No," Radisch replied.

"Would they be consistent with someone falling and hitting their head in a bathtub?"

"One of the five bruises could be consistent with that, but certainly not all five . . . They're in distinctly different locations, and that would just require too much bouncing around, I think, after the initial fall to account for that."

"Could she have suffered the bruises on her scalp during an attack or struggle, or if she was struck in the head with a blunt object?" Carroll wanted to know.

"That's correct," Radisch replied.

Radisch also said that, like the five bruises on Elaine's head, the bruises she observed on the inside of Elaine's upper arms were not consistent with resuscitative efforts. But because they, too, were "blunt traumatic injuries," they could be consistent with a struggle or an attack. Radisch, however, testified that she ultimately was unable to determine exactly what had caused Elaine's death. She added, however, that she did feel confident ruling out drowning or dry drowning, noting, "in my experience, an otherwise healthy young woman is not at risk of drowning in a bathtub." This was especially true in Elaine's case, Radisch said, because she wasn't impaired by alcohol or any other drug that might have resulted in her slipping. Elaine didn't have any seizure disorders, such as epilepsy, either, that might cause her to lose consciousness. As far as the possibility that Elaine might have fallen and hit her head, Radisch repeated it would be "very, very unusual" for a healthy woman of Elaine's age to do so. Finally, she again testified that while she could accept "a single bruise on the scalp as the result of a fall," she could not accept "five bruises as a result of a single fall."

Harris, too, began questioning Radisch by asking her about the three indented parallel lines stretching across Elaine's mid-section.

"Would the marks across the stomach be consistent with [someone] being put across a shower track in that manner so as to force out gastric contents and/or water? Would it be consistent with that?"

"Yes," Radisch agreed. "It could be."

Then, in an attempt to negate the suggestion that some type of struggle had taken place that morning in the bathroom, Harris asked Radisch about the fake fingernails Elaine was wearing at the time of her death.

"Is it true that every single one of them was intact, that is to say, not broken off or cracked in any fashion?"

"That's correct. They were all intact."

Finally, Harris asked Radisch about a number of possible scenarios that might explain how Elaine suffered the bruises Radisch observed on her head.

"If, when the firemen came in [the bathroom], Mr. Boczkowski moved Ms. Boczkowski's head forward so as to unblock the door . . . [but] as to hit her head on the top or the side of the tub, would that be consistent with the bruise that was on top of her head? Hitting the tub? Being moved up like that?"

"If that happened, it could be, yes," Radisch replied.

"Would the close quarters of the bathroom and the moving about of the body contribute to the possibility of bruises to the head? Could that be?"

"It could. It would indicate . . . several distinct episodes and somewhat rough handling."

"And if a wet, slippery body had been picked up by one person and placed over the tub, that might account for some of that rough handling, true?"

"Some of the bruises on the head or—"

"Sure," Harris said, cutting Radisch off. "And if a person did place another person who had either drowned or had some sort of gastric contents coming up over the tub in order to force out water or gastric content, if they then grabbed [the person] to pull them back away from the tub, if they grabbed their upper arms in order to pull them back, that would leave bruises consistent with the bruises [you observed], couldn't it?"

"It's possible," Radisch said. But, she added, beating Harris to the punch, "It doesn't seem all that likely because you're not going to move [somebody] very far by just grabbing [their] upper arms."

"Sure," said Harris. "It may be that the person grabbed them in the wrong place and had to reform their grip and get [their hands] in a better place. That could have happened, too?"

"That's possible."

CHAPTER 31

GREENSBORO POLICE Officer Steve Goode, who interviewed Tim the morning of Elaine's death, followed Radisch to the stand. Carroll had Goode read the lengthy
statement he took from Tim not long after they arrived at
police headquarters. At several points, Goode stopped to
note that certain comments Tim made that morning were
unprovoked, including his suggestion that Elaine might
very well have slipped and fallen in the bathtub that morning.

Harris, during his cross-examination of Goode, reminded
the officer that Tim voluntarily accompanied him to police
headquarters.

"Did he at any point refuse to answer any questions you
had?" Harris then asked.

"No."

"Was he free in telling you that he and his wife were
separated?"

"Yes."

"He gave you the names of various . . . witnesses who
could confirm where he was earlier that day and earlier that
evening?"

"Yes."

"Did he ever at any point say, 'I don't want to answer
that question'? Did he ever do that?"

"No."

"Did he ever say to you, 'I better get a lawyer over
here'?"

"No."

"Did he freely tell you that he and his wife had had
some arguments in the past?"

"Yes."

"Did he also give you the name of a person to talk to whom he had spoken about those arguments in the past?"

"Yes."

"[Those] are all the questions I have," Harris concluded. "Thank you, officer."

NEXT, CARROLL called Liz Maple, Tim and Elaine's next-door neighbor, to the stand. Within a matter of minutes, the fireworks began.

Maple testified that she had spent part of the afternoon of Saturday, November 3, sitting with a "very, very unhappy" Elaine on the deck behind Maple's townhouse.

"Do you know why she was unhappy?" Carroll asked.

Maple looked at both Carroll and Eagles.

"You can answer his question," Eagles instructed.

"She was afraid her husband was going to kill her."

"Oh, objection," Harris interjected, throwing his pen down on the defense table. He then immediately requested to be heard outside the presence of the jury.

"Your Honor," he began, "this is another episode of somebody who is just . . . quoting Ms. Boczkowski as [having said something]. There's no independent evidence [that she said] what the witness says she said."

Moreover, he argued, Maple, when interviewed by police following Elaine's death, never mentioned Elaine's fear that Tim was going to kill her. "This is the first time we've ever heard this in our lives," he said. "At some point, Your Honor has to reach a conclusion that what [the witness] is saying is . . . prejudicial."

"They can cross-examine her," Carroll countered.

"I'll overrule the objection," Eagles ruled. "You can bring the jury back in."

Back on the stand, Maple repeated that Elaine had told her she was afraid Tim might try to kill her.

"Did she make that statement to you, Ms. Maple, on more than one occasion, or just that day?" Carroll asked.

"On two occasions, sir."

"When was the other occasion?"

"It was about six days prior to that."

"In speaking with Elaine Boczkowski . . . on Saturday, November 3," Carroll wanted to know, "did she say anything to you at all, Ms. Maple, about any intention she had to harm herself?"

"Never."

"Did she say anything that would lead you to think she was inclined to harm herself that day?"

"Never."

WHEN IT was his turn, after Friday's lunch recess, to question Maple, Harris, hoping to portray her as an unbelievable witness, jumped on what he characterized as inconsistencies in both Maple's earlier testimony and her statement to police at the time of Elaine's death. He began by pointing out to Maple that she had testified that Elaine had drunk about a half a glass of wine Saturday afternoon. But about a month after Elaine's death, he reminded her, she had told Detective Ken Brady, "we each had a beer."

"I don't remember that," Maple said.

"You don't remember saying that?" Harris asked.

"No, I don't remember doing that."

Harris then asked Maple about her December 1990 interview with Brady.

"Now, you understood that Detective Ken Brady was attempting to ask you everything important that you could recall that might shed some light on Elaine's death. You understood that, didn't you?" Harris asked.

"Yes," Maple replied.

"And you tried to tell him everything you could possibly think of that would shed some light on her death, did you not?"

"Yes."

"Would it surprise you to know that there is no reference to Elaine being afraid, or Elaine being afraid that she might be killed, in your statement as recorded by Ken Brady?"

"Yes, it does surprise me," Maple insisted. "I have no

idea why he didn't put that down because we talked of it three different times."

"You're saying you said that back then?"

"Yes, sir, I am. Yes, sir."

Harris then returned to the discrepancy between Maple's testimony about what Elaine drank Saturday afternoon and what she told Brady that Elaine had drunk.

"Do you have any explanation as to why that's different?" he asked.

"No, I don't, sir."

"That's all I have."

AT THIS point, Marianne Rochford took the stand. As he had with each of the previous witnesses who'd been at the dance, Carroll asked if she recalled Elaine drinking that night. Rochford said her recollection was similar to that of the witnesses who testified before her: that she had had maybe two glasses of wine over the course of the entire evening and that she did not seem at all intoxicated.

Eventually, Carroll had Rochford read a number of entries from Elaine's journal aloud, among them the January 10, 1990, entry in which Elaine noted that her and Tim's "marriage is on the line." He also had her read the March 11, 1990, entry in which she wrote that their relationship had become "so strained that I'm not sure if it can be saved or if I want to be married to him anymore"; the April 6, 1990, entry in which she described the devastation she felt after learning that Tim had read her journal and confronted Father Jim Weisner; the October 27, 1990, entry in which she wrote about her and Tim's separation and how she was looking forward to the future; and the final entry, dated November 3, 1990, in which she again talked about the future—and the dream she had had about Father Jim.

Carroll would later say that he chose to have Marianne read from Elaine's journal not only because she had been Elaine's best friend, but because he knew how devastated she'd been by Elaine's death and felt that that sense of loss would come across to the jury. "It was like hearing the victim speak from her grave," he said.

Harris, during his cross of Marianne, attempted again to make an issue of how tired Elaine likely had been by the time she returned from driving babysitter Michelle Rotante home, and of how much alcohol Elaine may have consumed over the course of the last twenty-four hours of her life.

While questioning Marianne, Harris attempted, too, to eliminate money as a possible motive for Tim wanting Elaine dead. "In your interview with Detective Brady, it makes some reference to Tim getting money from his mom and dad," Harris said. "Do you remember saying that to Detective Brady?"

"Yes, I do," Marianne responded.

"And so," Harris continued, determined to drive his point home, "Tim had the ability to get money from his parents?"

"Yes."

"Therefore, if Tim Boczkowski needed money, he had somewhere to go, and that was to his parents. He could go to them and get money, couldn't he?"

"I'm not aware of his ability to receive money from them at all."

"But . . . Elaine told you that Tim, in fact, was receiving money from them."

"She was aware," Rochford confirmed, "that he had received money."

CHAPTER 32

BACK IN November 1990, Elaine's death had generated little media interest in Greensboro. In fact, other than a brief obituary that appeared in the Greensboro *News & Record*, it earned nary a mention. That changed once local reporters learned of Maryann's death.

"Police are reexamining the suspicious death of a Greensboro woman in 1990 after her husband's new wife died in similar circumstances in Pennsylvania this week," read the first paragraph of an article that appeared in the *News & Record* on November 9, 1994.

From that point on, local media reported all of the major developments in both the Greensboro and Pittsburgh cases. Tim's trial, naturally, was fodder for daily reports, but it wasn't just the day-to-day goings-on in Judge Eagles's courtroom that generated reporters' interest. It was the toll Elaine's and Maryann's deaths had taken on those they'd left behind. On Sunday, October 27, the *High Point* [NC] *Enterprise* ran a story about how four of Maryann's aunts had to go to Greensboro for Tim's trial and how they said they were seeking justice as much for Elaine as they were for Maryann. Not surprisingly, the foursome was quickly befriended by Elaine's Greensboro friends. The morning the *Enterprise* article appeared, Chris Cheek met Maryann's aunts at their Greensboro hotel so they could follow her to St. Paul the Apostle to attend Sunday mass. At one point, a member of the church's choir sang the song, "In His Presence," especially for the women. Tears began rolling down Ruth Schumann's cheeks as the woman's voice wafted through the sanctuary. "She sounded so much like Maryann," Schumann thought.

* * *

WHEN JUDGE Eagles took her seat behind the bench Monday morning following the weekend break, Carroll was prepared to call Marianne Rochford's sister, Gerri Minton, as his first witness of the day. But knowing that Harris was going to object to Minton testifying about the statements Sandy and Todd Boczkowski had made to her the morning of Elaine's death, Carroll suggested to Eagles that he and Harris present their arguments regarding the admissibility of her testimony prior to the jury being brought into the courtroom.

Carroll argued that Minton should be allowed to testify about Sandy's statements because they qualified as "excited utterances." An "excited utterance" is a statement made in the immediate or near-immediate aftermath of an unexpected incident or conversation, while the speaker is still in an "excited" state over what has transpired or what he or she has been told. In the courtroom, an "excited utterance" functions as an exception to the "hearsay rule," which is designed to prevent witnesses from testifying about statements or information they become aware of second-hand. The rationale behind the "excited utterance" exception is the belief that what a given witness's testimony may reveal sometimes outweighs the fact that his or her testimony may deal with second- as opposed to first-hand information.

Harris pointed out that he planned to call Sandy Boczkowski as a witness. Rather than risk "polluting the case" with Minton's testimony, he argued, why not simply allow Sandy to speak for herself? "You can hear it out of the witness's mouth," Harris said. "You don't need to hear it from someone who may well be making it up."

Carroll, in response, indicated to Eagles that he believed members of Tim's family had attempted to "brainwash" Tim and Elaine's children about their recollections of the morning Elaine died.

"I have talked to these children myself," Carroll noted. "I know that these children were living with the defendant's parents. I know that the defendant's father, Buc

Boczkowski, has been trying to brainwash these kids be cause each and every one of these children told me tha Buc Boczkowski had been talking to them about this ver issue, about whether or not they heard any screaming."

After listening to both Carroll and Harris plead thei cases, Eagles instructed Carroll to proceed with his ques tioning of Minton outside of the jury's presence.

Minton testified that a short time after arriving at Tin and Elaine's apartment with her sister, Marianne, the morn ing of Elaine's death, she noticed there were dirty dishe in the kitchen sink and decided to lend a hand. It was whil washing the dishes, she said, that she spoke briefly witl Sandy and her brother, Todd. Minton asked the childre how they were and whether there was anything she coul do for them. Sandy, Minton said, spoke first.

"She made the comment that she had heard some ar guing in the bathroom early in the morning hours becaus her bedroom was right next to the bathroom," Minton tes tified. "She heard conversation between her parents ani then she heard her mother saying, 'No, Tim, no. Stop. No Tim, no. Stop.' At that point, I was just shocked."

"Did Todd say anything?" Carroll asked.

"He just said he had heard some yelling."

"And that was in response to your just inquiring of then how they were doing [and] was there anything you coul do?"

"Yes."

"Did you have any further conversation with Sandy, Ms Minton?"

"At one point, I had gone upstairs with Sandy . . . ani again, she reiterated the same statement. We stood outsid the bathroom door looking into it . . . and she repeated wha she had said earlier."

During his cross-examination of Minton, Harris imme diately jumped on the fact that she never told the police about Sandy's or Todd's comments.

"When did you first tell this information to the police?" Harris asked, even though he knew she had not done so.

"I was never contacted by the police," Minton said. "I spoke about this with my sister, Marianne Rochford, and she [spoke] with Detective Brady. I was never contacted by Detective Brady."

"Even though you supposedly heard the daughter say there was an argument inside [the bathroom] and [that she] heard a voice, 'No, Tim, no,' your testimony is that Ken Brady never even contacted you?"

"That's correct . . . [but] everything was explained to him through my sister. He has been very much aware of my statement."

"[But] you never called the police," Harris noted with a tone of incredulity. "You never made a statement to the police."

"They knew where they could find me," Minton replied, clearly resentful of Harris's implication.

Once Harris finished questioning Minton, Eagles said she would take the matter under advisement. She then asked that the jury be brought into the courtroom, and instructed Carroll to proceed with the state's case. Eventually, he called the first witness for the prosecution who would testify about the circumstances surrounding Maryann's death: Dr. Leon Rozin, chief forensic pathologist for Pennsylvania's Allegheny County.

Rozin, who had performed Maryann's autopsy, testified that he found multiple external bruises and abrasions—fifty-three in all—on her body, including two on the front of her neck. He also said he found "multiple . . . severe contusions"—all "fresh and sustained in a short period of time prior to her demise"—inside the nape of her neck, in the front of her neck, and on the top of her head. Finally, he said he found numerous "signs of asphyxiation," including hemorrhages in her eyes, at the base of her tongue, and on her lips and gums. The cause of Maryann's death, according to Rozin: compression of the neck with subsequent asphyxiation. In other words, she was strangled.

At various points during Rozin's testimony, Carroll handed the jury photos taken during Maryann's autopsy.

They had the same reaction to these photos that they had
had when viewing photos of Elaine's autopsy. Most seemed
to be forcing themselves to look.

Because Rozin mentioned having discovered a minor
congenital defect in her heart during autopsy, Carroll asked
whether Maryann could have died of a heart attack or could
have accidentally drowned. Rozin dismissed both possibilities out of hand.

"She died," he insisted, "from trauma."

AFTER CARROLL finished his direct examination of Rozin,
Eagles recessed the court for lunch. When court reconvened
shortly before 2 p.m., Eagles heard additional arguments
from both sides regarding the admissibility of Gerri Minton's testimony, then issued her decision. There was legal
precedent for the children's statements to qualify as "excited utterances," she said. This meant Minton's testimony
was admissible as an exception to the hearsay rule. She was
going to allow Carroll to question Minton about her conversations with Sandy and Todd. It was a key victory for
the prosecution.

CHAPTER 33

As MONDAY afternoon's session began, the courtroom buzzed with anticipation over Gerri Minton's return to the witness stand. But first, it was Harris's turn to question Rozin.

Harris began his cross-examination by asking the Ukraine-educated pathologist about his credentials. At one point, for instance, Harris asked Rozin about his lack of board certification.

"Doesn't board certification mean you're recognized by your peers as being able to do what you do? Isn't that what it means?"

"That's correct," Rozin responded.

"So, as of now," Harris noted, "you are not recognized by your peers as being able to do what you do?"

"That's incorrect," replied Rozin, clearly perturbed by Harris's implication. "That's your opinion, not mine. I'm recognized by my colleagues."

"I don't mean that as an insult," Harris said. "I just mean to say that by virtue of not being board certified, that means no board has said you're recognized by your peers, true?"

"It's nothing to do about being recognized by the peers," the Soviet Union–born Rozin replied in broken English.

"Could some of the injuries Maryann sustained have been caused by the paramedics who treated her, or by other rescue or hospital personnel?" Harris asked Rozin.

"Number one," the pathologist insisted, "Ms. Boczkowski was delivered in hospital DOA. What means she was dead. Number two, CPR means resuscitation of the chest. People are not compressing the neck to do CPR. To compress neck means to prevent oxygen to go to the body."

Harris then brought up the fact that Maryann's blood alcohol level was .22 at the time of her death.

"Would you characterize that as between drunk and very drunk?"

"It's drunk," Rozin replied. ".22 is drunk."

"And would you agree that a person in that state would be expected to be suffering from mental confusion and disorientation?"

"Yes, sir."

"Would you agree they would have a tendency to lurch and fall?"

"Yes, sir."

"Would you agree that they might be suffering from vomiting?"

"Yes, sir."

"Would you also agree it would make a person who already had a problem more prone to a heart attack?"

"In this case, hypothetically, maybe. [But] I did not find any signs of a heart attack. Not at all. She was pretty healthy lady."

"But getting back to the hypothetical, being this drunk would make you more prone to a heart attack, true?"

"I never heard about this," Rozin insisted. "Maybe hypothetically in some cases—a person is old, and he is drunk, and he has occlusion of all coronary arteries. Maybe yes. But not in this case . . . She died from trauma."

Harris concluded his questioning of Rozin by asking the pathologist whether he had found any other injuries that might indicate an attack or struggle took place in the hot tub the night Maryann died. First, he asked Rozin if he had found any fractures, broken bones, or brain hemorrhaging while examining Maryann's body.

Rozin said he hadn't.

"Was there anything to indicate that any limb had been twisted around or bent back, any signs of damage to the muscle tissue?"

"I just found a cluster of contusions. How it occurred, I do not know."

"You don't know?"

"No."

Harris ended his cross-examination of Rozin with that final question, undoubtedly hoping to have at least raised the possibility in jurors' minds that the absence of a struggle suggested the absence of a murder. But while Harris may have gotten Rozin to concede that he didn't know "how" Maryann had died, Carroll, during his brief re-direct, made sure jurors knew exactly where Rozin stood on the question of Maryann's cause of death.

"Did Maryann Boczkowski die of natural causes?" he asked.

"No, sir. She died as a result of manual strangulation."

AFTER EAGLES dismissed Rozin from the stand, Carroll recalled Gerri Minton. His questions were direct and to the point. Near the end, knowing full well that Harris again would jump on Minton's failure to report the children's statements to the police, he asked her why she had not done so.

"Did you tell your sister Marianne what Sandy had said to you?" he asked.

"Yes, I did."

"Were you aware that Marianne had talked to Detective Brady at length and given him this information?"

"I was very much aware of the fact that my sister had informed Detective Brady of everything that I had heard."

As Carroll had correctly anticipated, Harris, on cross, came out swinging, attempting from the outset to cast doubt on Minton's testimony.

"Ms. Minton, would it surprise you to learn that Sandy Boczkowski herself tells a very different story and denies [this conversation] entirely and says that it never occurred?"

"Objection," Carroll interjected. "That *is* hearsay."

"Sustained."

"Mrs. Minton, did you take this to be an important statement when you heard it—when you claim you heard it?"

"Of course I did."

"And why don't you tell this jury the first time you ever told the police that story?"

"The first time I recounted this story to anybody other than my sister, who carried it to the police herself, was today in this—Well, when I spoke to Randy—Excuse me, Mr. Carroll."

"So even though it was an important story, from 1990 until late October 1996, you never said a word to the authorities?"

"No, I did not, because the police knew about it."

"Now what makes you think the police knew, since you didn't talk to them?"

"Because my sister and her husband spoke to them, to Detective Brady."

"And you relied upon them that they had told him?"

"Of course I did. They're my family."

"And you'd do anything to help your family?"

"Objection," Carroll interjected.

"Yes, I would," Minton responded.

"All right," Harris continued, "and if your sister believed that a man was getting away with murder, would you get up here and perjure yourself in front of this jury?"

"Objection," Carroll repeated.

Before Eagles could rule, Harris, seemingly pleased with the outcome of this latest exchange, informed her he had no further questions.

THE NEXT witness to take the stand for the prosecution was Dr. John Butts, chief medical examiner for the state of North Carolina. Butts testified that following Maryann's death, he had, at Ken Brady's request, reviewed the original autopsy report on Elaine. He spoke, too, he said, with Dr. Deborah Radisch, who had performed the initial autopsy, and with detectives in Pittsburgh who were investigating Maryann's death. The detectives, Butts testified, told him about the statements they had obtained from Randy, Sandy, and Todd about what the trio had heard the night of Elaine's death. Afterwards, he said, he re-certified the cause of death on Elaine's death certificate. His new conclusion: asphyxiation with aspiration of gastric contents due to, or as a consequence of, chest compression—or, in layman's terms, she choked to death while being beaten.

Butts testified, too, that the bruises found on Elaine's body were "consistent with some type of struggle." He noted, in particular, the indented parallel lines that stretched across Elaine's mid-section.

"Do you have an opinion as to how much force it would take to press down, say, on a shower door track to create those impressions?" Carroll asked.

"That type of pattern would not be caused simply by lying or sitting on that track. If you or I were to sit on one, we might get up after five minutes and we would see the creases, but, in all likelihood, there would be no bruising."

Carroll then asked Butts about Tim's explanation for the marks.

"Would that bruising pattern be consistent, in your opinion, with the defendant laying the decedent over the shower track and pressing her back to clear out the airway?"

"It wouldn't be consistent, in my opinion, with laying someone flat on it because the marks are more to the right side. If you were laid flat across it, they would be more across the middle. But someone laying heavily or pounding heavily on someone whose heart was still beating for some period of time, that could cause that type of a mark."

Later, Butts would dismiss the possibility that Elaine had suffered a heart attack or that she had drowned. "There were too many bruises . . . in different locations," he explained. "Typically, if one does slip and fall, you hit your head once. But Ms. Boczkowski had multiple bruises on the top and sides of her head."

Finally, at Carroll's request, Butts read the last paragraph of his report on Elaine's death aloud.

"On this basis," he began, "given the evidence of chest compression and the form of the imprint of the shower track on the lower chest and upper abdomen of Ms. Boczkowski, it is my opinion that her death was the result of asphyxia due to chest compression. The additional bruising present on the body was, in all probability, incurred during an accompanying struggle. The manner of death will be concomitantly changed from undetermined to homicide."

Fred Lind cross-examined Butts for the defense. As Harris had while questioning Radisch, Lind drilled Butts about the possibility that Elaine could have drowned.

"One possible scenario of this case could have been that Ms. Boczkowski had fallen and hit her head and been rendered unconscious and gone under the water," Lind began. "I know that's probably not your opinion, but that is a possibility, is it not?"

"Generally people fall face down. But, yes, if a person were rendered senseless for some reason, then happened to fall into the water with their face down in the water, or under the water, then drowning could occur."

"And that is a possibility in this case. It can't be excluded. Would that be fair to say? It's a possibility?"

Butts conceded it was. But, he added, "it wouldn't explain, in my opinion, the other injuries on her body."

Lind ignored Butts's last remark, continuing to focus instead on the possibility of Elaine having slipped and fallen. Could stress or fatigue have caused Elaine to fall? he asked. Butts answered that it was unlikely, but possible.

Shortly after Butts left the stand, Carroll recalled Greensboro Police Detective Ken Brady. He began his questioning of Brady by asking the lawman about the progression of his investigation into Elaine's death between November 1990 and November 1994.

"Did you ever close the investigation?"

"No."

"Did you ever take the file off your desk?"

"No," Brady noted matter-of-factly. "It was either on or in my desk the entire time."

Carroll asked Brady to recall the interviews he'd conducted with Tim at Greensboro police headquarters on November 28, 1990, and on January 16, 1991.

The first time they spoke, the detective said, Tim began

by recounting his version of the events of the evening of
Saturday, November 3 and the morning of Sunday, November 4. But when Tim reached the point where Elaine failed
to respond to his knock on the upstairs bathroom door, Tim
began rambling and then started crying.

"He started talking about [how] neither one of them was
seeing anyone else and that there had been no physical
harm done. I was finally able to get him back on [track]."

During the second interview, Brady said Tim began rambling when he started describing how he pulled Elaine out
of the bathtub.

Finally, Carroll asked Brady, "After Doctor Butts
changed the death certificate and filed a new death certificate ruling the death of Elaine Boczkowski a homicide,
what, if any, action did you take, Detective Brady?"

"I had a warrant issued for Mr. Boczkowski's arrest for
first-degree murder."

"At the earliest possible time after the new death certificate?"

"Fifteen minutes later."

CARROLL'S DIRECT examination of Brady spilled over
into Tuesday morning's session. Almost immediately, Carroll asked the detective why he had not obtained a murder
warrant against Tim in the months following Elaine's death.
Brady answered swiftly and succinctly, explaining that the
coroner had been unable to determine an immediate cause
of death. With that, Carroll quickly moved on.

Harris, during his cross-examination of Brady, focused
more on what Brady didn't do than what he did do during
the course of his investigation into Elaine's death. Not surprisingly, he jumped on the fact that Brady did not interview Gerri Minton. He also zeroed in on the absence of
any mention in Brady's report that Liz Maple had told him
Elaine was afraid that Tim was going to kill her.

Moreover, Brady himself conceded that Tim had talked
with him willingly, and had willingly—if two months be-
latedly—turned over Elaine's journal. He also testified that

much of what Tim had told him had checked out.

But under re-direct, Brady told Carroll that early on in his investigation, because of the injuries Elaine suffered and because of the suspicious circumstances surrounding her death, he "felt possibly" she had been asphyxiated.

CHAPTER 34

WHEN JUDGE Eagles ruled, prior to the start of Tim's trial, that Carroll could introduce evidence about Maryann's death, it set the stage for him to mount a prosecution that essentially amounted to two trials in one. And although the jury impaneled in Greensboro was charged with deciding Tim's fate only as it related to Elaine's death, because Carroll would be arguing that Tim was also guilty of murdering Maryann, the jurors' verdict would go a long way towards indicating how Tim might fare at trial in Pittsburgh.

It was Tuesday morning when Carroll began calling the parade of witnesses that his office had flown down from Pittsburgh. The first to take the witness stand was Tim and Maryann's next-door neighbor, Wes Semple, who testified that, being neighbors, he and his wife saw Tim and Maryann on an almost daily basis. He also noted that his son, Wesley Jr., and Todd Boczkowski, who were the same age, grew to become very close friends.

As he would with nearly all of the witnesses he called to testify about Tim's relationship with Maryann, Carroll asked Semple whether Tim had ever made any comments to him about Maryann's drinking. Semple recounted several, including the one Tim had made when the two men were away with their sons at a Cub Scout camp in the summer of 1994—that Semple shouldn't be surprised "if one of the kids comes to your house and says their mother has fallen down."

But Semple also testified that he considered Maryann to be no more than a social drinker—someone who might have a glass of wine with dinner or a drink or two at a party. He also said he had never seen her drunk.

As far as what Tim had told him about the circumstances surrounding Elaine's death, Semple said that although Tim never used the word "suicide," Tim's comments about Elaine having been depressed prior to her death had led him to conclude that she had killed herself.

Under cross-examination, Semple conceded that Tim and Maryann's marriage appeared to be a happy one. He also testified that while he did not have any specific knowledge of Tim and Maryann's financial status, they appeared to be doing well financially. It was clear from his line of questioning that Harris, as he had when questioning prior witnesses about Tim and Elaine's finances, was attempting to eliminate money as a motive for murder in the minds of jurors.

Semple would later recall that Tim avoided making eye contact with him the entire time he was on the stand and when he was led to and from the courtroom. "He either looked down or he looked away," he said. "He would not look me in the eye."

The next five witnesses called by Carroll were either Ross Township police officers or rescue personnel who had come to Tim and Maryann's house in the early morning hours of November 8, following Tim's call to 911. Ross Township Police Officer David Sysca testified about Tim's insistence that Maryann be transported to Allegheny General Hospital even after being informed by the paramedics that North Hills Passavant Hospital was closer and that "when the patient is as severe as this victim was," they normally go to the closest hospital.

It was during his cross-examination of Sysca that Harris would begin trying to justify Tim's preference for Allegheny General over North Hills Passavant. "Allegheny has a better reputation as a better hospital, does it not?" Harris asked.

"For accident and trauma victims I know they do," Sysca replied. "That's the only thing I know, that Allegheny has a better trauma or accident—"

"Well, in fact," Harris continued, cutting Sysca off, "Allegheny has a trauma unit just for that purpose, but the other hospital does not, true?"

"I don't know if Passavant does or not for sure."

"All right. So Mr. Boczkowski, if he knew the reputations of the hospitals, if he wanted his wife to go to the best hospital for trauma, he would want Allegheny, wouldn't he?"

"Objection."

"Sustained."

Ross Township Police Officer William Barrett, who arrived just behind Officers Sysca and Hess at the Boczkowski home that morning, was the next witness to take the stand for the prosecution.

Barrett testified about the conversation he overheard between Tim and his mother in which Tim stated, "I wish Gary Waters was here. I don't want none of this coming back on me."

"Did he say that to you or to his mother?" Carroll asked, referring to Tim's last comment.

"He said that to his mother and then, later, he said something similar to that to me and to Officer Hess: 'I hope this doesn't come back on me' or 'Hope this doesn't get put on me.'"

Harris, during his cross-examination of Barrett, touched briefly upon what the officer said he had overheard during the kitchen conversation between Tim and his mother. "In the statement that you overheard, with Mr. Boczkowski talking to his mother, he ended that statement by saying that even though they had had some sort of discussion earlier, that later on, everything was fine, everything was okay?" Harris asked.

"Yes," Barrett confirmed, "that they had made up in the tub."

WHEN COURT reconvened after the lunch break on Tuesday, Carroll called three of the rescue personnel who were dispatched to Tim and Maryann's home the morning of November 7. The first to testify was Scott Long, a volunteer paramedic with Ross/West View Emergency Medical

Services. Long, the first paramedic to arrive at the scene that morning, testified that after being directed to the back of the house by Officer Barrett, who was standing in the side yard, he was told by Officer Sysca that Maryann had just been lifted out of the tub. Sysca also informed him, he said, that the person on the deck attempting to perform mouth-to-mouth resuscitation on Maryann, using the kind of protective mask typically used by police and rescue personnel for protection against disease, was the victim's husband.

Long said Sysca told him that "he didn't believe any air was getting in" because Tim was using the mask improperly.

"He stated to me," Long testified, "that it had been turned over so that the tube that we generally blow into was actually inside the patient's mouth."

"For all practical purposes, was Maryann Boczkowski dead when you arrived?" Carroll asked.

"Based on other patients I've seen," Long replied, "that seemed to be the case."

Long went on to testify that it appeared to him that Maryann had been dead for some time. Her eyes, he said, were fixed and dilated, and the beds of her fingernails were purplish in color, an indication that she had not been breathing for a while. Her body, meanwhile, was cold to the touch.

Carroll then asked Long whether the bruises observed on Maryann's body during her autopsy could have resulted from rescue efforts. "In your ten years of experience," Carroll asked, "have you ever seen intubation cause any injury to the neck?"

"No," Long replied succinctly.

"And in your experience as a paramedic, have you ever . . . applied CPR by compressing the outside of the neck?"

"No."

"Would anything that you all did for Maryann Boczkowski in attempting to resuscitate her have left marks . . . on either side of the neck?"

"No."

During cross-examination, Harris was ineffective, too, in

getting Long to concede that some of Maryann's bruises could have resulted from Tim using the CPR mask incorrectly and from a rescue worker pounding on her chest.

"If [the breathing tube] were going in instead of out, it could bruise the lip and bruise the tongue and that sort of thing, couldn't it?" Harris asked.

"I can't say," Long replied. "I've never seen it used inappropriately."

"You've never seen it used inappropriately?"

"That's correct."

Stacy Tamburo, another paramedic with Ross/West View E.M.S services, followed Long to the stand. She testified that as soon as she arrived at Tim and Maryann's house, Tim, who was standing in the kitchen, directed her outside.

"She's out there," Tamburo said that Tim told her. "And I think she's very sick."

Tamburo also testified that a short time later, she asked Tim a number of questions about Maryann's medical history. She also asked him when the last time was that he'd seen Maryann alive. "He went into explaining what had happened during the evening," she said. "He explained that they were celebrating an upcoming event and that he and his wife were in the hot tub."

Carroll pressed Tamburo for more details about what Tim had said to her, knowing full well that what he told her contradicted statements he previously had made and would make later that evening.

"Did he tell you what they were celebrating?" he asked.

"He kind of rambled," Tamburo said. "He just said that they were celebrating an event that was going to happen on Wednesday."

Wednesday, of course, was the day the intervention for Maryann was scheduled to take place.

"What, if anything," Carroll continued, "did he say to you . . . about them having argued earlier, before they got in the hot tub?"

"He never stated that they argued."

Carroll then asked Tamburo, since she had spoken with both Tim and Buc, to describe their demeanor during the time Maryann was still at the house.

"In my opinion, they were very emotionless," she said.

"They were what?" Carroll said, asking Tamburo to repeat herself for good measure.

"They were non-emotional. Non-emotional."

Tamburo testified that after Maryann was loaded into the back of the E.M.S. ambulance, Tim declined the paramedics' offer to ride along with them to the hospital. "We were, I thought, waiting for him," Tamburo said, "but he never got in."

She testified that she also had the opportunity to observe Tim at the hospital after he was told that Maryann was dead.

"Describe the defendant's emotional state." Carroll asked the paramedic.

"He had no emotions," she replied matter-of-factly.

Harris, while cross-examining Tamburo, made a point of noting that because she wasn't there when Maryann was lifted out of the tub or moved to a drier spot on the deck, she was not in a position to say whether or not Maryann could have sustained any injuries during the rescue effort. He also suggested that Tim's statement to Tamburo that Maryann was "very sick" was an expression of concern.

"So, he didn't say anything [like], 'She's dead' or 'It's too late' or anything like that, did he?" Harris asked.

"No, he didn't," Tamburo conceded.

"And he showed you the way out [to the deck]?"

"He motioned to the door."

"That's all I have," Harris concluded. He was apparently convinced he had made his point: that Tim's directing Tamburo to the deck suggested he very much wanted Maryann to be revived, and that his comment to the paramedic that Maryann was "sick" could be seen as an indication that, at that point, he believed Maryann was very much alive.

CHAPTER 35

As Tuesday morning wore on, Carroll continued calling witnesses who had been at Tim and Maryann's home the morning of Maryann's death. Allegheny County Police Detective Kevin McCarthy described arriving on the scene at approximately the same time as fellow ACPD Detective Jim Cvetic. After listing the items he removed from the hot tub later that morning—Maryann's eyeglasses, a brown hair band, a piece of the thermometer, a clump of human hair, and a white handkerchief—McCarthy recalled his initial conversation with Greensboro Police Detective Ken Brady.

"He was a little surprised because he had a similar situation with the defendant down there," the detective testified, describing Brady's reaction upon learning of Maryann's death. "The defendant's first wife had died . . . in [their] bathroom . . . in the bathtub. He said he was [still] investigating her death as a possible homicide."

Carroll then asked McCarthy about his having been present during Maryann's autopsy and about what he observed.

"There were a large number of small black-and-blue marks all over the left side of the body, the arms, up underneath the jaw line, and on top of the chest. There were larger and smaller black-and-blue marks on the back on the left side and on the back of the legs."

"Have you ever [known] those types of injuries [to be] caused by resuscitative efforts?"

"No, sir."

"Were the injuries and pattern of injuries that you observed on Maryann Boczkowski . . . consistent with someone who [has] been in a struggle or been attacked?"

"Yes," McCarthy said. "They were."

Harris, during his cross-examination of the detective, ignored the autopsy issue completely, focusing instead on the items McCarthy testified he'd retrieved from the hot tub.

"You examined those glasses," Harris stated matter-of-factly. "Were they broken in any way or harmed in any way?"

"No," McCarthy conceded.

Harris then referred to a series of photographs that were taken at Tim and Maryann's house by a police photographer sometime between 4 a.m. and 6 a.m. the morning of Maryann's death, noting that the close-ups of the hot tub and the deck could not have been taken without Tim's permission.

"If he objected," Harris asked, "you'd go get a warrant?"

"If he objected," McCarthy replied, "we would have left officers there and gone to get a warrant."

"But in point of fact, he voluntarily signed papers allowing you to take whatever photographs you wanted and however many photographs you wanted, true?"

"Yes," McCarthy acknowledged.

Harris was pleased with the exchange. Even the police had to admit that up until the time Tim asked to speak to his attorney, he had cooperated with them fully. It was a point the defense attorney knew could only help stem the tide of what was starting to seem, to many courtroom observers, like a one-sided case in favor of the prosecution.

Ross Township Police Detective Gary Waters followed McCarthy to the stand. Waters described being summoned to Tim and Maryann's house the morning of November 7 after one of the uniformed officers on the scene overheard Tim say, "I wish Gary Waters was here."

Carroll asked Waters about the interviews he, Detective Cvetic, and Pennsylvania State Trooper Richard Ealing conducted with Tim at Ross Township police headquarters.

"During those interviews, did Trooper Ealing say to the defendant, 'There is now no question but you were involved in your wife's death,' or some words to that effect?"

"Yes," Waters replied.

"And what was the defendant's response?"

Harris immediately objected and asked to be heard outside the jury's presence.

"Your Honor, there are two issues I want to raise here," he began. "The first is that I believe the gentleman is going to testify that my client then nodded his head. I believe he's further going to give the opinion that he was giving an affirmative response. Keeping in mind, Your Honor, my client had been up all night, I would suggest to Your Honor that if he wants to say he nodded his head and show the jury in what manner, that's one thing. But he ought not be able to give an opinion as to what that meant. Number two, the next thing my client says is, 'I want to talk to an attorney first.' [Even though] my client has a right to remain silent [and] has a right to talk to an attorney, a jury might well interpret that as a guilty mind, even though, of course, in law, that means nothing. So I would ask that he not be allowed to say that he then asked for an attorney."

Carroll, in turn, argued that nodding one's head up and down is a universally understood gesture. "I would say that it's just universal common sense that nodding your head up and down indicates affirmative," Carroll said.

As far as Tim's having asked afterward to see an attorney, Carroll contended that because Tim made the request immediately after nodding his head, Waters's testimony to that fact should be allowed, too.

Judge Eagles issued a split decision. Waters could testify about Tim having nodded his head, but not about his request for an attorney.

During his cross of Waters, Harris, rather than arguing about the meaning of Tim's nod, focused instead on his state of mind.

"At that point . . . , he had been up all night, hadn't he?" Harris noted.

"Yes," Waters replied. But the Ross Township detective went on to make the point later on that at no point did Tim ever complain about being tired. Moreover, he said, "He didn't appear tired to us."

Harris then turned his attention to Maryann's blood-alcohol level at the time of her death, attempting to establish that she would have been falling-down drunk. But Waters replied that different people handle alcohol differently and that there was no way of knowing Maryann's state.

With this line of questioning, Harris managed, for a few moments at least, to switch this part of the trial's focus from Tim to Maryann. He also was laying the groundwork for the defense's argument that Maryann's alcohol intake at the dance and before played a role in her death. Harris knew, though, that he was walking a thin line. While he wanted to plant this seed in jurors' minds, he had to be careful not to make it seem as if he were blaming the victim.

Waters was Tuesday's final witness. When court resumed Wednesday morning, Carroll called Pennsylvania State Trooper Richard Ealing to the stand. After summarizing the interview he'd conducted while alone with Tim—he couldn't mention administering the lie-detector test because the results of polygraph tests are not admissible in court—Ealing testified as to what transpired after Detectives Jim Cvetic and Gary Waters returned to the room.

"I told [the defendant] that I knew that he had caused the death of his wife," Ealing said. "He nodded his head slowly up and down while looking down. [And] he seemed neither surprised nor agitated that I had arrived at that conclusion."

"Did he ever, in the course of this interview, deny killing his wife or being responsible for her death?" Carroll asked the state trooper.

"No, sir," Ealing replied. "He did not."

Carroll also questioned Ealing, as he had Waters, about Tim's complexion. Tim, after all, claimed he had asked Maryann to give him a scratch massage Sunday night. His back was itching, he said, thanks to the sunburn he'd suffered on the October cruise.

"Did he appear to you to be sunburned?" the prosecutor asked.

"No, sir. Not at all," Ealing replied.

"How would you describe his complexion on that date?"

The state trooper offered a characteristically laconic reply: "Pale."

During his cross-examination of Ealing, Harris tried to lessen the impact of the statements Tim made to Cvetic, Waters, and Ealing the morning of Maryann's death by asking the state trooper why the interview with Tim wasn't tape-recorded or videotaped. He also asked Ealing how he could say with 100 percent certainty that Tim knew exactly what he meant when Ealing had said to him, "We know you caused the death of your wife."

"He knew precisely what I was speaking about when I said, 'caused the death,' " Ealing said.

Detective Jim Cvetic, who sat by Carroll's side throughout the length of the trial, followed Ealing on the stand. He testified about having observed a number of scratch marks on Tim's body after asking him to remove his sweatshirt and drop his pants. He also recounted his interview with Tim at Ross Township police headquarters.

Most noteworthy about Cvetic's testimony was his contention that each time Tim repeated his account of what had transpired after he and Maryann went in the hot tub, he offered not only conflicting times as to what happened when, but times that seemed a little too exact. Cvetic testified, too, that Tim refused to explain why he was drinking wine with Maryann in the hot tub if he believed she had a drinking problem and had scheduled an intervention for later that week; and that Tim's demeanor changed significantly after Cvetic asked about his marriage to Elaine and about her death.

"When we spoke about Elaine Boczkowski," the detective testified, "Timothy Boczkowski, from my observation, became somewhat nervous and evasive."

In yet another pre-emptive strike, Carroll asked Cvetic about Tim's state of mind and the manner in which he was treated while being questioned the morning of Maryann's death.

"During the time that you were [interviewing the defen
dant], before Trooper Ealing got involved, did the defen
dant indicate that he was tired and wanted to go home?
the prosecutor asked.

"Not to me, sir," Cvetic replied.

"Did he appear to be nodding off to you?"

"Absolutely not."

"Was he provided anything to drink in addition t
having breakfast?"

"He had coffee."

"Was he allowed to use the bathroom if he needed to?

"Anytime he wanted."

"Did you or anyone in your presence threaten him o
promise him [anything] in order to get him to make an
statements to you?"

"No, sir. He was told he could leave anytime that h
wanted. We appreciated his cooperation, and he was mor
than reciprocal to our requests."

Harris, during his cross-examination of Cvetic, imme
diately jumped on Cvetic's characterization of Tim as bein
"evasive" whenever he was asking about Elaine, noting tha
the detective's testimony conflicted with the report he'
written two years earlier, following his interview with Tim

"Isn't it true that in the five-page detailed report on you
interview with Tim Boczkowski, the word 'evasive' doe
not appear anywhere?" Harris asked.

"If you're saying it's not there, I will take your word o
it, sir," a diplomatic Cvetic replied.

Harris made a point of noting that Cvetic also failed t
note the scratches he observed on Tim's body in his report

"I asked him about the scratches at his residence becaus
that's where I first saw them," Cvetic said, explaining th
discrepancy.

"Well, nevertheless," Harris insisted, "in your report, i
doesn't say anything about scratches, does it?"

Cvetic asked to review his report.

"Yes, sir. You're correct."

Harris then shifted gears. As he had Ealing, he aske

Cvetic why the interview he'd conducted with Tim wasn't tape-recorded. In doing so, he was suggesting that Cvetic's recollections may have been faulty or, at the very least, unsubstantiated.

Perhaps realizing he was making little headway, Harris next began asking Cvetic a series of not especially relevant questions about the photographs that were taken of Tim and Maryann's hot tub—he even mistakenly referred to it twice as their bathtub—on the morning of Maryann's death. Then, almost as if admitting defeat, he informed Judge Eagles that he had no more questions.

Carroll, seizing on the momentum that seemed, at this point in the trial, to favor the prosecution, then called, in rapid-fire succession, Eileen Datt and her husband, Chuck, and Gay Barbiaux and her husband, Bob.

"I was a nervous wreck," Eileen would later say, describing how she felt upon taking the witness stand. "I thought my heart was going to jump out of my chest. Then, I pictured Maryann, and I said, 'Maryann, please help me get through this.' It got a little easier after that."

Eileen and Gay both testified about Tim's attempts to convince them that Maryann had a drinking problem and about the intervention he had planned for November 9. Eileen testified, too, about what Maryann had told her about Elaine's death shortly after she and Tim had started dating.

"Maryann told me when she first met [Tim] that he told her that he was a widower with three children, that his first wife was an alcoholic, and that she was at a party the night she died," Eileen said. "She was drunk, they came home, she went to take a bath and she either vomited and choked on her own vomit or she drowned."

Moreover, Eileen said, "[Maryann] asked me never to talk to him about [what happened]."

During his cross-examination of Eileen, Harris asked her about Maryann's ultimate willingness to let Tim buy the hot tub. It was a roundabout way of trying to deflate the prosecution's argument that money problems had led Tim to kill Maryann—and Elaine.

"She expressed that she had better ways to spend her money, is that right?"

"Correct," Eileen replied.

"But she didn't indicate that she was short of money or this would deprive them of anything, did she?"

"No, she did not."

"And, in fact, they were getting along reasonably well financially, weren't they?"

"As far as I know," Eileen conceded, "yes."

Finally, Harris asked Eileen about the DUI Maryann received one night in the early eighties after the two of them had spent the evening drinking.

"It was one of those things," Eileen said. "If it [had been] me driving, I probably would have gotten [the ticket]."

Under re-direct, Carroll asked Eileen about the sunburn Tim alleged he suffered while on the cruise. "Ms. Datt," he inquired, "what, if any, efforts did Mr. Boczkowski make on the cruise to keep from getting too much sun?"

"He bought a hat at the very beginning, one of those straw hats that they make on the islands. He wore that the whole time. And he always had his T-shirt on. Even when he was in the water, he had a T-shirt on."

"Did you notice whether or not he used any sunscreen or sun block?"

"I believe he did. Yes. Sun block."

Carroll asked Gay, too, about Tim's attempt to protect himself from the sun's rays during the cruise. Her answer provided an unexpected moment of comic relief.

"Did you notice whether or not the defendant wore a hat at times?" Carroll asked.

"Yes, he did," Gay replied. "We joked about it. It was a woman's hat."

Not surprisingly, the image of Tim wearing a straw hat designed for a woman elicited snickers from more than a few observers seated behind the prosecutor's table.

Gay also testified about what Maryann had told her about Elaine's death. "She said she drowned in the bathtub.

She [also] said that Elaine used to lock the kids in their rooms all day and just sit around and drink. She was an alcoholic."

But while being crossed by Harris, Gay conceded that Tim and Maryann had a strong, healthy relationship.

"As far as you could see," he concluded, "Maryann was happy in her marriage and was making plans for the future, true?"

"That's true."

After testifying, Gay would say that the entire time she was in the courtroom, she tried to avoid looking at Tim. "The only time I did was when I was on the stand," she said. "Randy Carroll wanted me to describe how Tim's appearance had changed since Maryann's death. I said, 'Can you have him stand up?'" After he did, Gay realized just how different Tim looked. "He was thin, he was pale ... He looked like he was on his deathbed," she said. "I looked him right in the eyes for a second," Gay added. "He just stared back. He was like a zombie. That's how he was the whole trial. He never showed any emotion. Nothing fazed him."

Chuck Datt and Bob Barbiaux, meanwhile, testified about the comments Tim had made to them about Maryann's drinking while they were all cruising in the Caribbean a few weeks before Maryann's death. They also testified that they had never really liked Tim. They only tolerated him, each said, because he was married to Maryann.

"I never really cared for him," Chuck noted.

Bob was even more blunt. "Personally, I never liked the guy," he said. "I thought he was a jerk."

CHAPTER 36

Next, Carroll called Maria Crendall and Angela De Marco, Tim and Elaine's oldest friends from Pittsburgh, to the stand. Both testified about Tim's request to meet with them upon his return to Pittsburgh over the 1990 Christmas holiday so he could tell them "what really happened" the morning Elaine died.

Maria and Angela described how Tim had read passages from Elaine's journal to them and how he'd shown them the Polaroids his father, Buc, had taken of him standing in underwear shortly after Elaine's death.

"The purpose of them was what?" Carroll asked Maria.

"To show that there were no scratches on him," she replied.

Harris asked Maria only a few questions under cross, demonstrating again, to some courtroom observers, that grilling witnesses was not Harris's greatest strength. At one point, for instance, Harris asked Maria about her assertion that Tim had said Elaine arrived home before him after the dance, testimony that supported the prosecution's contention that Tim constantly changed his story.

"Did I understand you to say that you believe he said that Elaine came home before him?" Harris asked.

"Yes," Maria replied.

"Could it have been the other way around?"

"No."

"Okay," Harris noted nonchalantly, before moving on to another subject entirely.

Maria would later say that while she was testifying, Tim's eyes did meet hers more than once. "I'd look at him, he'd look at me, then I'd look away," she said. "It was so strange," she added, describing the mixed emotions that testifying against Tim generated in her. "I was up there for Elaine, because I loved my friend and because I wanted the truth to come out. But the guy sitting at the defense table had been my friend, too."

AFTER HARRIS finished cross-examining Angela, Carroll called his last witness—his trump card, so to speak. At the time, 39-year-old Randy Erwin was serving time at the Somerset Correctional Institution in Aliquippa, Pennsylvania, on shoplifting charges. But in December 1994, he had been incarcerated at the Allegheny County Jail, on the same "range," or cell block, as a suburban Pittsburgh man who had been charged the month before with his wife's murder. The man's name was Timothy Boczkowski.

Erwin, who was dressed in an orange prison jumpsuit, testified that the jail's inmates at times were allowed to move freely within their cell blocks, and that over the course of a couple of weeks, he and Tim talked "periodically throughout the day."

"Did there come a time when the defendant told you why he was in jail?" Carroll asked.

"Yes, sir," Erwin politely replied.

"Why did he say he was in jail?"

"At the beginning, he said he was accused of killing his wife."

"And if you remember, Mr. Erwin, how long were you in the Allegheny County Jail with Mr. Boczkowski before he said that to you?"

"About three or four days."

"Did he say anything to you about his case?"

"Yes, sir."

"What did he say?"

"He said that there was another death in North Carolina. His first wife. He said that he had an ice cream business along the highway [but] that the roadway was ripped up [so] there was no access to get to [it] and that the business started going bad and that he was going to lose his business. He said she was in a car accident—"

" 'She' being who?" Carroll asked for clarification's sake. "His first wife?"

"Yeah," Erwin replied. "I don't know her name, but his wife and children. He said she kept complaining about injuries to her back and neck and it was something different every day and she just kept getting on his nerves. And he said he was mad that money from the insurance was put in a trust in his kids' names."

"How were you able to remember any of these things, Mr. Erwin?" Carroll asked the inmate.

"Because I wrote them down as he was telling me," Erwin explained.

"Did he say anything in the course of y'all talking about the death of his second wife in the hot tub?"

"Yes. [One day] I was reading a newspaper that his picture [had come out in], and he came running down the range cheerful and smiling. He says, 'I should charge you for reading that,' and I says, 'What do you mean?' He said 'That's me. I'm the hot tub man. I'm famous,' like it was a joke or something. And we got to talking—I don't know if it was the next day or later that day—and I says, 'Well, why did you kill both women the same way?' And he said 'I don't know. That was stupid, wasn't it?' "

An audible gasp could be heard throughout the courtroom.

"Do you see the person in the courtroom who made that statement to you?" Carroll asked, wanting to leave no room for doubt.

"Yes, sir."

"And would you point him out, please?"

Erwin pointed toward the defense table, to Tim in particular.

Carroll asked Erwin how he happened to bring what Tim had told him to the attention of authorities. Erwin testified that he had contacted Detective Jim Cvetic after being

picked up on another shoplifting charge following his re-
lease from the county jail.

"Did you make a statement to Detective Cvetic and Detective McCarthy?"

"Yes, I did."

"And did either of them or anyone make you any promise in exchange for that statement?"

"No, sir."

"And what, if any, promises have you been made in
exchange for your testimony here in North Carolina?"

"None."

"And do you know whether North Carolina even has
any jurisdiction over your case?"

"I know that they don't."

"And have you talked to me at any time concerning this
statement and your testimony?"

"Yes, sir."

"And what, if any, promises have I made to you of any
nature concerning your testimony in this case?"

"None."

"I believe that's all."

It was clear from the looks on the jurors' faces that Erwin had come across as a credible witness. This meant that
Harris, during his cross-examination, was going to have to
strike hard and fast. Harris addressed Erwin in an almost
contemptuous manner. But by the time Erwin left the stand,
there would be little doubt that the defense attorney had
made a serious tactical mistake.

Harris began by suggesting that Erwin was testifying in
order to get out of jail for two days, but Erwin said the trip
had been anything but enjoyable. Harris then asked Erwin
about his criminal record.

"Now, in 1994, you were convicted of obstructing justice, too, weren't you?"

"Obstructing justice?"

"You the Randy Lee Erwin convicted of obstructing justice?"

"Probably. I've been convicted of several minor charges."

"You the Randy Lee Erwin convicted in 1994 of false reports to the police?"

"Yes, sir."

"So when you made this report to the police, you had already made false reports to the police?"

"Objection," Carroll interjected.

"Overruled."

"I gave them my brother's name for a shoplifting charge because at the time, I knew that they would let me go at the scene. I was on drugs."

"And, as a matter of fact, you've been convicted of drug dealing down in Florida, haven't you?"

"Of drug dealing?"

"Drug dealing."

"No, sir."

"Drug possession?"

"Probably."

"You've been convicted of possession—"

"I don't think I have any drug convictions," Erwin said, cutting Harris off. "I have several convictions. I don't believe none are drugs."

"All right. And you were convicted of assault and terroristic threats in 1986, were you not?"

"Yes, sir."

"Now, you've talked about shoplifting, but your recent shoplifting convictions have been felony shoplifting convictions because you have such a long record of it, true?"

"That's why I'm in the penitentiary. Yes, sir."

"And you've been convicted of burglary, I believe you said?"

"Yes, sir."

"Burglary, for those of us who don't know, is what?"

"Objection," Carroll interjected.

"Sustained."

"All right. You were convicted in 1987 of receiving stolen property, true?"

"Probably."

"Where did you live between 1987 and 1990?"

"In prison."

"Where did you live most of the last decade?"

"In prison."

"Can you tell us [about] any gainful employment you've had in the last decade?"

"Yes. I worked for my brother's construction company and trucking company, and my father has a sixty-three-room motel we're remodeling."

"Anybody besides family?"

"A brother-in-law. I worked at his printing company."

"All right. Now, in point of fact, you were given special consideration when you were sentenced this last time. Your sentence was reduced, and the charges were reduced. True?" Erwin denied that he'd cut any deals with prosecutors and Harris chose to move on.

"Now, did I understand you to say that Mr. Boczkowski told you that his business was losing money and [that] he was worried he was going to lose it? Did you say that?"

"Yes, sir."

"And if there is evidence that the business was, in fact, sold in May of 1990, before his wife's death, then that's wrong, isn't it?"

"I've never been in North Carolina. And had no way of knowing. That's just what he told me."

"Now, in your statement, you said, 'Then, he said a day or two later, the detectives came over to the house to check the hot tub for evidence but he had already drained and scrubbed it.' Was that your statement?"

"Yes, sir. That's what he told me."

"Now, by that, you mean that the detectives came to take photographs and take evidence, and it was already drained, I take it?"

"I mean that's what he told me."

"And so if there are photographs in this courtroom right now entered into evidence which were taken on the very morning that Maryann Boczkowski was taken out of the tub, then that would be wrong, wouldn't it?"

"Objection," Carroll declared. "That's arguing with the witness."

"Sustained."

"I don't know," Erwin replied despite Eagles's ruling.

"Sustained," she repeated. "You can argue the case to the jury later."

"Do you know when photographs were taken of the tub where Maryann Boczkowski died?"

"All I know is what he told me."

"And . . . ?"

"He said when they came over to the house that he had already drained and scrubbed the tub so they wouldn't find any evidence. For whatever reason, he told me that. [What] that meant, I don't know. But that's what he said."

"So you say that when detectives got there, he had already drained and scrubbed it. That's what you say?"

"Yes, sir."

Harris then asked Erwin if he had any idea why Tim would talk to him after having sent a letter to neighbor Wes Semple saying that his lawyer had instructed Tim not to speak with anyone about the case.

"Yes, I do," Erwin said.

"What is it?"

"During our conversation, I brought up the fact that my mother was killed in front of me when I was five years old. She was stabbed thirty-seven times and it kind of, like, hit him funny. And he asked me if his son would still love him. I [said], 'What are you talking about?' Do I still love my dad? he asked me. I said, 'Yeah,' and then he [said], 'Do you think my son will still love me?' And I [said], 'What are you talking about?' That's when he started telling me about the circumstances of the case and everything. That's what triggered mostly why I'm here, okay? So his son won't have to grow up the way I did."

Erwin's explanation brought tears to a number of courtroom observers, including a couple of jurors. Harris, though, wasn't the least bit moved.

"And you contend that he's saying all of this to a stranger?"

"Don't ask me why, but he did. Maybe it was bothering him."

"You contend he's doing this even though his attorneys told him not to?"

"Objection," Carroll declared. "He's not contending."

"Sustained."

"And you're down here testifying out of what? A sense of public duty? Why are you here?"

"You know, sir, I don't know that myself, because I'm in a maximum-security prison right now. This is probably going to be on the news, and I'm probably going to have a pretty hard time when I get back. I've got 120 days left until I'm released."

"So this is what? A public service?" Harris repeated.

"No, it's more like for his son, I believe, I'm doing it."

"So you're concerned about his son?"

"And my mother."

"That's all the questions I have of this witness," Harris informed Eagles.

Carroll then got up from the prosecutor's table, walked toward the witness stand, and asked Erwin a single question.

"Who killed your mother?"

"My father," Erwin replied.

By asking Erwin his rationale for testifying, Harris opened the door for Carroll to ask the inmate who had killed his mother. Harris, in effect, had thrown Carroll a fat, juicy fastball right over the plate, the kind that make major league sluggers drool, and Carroll, in turn, hit it out of the park. After allowing a few moments to pass for dramatic effect, Carroll informed Eagles that he had no more witnesses.

"The state," he announced, "rests."

Later Carroll would explain how Harris had played right into his hand.

"I knew his father had killed his mother," he said, "but

I'd made an intentional decision not to ask him about that while he was testifying for the state. I thought it would be more effective if that came out while Harris was questioning him."

"When he answered 'My father' after I asked him who killed his mother, you could have heard a pin drop. In my mind, that was the final nail in Boczkowski's coffin."

CHAPTER 37

AFTER ERWIN stepped down from the witness stand, Carroll declared he had finished presenting the state's case. Eagles then excused the jury from the courtroom.

"Anything for the defendant at the close of the state's evidence?" she asked.

Co-defense counsel Fred Lind stood up.

"We would respectfully move to dismiss due to insufficiency of evidence . . . and under the due-process clause of the Fourteenth Amendment," he said, employing a common defense tactic after the state rests.

"Do you want to be heard, Mr. Carroll?" Eagles asked the prosecutor.

"No, Your Honor," Carroll replied.

"All right," Eagles noted. "The motion is denied. Are y'all ready to proceed?"

HARRIS CALLED Sandy Boczkowski as the defense's first witness. The bespectacled 13-year-old, her blonde hair pulled back in a ponytail, climbed somewhat unsteadily onto the witness stand. That the teenager had not been called by Carroll puzzled observers who'd been in court the day the prosecutor delivered his opening argument and had heard him state his intention to call the Boczkowski children as witnesses. Once the trial began, though, Carroll reconsidered, in part because he felt they'd been through enough, in part because Eagles had allowed Gerri Minton to testify about the statements Sandy had made to her in Tim and Elaine's kitchen the morning of Elaine's death, and in part because of a conversation he'd had with his own children.

"Would you want to testify against me even if you knew
I murdered your mother?" he asked them one morning over
breakfast.

Their answer: a unanimous "no."

Although tears began to well in her eyes when Harris
asked her about her birth mother, Sandy, for the most part,
retained her composure while being questioned.

"Do you understand the importance of telling this jury
here the truth?" Harris asked the North Hills Junior High
eighth-grader.

"Yes," she answered solemnly.

"Now, Sandy, do you remember the night your mother
died?"

"Yes."

"Would you tell the jury what you remember about it?"

"My bedroom was right beside the bathroom, and I
heard a noise, like something fell. The water was running,
so I got up and I went into my parents' bedroom, and my
father was the only one there. So I woke him up, and I had
to shake him to wake him up because he must have been
sleeping. Then he went to the door of the bathroom and he
started banging on it. First, he tried to turn the knob. But
it wouldn't unlock, it wouldn't open, so he woke my brothers up and, at some point, we went downstairs, and either
my brother or my father called 911. Then we went outside,
and we went to our neighbor's house. And as we were
going outside to a neighbor's house and ringing the doorbell, the paramedics and the fire and police and everyone
was getting there."

"Were there emergency vehicles and things of that sort
outside?" Harris asked.

"Yes."

"Now, tell the jury what, if anything, you remember being told about your mother's death."

"I remember . . . my father told me that—how they were
supposed to get a divorce. Then he told me that they
weren't because my mom died."

"Had you known before that time that your parents were thinking of getting divorced?"

"Yes."

"How had you been told that?"

"My parents talked to me and my brothers and told us that they were thinking about getting a divorce."

"As far back as you can remember, do you ever recollect your mother and your father getting physical? That is to say, pushing each other or hitting each other or doing something that would [involve] physical contact?"

"No."

Harris asked Sandy if she'd ever met Marianne Rochford's sister or if she remembered having a conversation with her the day her mother died. Sandy answered that she hadn't, and she didn't.

"If someone says that they talked to you that day and you told them that you heard your mother and father arguing in the bathroom that morning before her death, would that be true?"

"No."

"Did you ever say words to the effect of 'My mother and father' or 'My parents were arguing in the bathroom on the morning of her death'? Did you ever say that to anyone?"

"No."

"Did you ever say to anyone that you heard you mother crying out on the morning of her death, crying out any words?"

"No."

Harris then asked Sandy a series of questions designed to support Tim's contention that the scratches police saw on his back were the result of a "scratch massage" Maryann had given him shortly before her death.

"Have you ever had occasion to give your father back scratches or back rubs?"

"Yes."

"Have you ever had occasion to see your brothers give him back scratches and back rubs?"

"Yes."

"Have you ever had occasion to see others give him back scratches and back rubs?"

"Yes."

"Is that a common thing with your father?"

"Common," Sandy confirmed.

"Tell the jury about that."

"Usually, my father, when he's tired or something, he would ask either me or my brothers or someone if we would give him a back rub."

"And do you do that?"

"Yes."

"Now, I'd like to talk about your stepmother, Maryann, a little bit, too," Harris said, shifting gears. "Did you ever have occasion to see your stepmother, Maryann, drinking?"

"Yes."

"Alcoholic beverages?"

"Yes."

"Tell the jury about that."

"Well, our [recycling] bin usually got picked up every week, and it was usually filled with beer bottles or jugs of wine."

"Do you know if your father or your stepmother was drinking [those]?"

"Well, I always saw my stepmom drinking, so I sort of knew it was her."

"How much did you see her drinking?"

"Pretty much," Sandy estimated.

"Did you have occasion to see her drink in the morning?"

"Yes."

"Tell the jury about that."

"Well, my mom, she sang at church, so on Sunday, usually, or on any other day that she would practice her singing, she would get up and usually come down and get, like, wine or beer . . . Sometimes, she would mix it with ginger ale and she would go upstairs and practice."

"Now, tell the jury what you recollect about your stepmother's death."

"Well, I just remember that I went to bed probably around 8:30 or so. I woke up the next morning, and my grandma was there. She took us out to breakfast at Eat 'n Park. We usually go upstairs and say goodbye to my mom before we leave for school, but we were running late that morning and we were already downstairs and had our shoes on. That's when it came to me that we forgot to go upstairs to say goodbye. [But] we were just in such a rush that we didn't."

"Were your father and stepmother getting along well?"

"Yes."

"Did you ever see your stepmother and father have any physical problems before, like hitting, pushing, shoving, that sort of thing?"

"No."

"Have your grandparents at any time ever had occasion to instruct you or tell you what to say to the police or anybody else concerning your mother's death or your stepmother's death?"

"They always told us to tell the truth."

Harris sat down after asking Sandy a few brief questions about how Maryann had adopted her and her brothers. Now it was Carroll's turn. Carroll would later say that Sandy's testimony directly contradicted everything she had told him in Pittsburgh, but that did not catch him off guard.

As he had argued before the judge, he believed that she and her brothers had been "brainwashed" by Buc, and was not surprised by her testimony.

Still, Carroll was disappointed.

"I had hoped that once she was up on the stand, she would do the right thing," he said.

Whatever her testimony, Carroll wasn't about to approach the teen with anything but kid gloves. Still, he had his own points that he needed to communicate to the jury.

"Sandy, do you remember me coming up to Pittsburgh?" Carroll asked.

"Yes."

"And do you remember talking to me that day?"

"Yes."

"And do you remember telling me, Sandy, that you grandfather had been talking to you about your testimon and wondering what you were going to say to the jury whe you testified?"

"No."

"You don't remember that?"

"No."

"That could have happened, couldn't it? You could have told me that?"

"No."

"You deny making that statement?"

"Yes."

"Do you know a girl named Johanna Cain?"

"No."

"You don't remember a nine-year-old girl, Johanna Cain, that lived next door to you on Noring Court?"

"Oh, yeah. Okay."

"And she was a friend of yours?"

"A little bit."

Johanna Cain was a neighborhood playmate of Sandy's. Allegheny County Homicide Detective Jim Cvetic interviewed the Cain family after receiving a tip from Maryann's aunt, Ruth Schumann. Schumann had heard that Sandy may have spoken to Johanna about her mother's death.

"You talked to her some about this situation concerning your mother and your father, didn't you?"

"Yes."

"And didn't you tell her that your dad didn't want you to say anything because he would get mad at you for telling?"

"No."

"You didn't tell her that?"

"No."

"Okay, when you were living in Greensboro at the time
his happened, how old were you?"

"Probably six."

"Were you going to Joyner School?"

"Yes."

"Do you remember the police coming out to Joyner
School and talking to you?"

"No."

"You don't remember that?"

"No."

"And do you remember at some point after you talked
o the police, after your mother died, that your daddy told
you not to talk to the police any more?"

"No."

"Your daddy never told you that?"

"No."

"You never knew your natural mother to drink anything,
did you?"

"No."

"I believe that's all," Carroll said. "Thank you, Sandy."

With Eagles's permission, Sandy carefully stepped down
rom the witness stand. Tim showed little emotion during
his daughter's testimony, maintaining the same single facial
expression he had been wearing since the trial began. He
did, however, smile and wink as Sandy passed the defense
able.

CHAPTER 38

SHORTLY AFTER 9 a.m. on Thursday, October 31, Dou
Harris called his first expert witness: Dr. Donald Jason. A
assistant professor at the Bowman Gray School of Medicir
in Winston-Salem, NC, Jason boasted a solid résumé. .
1970 graduate of New York University Medical, he serve
for two years as a U.S. Navy pathologist. He also serve
as a staff pathologist for New York City's chief medic;
examiner. A veteran of some 4,000 autopsies, Jason, at th
time of Elaine's trial, also held the position of Forsyt
County [NC] medical examiner in addition to his academi
post.

Jason testified that he disagreed with Dr. John Butts'
conclusion that Elaine's death was a result of asphyxia du
to compression of the chest. The three indented lines o
Elaine's mid-section, which Butts testified were a result c
her being held down against the track for the sliding showe
doors, were, he said, "fairly faint" and "about as obviou
as a mark near her breast which was left by an electr(
cardiograph pad."

"Would you find those marks to be consistent or incor
sistent with a person being placed across a tub so as t
expel water or vomit?" Harris asked.

"They are perfectly consistent with someone bein
placed across the tub in that position," Jason replied withou
any hesitation.

"Would you find those marks to be consistent or incon
sistent with somebody being positionally asphyxiated? I
other words, held across those [tracks] on the tub and hel
down and pressed until such time as she ceased to breathe?

"Inconsistent."

Jason went on to contend it was unlikely the marks would appear as they did—one single, parallel set—if Elaine had been engaged in a struggle. "I would have expected a conscious woman to be able to move even just a little bit," he said.

Jason cited two other factors that made him doubt that a struggle had taken place: a lack of evidence of rib fractures or hemorrhages in the muscles around Elaine's midsection, which, he said, suggested she "was not conscious when she was placed on the side of that bathtub," and the fact that Elaine's fingernail on-lays were still intact at the time of her autopsy.

So what, in Jason's mind, was the cause of Elaine's death?

The pathologist offered two potential theories. The first was that Elaine had drowned.

"First of all," he testified, "this was not a normal, healthy woman. She had some significant coronary artery disease. The autopsy describes a thirty to forty percent blockage of one of the main coronary arteries. [This] is not normal for a young woman of her age."

Jason added that while Elaine's heart muscle did not show "any absolute signs of a heart attack," if she had suffered an acute heart attack just before she died, there would be no such evidence of that in the heart muscle.

"Second, Ms. Boczkowski had a fatty change of the liver," he said. "This indicates a previous history of drinking. Even though she was not intoxicated at the time she died, a person who drinks enough to have a fatty liver would have been doing some microscopic damage to his or her heart all along.

"Third," he concluded, "she had had a very long day. She woke up early. She had been drinking earlier in the day. She went to a party. She came home late. She would have been tired, exhausted. That would also lead to the heart being more susceptible to an abnormal rhythm. So she may have had an abnormal rhythm, passed out, gone under the water, and drowned."

Jason's alternative theory was that Elaine had slipped
the tub's smooth bottom, hit her head, and then drowne

Finally, he testified that the absence of petechia
Elaine's eyes made it unlikely that she was a victim
positional asphyxia. "In any type of traumatic asphyxi
the pathologist explained, "there is an increase in blo
pressure which causes [the] bursting of small blood vess
in a number of places and, particularly, in the lining of t
eyes, the inside of the eyelid, and over the whites of t
eyes. There is no mention of that whatsoever [in the a
topsy report]."

While cross-examining Jason, Carroll quizzed the p
thologist about both of his theories. He asked Jason fi
about his hypothesis that Elaine could have suffered cardi
arrhythmia, or an abnormal heart rhythm, that could ha
resulted in her becoming unconscious and then drownin

Jason suggested there could have been evidence of
blood clot or blockage in Elaine's heart but that Dr. Radis
might have missed it while performing Elaine's autops
"When you do an autopsy and look at each of the corona
arteries, you make multiple cuts across each," he explaine
"It's always possible, if you [leave] three or four millim
ters between cuts that you may miss something . . . That
a possibility."

Carroll then began focusing on the "30 to 40 perce
blockage of the coronary arteries" that Radisch noted in h
initial autopsy report.

"Doctor, would you agree that a thirty to forty perce
blockage of the coronary arteries would be considered,
your profession, to be a mild to moderate blockage?" Ca
roll asked.

"That's the way we usually describe it, yes," Jason r
plied.

"Isn't it true that a thirty to forty percent blockage
the coronary arteries is not usually symptomatic of cardi
arrhythmia?"

"That's right. Not usually . . . But you see, there's mo
here than just the thirty to forty percent blockage of or

coronary artery alone. There's also the fact that she was exhausted [and] the fact that she had a fatty liver, indicating drinking in the past. Altogether, that makes her not a normal, healthy woman."

"Doctor, would it be your testimony . . . that asphyxia, secondary to chest compression, is not even a possible [cause of death]?"

"I think it's a very far out possibility," Jason maintained. "I don't think it's near as probable as the other two [possibilities] I've described. I would be very surprised if it were, in fact, the case."

Finally, Carroll asked Jason to turn his attention to the five contusions found on different areas of Elaine's scalp during her autopsy. If any one of these bruises could have rendered Elaine dazed and unconscious, Carroll wanted to know, how would Jason account for the remaining four?

"I can account for two of them: one on the way down and then, when she lands, easily," Jason testified. "As far as the other injuries are concerned, they could have happened during the actual drowning act or during resuscitation [attempts]."

As HIS next witness, Harris called Beth Elder, an employee of the office of the Superior Court Clerk for North Carolina's Eighteenth Judicial District, which includes Guilford County. According to Elder, in August 1992, after Elaine's will was probated, Tim received $2,500 worth of household goods from his late wife's estate, while Randy, Sandy, and Todd each received $747.90, which was then deposited in a trust being held for them until they turned 18.

Harris again was clearly aiming to convince the jury that Tim had little financial motive for wanting Elaine dead. But Carroll, during his cross-examination of Elder, succeeded in suggesting that her testimony, through no fault of her own, was misleading.

"Ms. Elder, any life insurance does not go through the estate, is that correct?" Carroll asked.

"Not if it's to a named beneficiary," Elder replied.

"And if Timothy Boczkowski was named a beneficiary on Elaine Boczkowski's life insurance, that would not have gone through the estate, would it?"

"No, sir. It would not."

Court recessed for roughly fifteen minutes following Elder's testimony. When it resumed, Harris called Tim's chiropractor, Dr. Russell Cobb, to the stand. Cobb testified that he had begun treating Tim on December 8, 1990, a little over a month after Elaine's death. Cobb said Tim came to him complaining of low back pain and discomfort, explaining that he had injured his back while pulling his late wife out of the bathtub after she had drowned.

Cobb, who saw Tim a total of five times in December and once in January 1991, testified that he examined Tim and took x-rays. He said the injuries he found were consistent with someone who had performed a "pulling-type motion."

Carroll, however, needed no more than a few minutes to destroy whatever credibility Cobb might have had in jurors' eyes. Harris didn't come out looking too good either.

"Doctor Cobb," Carroll began, "what have you been tried and convicted of in the last ten years that carries [a sentence of] more than sixty day's imprisonment?"

"Well, back in the late eighties, I had some trouble with the federal government where I had a conviction of—where I had filled out some loan applications for leases."

"Were you convicted in federal court for that?"

"Yes."

"Three counts of wire fraud?"

"Yes."

"Would that have been on May 23, 1989?"

"Yes."

"Was Mr. Harris your lawyer in that case?"

"Yes."

"Elaine Boczkowski had been a patient of yours as well, wasn't she?"

"I believe she was."

"Do you have a recollection or not, Doctor Cobb, that Elaine Boczkowski had been in an automobile accident [a] year or so before her death and was coming to see you about some complaints she had as a result of that [accident]?"

"I can't remember exactly what her complaints were, but that's very possible."

"And do you recall that, as a result of that automobile accident, there had been a lawsuit filed against the driver of the other car?"

"I don't remember that."

"So I take it you don't remember that Mr. Harris was the lawyer that filed that suit for her?"

"No, I don't remember. No."

"And do you recall how Timothy Boczkowski got referred to your office?"

"No, I don't."

"Did Mr. Harris refer him to your office?"

"Not according to the records, he didn't. No."

"Have you had referrals to your office from Mr. Harris?"

"I probably have. More in the realm of people in accidents. Car accidents."

Rather than pressing Cobb for more information on the relationship between the chiropractor and Harris, Carroll returned to the prosecutor's table. The expressions that crept across jurors' faces following Cobb's last reply left the prosecutor with the distinct impression that little more needed to be said.

CHAPTER 39

FOLLOWING ELAINE'S death, Tim cut himself off from nearly all of the friends he and Elaine had made through St. Paul the Apostle. Jim and Celia Borowicz were the exceptions.

After being called to the stand by Harris, Jim Borowicz testified that he and his wife had watched Randy, Sandy, and Todd from about 2 p.m. to 8 p.m. the day Elaine died, taking them to the park, for ice cream, and then to church.

Harris asked Borowicz if the children, during the time they were with him and his wife, had said anything to them about Elaine's death.

"No, sir," Borowicz replied. "We didn't speak about what had happened other than in general."

Harris also asked Borowicz about meeting Maryann when Tim brought her to Greensboro in the fall of 1992.

"They came to visit us one evening at our home while they were in town," Borowicz said. "Tim wanted to introduce her."

"So Tim Boczkowski brought his new wife by to see his old friends from his old life?" Harris asked, placing emphasis on the phrases "old friends" and "old life" in order to imply that Tim never tried to hide his past from Maryann.

"Yes, sir," Borowicz replied.

Celia Borowicz's testimony about the night of the St. Paul's dance was significantly more explosive than her husband's had been.

"I told her when she got there how beautiful she looked," she recalled. "She had a beautiful white outfit on and her hair was very pretty . . . She told me she was determined to have a good time that night and that she had just finished a bottle of wine by herself in order to start that night out well. Because I saw her drinking further that night, at one point in the evening I offered to give her a ride home. I wasn't drinking. I had bronchitis, so I knew that I was the designated driver for my husband and me. Anyway, I was concerned about her driving, having had that much."

"What was her demeanor most of the night?"

"I think she was determined to have a good time and for most of the night, seemed to be happy-go-lucky."

"Did you have occasion to see her when she was unhappy or crying or anything like that that night?" Harris asked.

"There was a period of time that she was very unhappy," Borowicz replied. "She was outside underneath a tree crying. There were two people outside. One was Elaine. She was very easy to identify in her white outfit. It was audible that she was crying, and it was visible that she was being comforted. I went to see if I could help, and the other person with her kind of waved me away, so I didn't disturb them."

"And who was the other person with her?"

"Gerri Minton."

"Did Elaine Boczkowski ever discuss with you anything about any kind of spousal abuse or any problem in [her] marriage?" Harris asked.

"No."

"Do you know of any reason that she would have confided to you or you would have expected her to?"

"Yes."

"Tell the jury what that reason is."

"During the years Elaine and I were friends and confided quite a bit to each other, she knew that, in 1983, I had left an abusive husband and was still in hiding from him at that point."

"And Elaine knew that?"

"Elaine knew that."

Harris asked Celia, as he had Jim, if she ever felt Tim had made an effort to hide his "old life" from Maryann. She said she never felt that way.

"He wouldn't have made an effort to bring [Maryann] to our home and introduce us [to her] if he was trying to [keep his lives] separate," she said.

Finally, Harris asked Borowicz about Sandy Boczkowski, hoping to erase any doubts jurors might have had regarding the truthfulness of her testimony.

"Did Sandy have occasion to stay at your house last night?"

"Yes."

"What sort of girl is Sandy? Tell the jury."

"She has a great sense of humor. She's kind. She's patient. I have three young children now, and she's great with them. She's doing her homework today. She's conscientious. I'd be glad if she were my daughter or if my daughters turn out to be like her."

Exactly how Sandy Boczkowski's testimony had played to the jury was unclear, courtroom observers agreed. She was not, however, the only Boczkowski the defense turned to in the hope of winning Tim's acquittal. Ron Boczkowski, Tim's older brother, followed Celia Borowicz to the witness stand. An operations technician for an Alvin, Texas, petrochemical company, Boczkowski testified that he was capable of providing his brother with financial help.

"Was your father financially capable of helping your brother if he needed it?" Harris asked. Yet again, he was attempting to erase money as a possible motive in jurors' minds.

"Yes, sir, he was," Tim's brother replied.

Harris also asked Boczkowski about a visit he made to Pittsburgh prior to Maryann's death. "You had a chance to see the house [Tim and Maryann] were living in?"

"Yes, sir. Yes, I did."

"Tell the jury about the house. What sort of house was it?"

"It was a brand new house. Two stories. Nicely furnished. I recollect the dining room set. It was real nice. It was a dark cherry mahogany."

Harris asked Boczkowski what he knew about his brother's dental products business at the time.

"Apparently, he was doing very well, from what I saw," he said. "I visited him over at his dental lab. Talked to some of the doctors. They were real pleased with him."

Boczkowski testified, too, about Sandy, describing his niece as "a very nice person raised in a Christian atmosphere." He also noted that she was "very smart."

"Smart how?" Harris asked.

"Academically," Boczkowski replied, explaining that Sandy was studying four foreign languages.

"She takes four foreign languages?"

"Yes."

"Does she do well in school?"

"Yes, sir. She's a straight-*A* student."

Carroll's cross of Tim's brother was brief, but effective.

"Mr. Boczkowski," Carroll asked, "did you go to your brother's and Maryann's wedding?"

"No, sir."

"Did you go to [Maryann's] funeral?"

"No, sir. I did not go to the funeral."

Carroll then pointed to Kevin Rochford, who was sitting in the row directly behind the prosecution table.

"Do you know this gentleman here in the gray suit?" Carroll asked. "You've met him before, haven't you?"

"The first time I saw him was in the courtroom here," Boczkowski replied.

"Don't you recall when y'all were putting in the miniature golf course up there at King Kones that he was helping with that and he worked alongside of you? Don't you remember that?"

"I don't know. I don't know if he had a beard then or not. I really don't recollect."

Carroll's point here was clear. Tim's brother hadn't gone to Tim and Maryann's wedding or Maryann's funeral and couldn't remember having worked alongside one of

Elaine's closest friends. Maybe, the prosecutor was suggesting, the Boczkowski brothers weren't quite as close as the defense would have liked the jury to believe.

AFTER THURSDAY'S lunch recess, with the jury still out of the courtroom, Judge Eagles, Carroll, Harris, and defense co-counsel Fred Lind discussed the charges the jury would be allowed to consider. Although the defense asked that both voluntary and involuntary manslaughter be included, Eagles ultimately ruled that the jury would be given three possible verdicts to choose from: guilty of first-degree murder, guilty of second-degree murder, and not guilty.

A short time later, Eagles addressed the issue of Tim's right to testify in his own defense. "I assume that y'all have told him he does have the right to testify, and he knows that it's his decision?" she asked the defense team.

"Yes, Your Honor," Harris replied. "Let me state that on the record."

Harris then turned to Tim. "Mr. Boczkowski, you and I have discussed on a number of occasions over at the jail and in lock-up here, too, that you understand that you have the right to testify if you wish to. Do you understand that, Mr. Boczkowski?"

For the first time since the trial began, Tim spoke aloud in the courtroom.

"That is correct," he said in a flat, monotone voice.

"And it has been my recommendation that you not testify in this particular case, but do you understand that that's only my recommendation, and you could, if you wished, take the stand no matter what I said or what Mr. Lind said? Do you understand that, sir?"

"That is correct," Tim repeated.

"Do you wish to take the stand and testify for yourself?"

"I do not," Tim replied. "I wish to take your advice."

Tim's decision not to testify did not surprise Carroll. "At first, I thought he might, because he wasn't your typical

urder defendant," he would later say. "He was an edu-
ted family man. On the other hand, he'd told so many
es, they had to keep him off the stand. More often than
ot, murder defendants convict themselves."

CHAPTER 40

A LITTLE before 9:30 a.m. on Friday, November 1, tl
defense called its final witness: Dr. Louis Roh, the depu
chief medical examiner for Westchester County, New Yo
Like Dr. Donald Jason, the defense's expert witness fro
the day before, Roh, at one time, had worked as a forens
pathologist for the New York City Medical Examiner's O
fice. Roh testified that over the course of his twenty-si
year career, he had performed some 7,000 autopsies ar
had testified as an expert in the field of pathology son
200 times, mostly for the prosecution.

Roh, whose testimony Harris hoped would shoot hol
in the state's argument that Maryann, like Elaine, had bee
murdered, said that after reviewing the report on Maryann
autopsy and microscopic slides made during the procedur
he concluded that Maryann, at some point in her life, ha
suffered a "silent heart attack."

Typically, Roh explained, as people get older and chc
lesterol and fatty acids deposit inside the coronary artery-
the artery that supplies blood to the heart—the artery na
rows. This can result in an insufficient amount of bloc
reaching the heart, which, in turn, can result in a heart a
tack.

"Unfortunately, in this case, she was born with a sma
coronary artery . . . and as a result, she had a silent hea
attack," said Roh, who, at this point, was standing in fro
of the jury, beside a photograph of a microscopic image c
Maryann's heart magnified many times over.

Roh then began pointing to a similarly-sized photograp
of a section of Maryann's heart muscle—an image, he sai

at "clearly illustrates that all the heart muscles are broken to pieces."

When one suffers a "silent heart attack," Roh continued, all the heart muscles are broken into pieces. So clearly, at the time of, or just before her death, she suffered another heart attack . . . and this time, the damage to her heart was serious enough that her heart failed to function, and she died."

Roh, however, testified that it was his opinion that it wasn't just that Maryann had a small coronary artery that caused her fatal heart attack. There were other contributing factors, too. According to Roh, Maryann had an enlarged liver—almost twice as large as one would expect to find in a healthy woman her age.

"And it has these round clear holes known as fat vacuoles," Roh explained. "This fatty change, almost always, is a result of alcohol trauma . . . In order to have this type of fatty change in the liver, one has to drink a lot for a long period of time."

"Are there other possible causes of a fatty liver?" Harris asked.

"If a person is obese, you can have a little fatty change," Roh replied, "or a person with longstanding diabetes can have some fatty change. But the most common cause of fatty change in the liver is drinking."

"Are you aware of Maryann Boczkowski being diagnosed with any other condition that would be known to cause a fatty liver?"

"No, not other than the drinking problem."

Roh then testified that he disagreed with the state's theory that Maryann had been asphyxiated, noting the presence of food particles in Maryann's lungs.

"Doctor, is food found down in the lungs like that consistent or inconsistent with a person who was strangled by the neck and asphyxiated?" Harris asked.

"If the person was asphyxiated and strangled and died, then [that] person cannot have these food particles aspirated into the lungs," Roh replied.

Roh also said that when reviewing the slides taken during Maryann's autopsy, he found a tear in the inner-lining of the larynx, or in the area of the vocal cord. This tear, he said, likely was the result of an object—such as the intubation tube used by the paramedics who tried to resuscitate Maryann—"going through and touching and ripping the inner-lining."

Harris asked Roh how he could tell the tear wasn't the result of pressure from the outside.

"If the person was strangled by hand," Roh explained, "you invariably find finger marks in the neck area. You don't have those here. The only markings found were under the chin, which could have been a result of the paramedic holding her chin [while intubating her]."

Roh also testified that he did not find any evidence two other tell-tale signs of strangulation: the presence petechia, or fine pinpoint hemorrhages, in the eyes, and fractured hyoid bone. "The hyoid bone is a small C-shape bone that sits on top of the Adam's apple," he explained. "When the neck area [is compressed], that bone breaks. We don't have that here."

Finally, Harris asked Roh about the role Maryann blood alcohol level might have played in her death.

"A high level of alcohol . . . can trigger a heart attack there is already a pre-existing heart condition," Roh replied.

"And did Maryann Boczkowski have a pre-existing heart condition?"

"Yes."

During his cross-examination of Roh, Carroll, after establishing that the pathologist was being paid a total of $3,600 to testify on behalf of the defense, asked him about his testimony that most of the fifty-plus contusions found on Maryann's body during her autopsy were the results of resuscitative efforts.

"What about the contusions to the top of the head? How did you account for those?" Carroll asked.

Roh suggested these bruises could have occurred while Maryann was being transported to the hospital or removed

om the ambulance. "These bruises are very minor," he
ted. "An inch or so in diameter. They were not fatal."

Carroll, however, did succeed in scoring a point for the
ate when Roh was forced to concede that he had never
viewed Maryann's medical history.

"Did you have access to her medical records?" Carroll
ked.

"No," Roh replied.

"So, [even though] you testified as to whether she had
y other medical condition, such as diabetes, you don't
ally know whether she did or not, do you?"

"Diabetes starts from the pancreas," Roh explained.
But] since her pancreas [was] normal, it is clear that she
dn't have diabetes."

Carroll asked Roh whether it was possible that the scar-
ng he observed on Maryann's heart could have been the
sult of a heart condition known as myocarditis, an inflam-
ation of the heart that can cause small scarring.

"There's no history of her having myocarditis," Roh shot
ack.

"Well, you never saw her history, did you? You never
w her medical records?"

Roh acknowledged that that was the case, but added,
'm sure I would have been told. Myocarditis is very se-
ous."

Finally, Carroll tried to sneak in a question he knew
agles wasn't likely to allow. But he felt just asking it
ould raise a red flag in jurors' minds.

"Doctor Roh, would you find it extremely unusual for
wo women married to the same man, one thirty-four and
ne thirty-five, to die of heart attacks?" Carroll asked.

"Objection," Harris declared.

"Sustained," Eagles said.

"Thank you, doctor," Carroll said. "That's all."

CHAPTER 41

AFTER EAGLES excused Roh from the stand, Harris [ ]
formed the judge that he had no additional witnesses.

The defense, he announced, "rests."

Judge Eagles then called for a brief recess, during whi[ ]
an incident occurred in the hallway outside the courtroo[ ]
that almost resulted in her calling a mistrial. One of Ma[ ]
ann's aunts, Ruth Schumann, and two of her sisters, we[ ]
on their way to the ladies' room when they walked pass[ ]
Buc Boczkowski and Louis Roh. Schumann was feeli[ ]
slightly disheartened. Roh had made for a strong defen[ ]
witness. What if the jury bought his testimony? s[ ]
couldn't help but wonder. Then, just as Buc and Sch[ ]
mann's eyes locked, he flashed what she would later d[ ]
scribe as a "gloating grin." Within seconds, Schumann[ ]
temper got the better of her.

"Oh, you were good, Doctor Roh," she shouted at t[ ]
defense witness. "Maybe you'll get him off with your lie[ ]
Maybe you'll get him off, and, when he gets out, he[ ]
marry your daughter next. Would you like that? Would y[ ]
like him to be married to your daughter? Then when [ ]
kills again, you can see what it feels like. Your family c[ ]
go through what mine's going through."

Roh, clearly caught off guard by the ambush, respond[ ]
with stunned silence. Schumann, having surprised herse[ ]
as well, dashed into the women's restroom, emerging on[ ]
after taking a few moments to regain her composure. B[ ]
just as she stepped out into the hallway, she saw Kev[ ]
Rochford and Bob Barbiaux gesturing for her to go ba[ ]
inside. Confused, she waited inside for a couple of minute[ ]
then opened the door and poked her head out.

"What's going on?"

"You may have caused a mistrial," Rochford replied.

It turned out that one of the jurors had been standing in the hallway during Schumann's tirade and had heard every word.

Schumann retreated inside the restroom and remained there until Randy Carroll's wife, Sharon, retrieved her and escorted her to her husband's office.

"You're not the first family member to lash out at a witness, and you won't be the last," Sharon Carroll said, trying to comfort Schumann.

Sharon told Schumann that her husband and Tim's attorneys were in Eagles's chambers at that very moment discussing the incident. A few minutes later, Jim Cvetic walked into Carroll's office.

"Is she going to call a mistrial?" an anxious Schumann asked the detective.

"No," he said, "and you're allowed back inside. But the judge said if you say another word, she'll bar you."

Moments after Cvetic and Schumann returned to their seats in the courtroom, Carroll made a brief statement to the jury, a kind of precursor to his closing argument.

"I believe the defense is going to contend to you that the death of Elaine Boczkowski occurred accidentally," he began. "They're going to say that she apparently hit her head while falling in the bathtub, was dazed or unconscious, and drowned. And if you believe that, it would be your duty to return a verdict of not guilty. I say and contend to you that when you consider all the evidence, you will agree with me that there is simply no doubt, there is no question, that Timothy Boczkowski committed this murder, that he did it with premeditation and deliberation."

Carroll reminded the jury that it could—and should—take Maryann's death into account when deciding its verdict.

"Look at [the] two cases," he said. "The sheer coincidence is just too hard to swallow."

It was Harris's turn next. He began by referring back to

something from Carroll's opening argument. The prosecu
tor had argued at the trial's start that he was there for Elain
because she could no longer speak for herself. But Harri
contended that in a way she could—and that her voic
could be heard loud and clear through her journal.

"Don't take another person's word for what happene
or didn't happen," Harris urged the jury. "Read about it i
[Elaine's] diary. It's right here. We have a unique viev
here. In so many cases where the person is dead, by defi
nition, they're not here to talk to you. They can't tell yo
what they really said. They can't tell you what they reall
felt. They can't tell you what was really going on in thei
life. We have her own diary in her own words and her ow
hand."

Harris also said he agreed with Carroll's characterizatio
of the case as unusual, but for a very different reason. "Hov
unusual is it when a man who has a family, has three chil
dren who he treats well, goes to church regularly, work
for a living, keeps a home . . . who seems to be a good ma
in every way that we judge a good man, how unusual is i
when a man like that kills?

"Not unheard of," Harris said, answering his own ques
tion, "but unusual. That's just one reason that you ought t
look at this case beyond a reasonable doubt. We're no
talking about some sleazeball who's been in prison most o
his life, like Randy Erwin. We're not talking about som
person who has been violent and you can see it buildin
and you can see it coming. Nobody, nobody, on that stan
has testified that Tim Boczkowski ever hit Elaine Bo
czkowski. Nobody has told you that he ever punched her
touched her, shoved her, nothing like that. [There's] no evi
dence whatsoever, none, of domestic violence. No evidenc
of any criminal behavior of any variety.

"Every [crime] has to have a motive," Harris continued
"The prosecution would have you believe the [motive was
money, that this [was] a money killing. But here again, look
at the man. This man is a trained dental technician. He
makes good money. When he was in Pennsylvania, before

he came to North Carolina, he made enough money to buy
a business and buy land up on [Highway] 220 and open up
an ice cream parlor. Now, it's true enough the ice cream
parlor wasn't doing as well as he had hoped, what with the
widening of 220 and everything. But you also heard that
he had sold this business [and] although [that sale] was not
consummated before Elaine Boczkowski was killed, he had
money coming in. It was coming.

"Furthermore, you heard that he could go back to being
a dental technician. Indeed, he did, and when he went back
to being a dental technician, you heard he was making good
money. If this is a money crime, how could it be that [this]
man goes up to Pennsylvania and makes enough money to
build a new house, buy nice furniture, buy a nice vehicle,
buy dental equipment? How can it be that he can make that
kind of money, but, at the same time, [be] killing people
because he needs money? How much sense does that
make?"

Harris also dismissed the notion that Tim had his eye
on the money he would receive as the beneficiary of
Elaine's life insurance policy.

"Now how much money is $25,000 to a man who can
buy a new house, a man who can afford to buy things on his
own? It's a lot of money. I'm not making $25,000 small.
But you ought to ask yourself how much it took to bury
Elaine Boczkowski. How much money got spent on that.
You ought to ask how much money it took to move back to
Pennsylvania, how much money it took to [move Elaine's]
body out of a mausoleum in North Carolina and ship it to
Pennsylvania and re-inter it in a plot that had to be pur-
chased [there]. When it comes right down to it, $25,000
wouldn't go very far toward that, let alone any kind of nor-
mal living expenses.

"Now, that seems to be the prosecution theory. But let's
suppose there's another theory. Let's suppose their theory
is that things are really getting ugly in [Tim and Elaine's]
separation. People getting separated sometimes kill each
other. People getting divorced sometimes kill each other.

Maybe they couldn't agree on how to divide up the money. They couldn't agree on who was going to have custody of the kids. Well, here's what's wrong with that. You can read right in Elaine Boczkowski's own hand, written not long before she died, [that] everything was fine. Everything was worked out. The lawyers who were intimately involved in the case told you that things seemed to be moving along. Tim Boczkowski didn't even have an attorney."

Harris then began talking about a few witnesses in particular and the likely veracity of their testimony, starting with Sandy Boczkowski.

"If Sandy Boczkowski is telling the truth," Harris said, after summarizing her testimony about what she heard and saw in the bathroom the morning of November 4, 1990, "then Elaine Boczkowski cannot have been murdered because she was inside the bathroom, and the door was locked from the inside. She cannot have been murdered." But, he added, "if Sandy Boczkowski is lying about that, she is one disturbed little girl. She is one sicko case. She's got to be. Why? Because Sandy Boczkowski knows or has reason to know that her father killed her mother. If she has been asked to tell that story by anybody, by Tim Boczkowski, her grandparents, or anyone else, she knows that's a lie. I suggest to you that would make one sick little girl, not a girl who makes straight A's, not a girl who learns four languages, not the girl who testified before you and you saw with your own eyes, not a girl who people on both sides, even people that want to see Tim Boczkowski convicted, describe as a normal, healthy girl.

"Now what about the fact that Marianne Rochford's sister got up on the stand and said that Sandy Boczkowski said to her she heard her parents arguing and she heard her mother say, 'No, Tim, no'? What is that all about? What does that make Marianne Rochford's sister? Am I suggesting she's a bad person? I am not. What's basically going on here is that she believes Tim Boczkowski is guilty and, therefore, wants to help to do justice. She doesn't want to see a guilty man go free. Well, ladies and gentlemen, you

don't help justice by standing here and putting your hand
on the Bible, swearing an oath to tell the truth, going up
[on the witness stand] and then exaggerating or saying
things that aren't true. If you want to help justice, you stick
to your oath."

Finally, Harris reviewed some of the physical evidence
he said supported the defense's theory that Elaine's death
was an accident, including the three perfectly even, indented parallel lines found across Elaine's mid-section and
the fact that Elaine's fingernail extensions were completely
intact despite the prosecution's claim that Elaine struggled
against Tim in the bathroom that night.

"Now, if Elaine Boczkowski did not die by positional
asphyxia, how did she die?" Harris continued. "Doctor
Donald Jason said she had a [contusion] on the back of her
head which was consistent with someone hitting their head.
How could she have fallen in the bathtub? If she was step-
ping in the bathtub after filling it up, she could have slipped
on the slick tub bottom. She could have fallen in the process of turning off the faucets. She could have had a moment of dizziness and she could have dropped straight
down." However she sustained the bruises on her head,
Harris reminded the jury, the injury was serious enough to
leave Elaine dazed and unable to keep her head above the
bath water and thus prevent herself from drowning.

"The burden is upon the state to prove its case," Harris
concluded. "You've heard the witnesses. You've heard the
evidence. You've seen the exhibits. If you get their full
meaning, you'll find Tim Boczkowski not guilty."

SHORTLY BEFORE 2:30 p.m., following a one-hour lunch
recess, Randy Carroll got up from his seat, walked out to
the middle of the courtroom, turned toward the jury, and
then pointed to a framed 8×10 photo of Elaine sitting on
the prosecution table in front of an empty seat.

"It's my job to represent innocent victims of crime,"
Carroll began, echoing his own opening statement. "It's my
job to speak for Elaine, because she's not here. Her chair

is empty. Her chair will be forever empty. She'll never have the opportunity to see Sandy drive, to spend Christmases with her, birthdays with her, because he took it all away. She wasn't given a right to sit at the table with her lawyer. She wasn't given a right to confer with her lawyers, to have pictures made of herself. I have to talk for her."

Almost immediately, Carroll responded to defense co-counsel Fred Lind's remarks in his closing—both Lind and Harris addressed the jury—about Carroll's stating in his opening argument that he was going to call the Boczkowski children as witnesses, but ultimately failed to do so. "You know, there comes a point where you use a little common sense, even as a lawyer," Carroll explained, "and there comes a point where you ask, 'Haven't these children been through enough?' "

Tim, on the other hand, the prosecutor suggested, apparently could not be bothered to ask himself that question, especially as far as Sandy was concerned.

"Why," Carroll asked, "after he has put her through the death of her mother and the death of her stepmother, why in God's name does he put her up on the witness stand to [testify] to something that's already [on the record]? Because it shows just how cold-blooded he is."

Carroll reeled off the names of witnesses who described how unemotional Tim appeared in the face of the deaths of both of his wives: Charlie Connolly, his friend from Greensboro, Stacy Tamburo, one of the paramedics who responded to Tim and Maryann's home.

"Have you watched him in the courtroom?" he then asked the jurors themselves. "Throughout the course of this trial, he's showed no emotion, no remorse, just like he did November 4, 1990, just like he did on November 7, 1994."

Carroll asked the jury, too, to think back to the testimony offered by a few witnesses in particular, starting with Marianne Rochford's sister, Gerri Minton. Although Harris suggested in his closing argument that Minton had perjured herself on the witness stand, "There wasn't any reason offered [as to] why she might do that," he noted. "There's no evidence that Gerri Minton was close to Elaine, that she was close to the Boczkowskis. There was no reason offered as to why she would just come in and flat out commit perjury, other than the defense's [theory that she was part] of a conspiracy, which just doesn't hold water.

"Then you've got Randy Erwin," Carroll continued. "Now, I say to you, they've got a lot of nerve to call my witness a sleazebag when they bring in a chiropractor who is a convicted felon." As far as Cobb's contention that Tim hurt his back pulling Elaine from the tub, Carroll contended he just as easily could have injured his back "killing his wife."

Carroll then turned his attention to the circumstances surrounding Elaine's death—most notably, the conflicting accounts Tim gave as to what transpired in the early morning hours of November 4.

"Look at how many different things he said," the prosecutor pointed out. "Depending on who he was talking to, he said he pried the [bathroom] door open, or he popped the lock, or he took the door off its hinges, or he knocked. Now this doesn't prove that he killed his wife. I agree with that. But why did he tell [so many] different stories about how he got in the bathroom? If he's telling the truth, and [Elaine's death] was an accident, he didn't need to lie about anything. But he told different stories, [which means] he didn't tell the truth [to someone]."

Equally suspicious, Carroll insisted, was Tim's habit of implying different things to different people about how Elaine died.

"He leaves the Crendalls and the Di Marcos with the impression that Elaine killed herself," he said. "[But] he tells other people in Pennsylvania that she died because she had psychological problems, that she suffered from depression. [And] he tells people in Greensboro—the Rochfords, Chris Cheek, Charlie Connolly—the same story he told the police: that she drowned."

Carroll mentioned, too, that he thought it curious that Tim was in the bathroom with the door closed when Greensboro firefighters Willie Jones and Bobby Mitchell arrived on the scene.

"Why would he have the door closed?" Carroll asked the jurors to consider. "Wouldn't he want them to get in there real quick? No, he tells the firemen when they yell out to find out where he is, 'Hold on a minute. Hold on.' Why does he want them to hold on? What position is he wanting to get Elaine in while they're holding on? What would a reasonable person do in that situation? [They'd yell], 'I'm upstairs. My wife is dying. Get up here now.' Not him. Not this man. He wants them to 'Hold on.' "

Carroll then asked the jury to think about Tim's behavior the morning of Maryann's death.

"The defendant says, 'I want Gary Waters here. I don't want any of this coming back on me,' " Carroll notes. "Now, isn't that a strange comment to [hear] from an innocent man—or is that the voice of a guilty conscience, of someone who knows he got away with murder four years before and wants to cover himself again? He doesn't even know Gary Waters.

"Why is he getting them both wine [for the hot tub] . . . if he is planning this intervention for her alcohol abuse the next Wednesday? Why, if she's had fourteen beers and is drunk, does he leave her in the hot tub alone for twenty minutes? And why, after finding her with her head turned over in the water, does he immediately go down to the basement to get this mask? He knows how to do CPR. He was a volunteer fireman. Then he puts it on upside down? . . . Probably, y'all can figure it out."

Finally, Carroll pointed to a large piece of poster board that he'd tacked to a spot on the courtroom wall between Judge Eagles and the jury. It read in large black letters:

Money
+ Control
+ *Jealousy*
= Murder

"This is a man who is driven by money," Carroll stated matter-of-factly. "Look how lawsuit-happy he is. I mean, just to give you an example, he talks to Kevin Rochford about bringing suit against the woman [who rear-ended] Elaine, because after the accident, she wants to have too much sex. I ask you, in thinking about how plausible that story is, what red-blooded American male thinks their wife wants too much sex?

"Control is the second thing. You remember what Marianne Rochford read to you from [Elaine's] journal. She talks about how her life is changing. She's getting more independent. She's getting a job. He's losing control over her. And then there is the jealousy thing. You know from the evidence that Timothy Boczkowski was reading Elaine's journal. She even has an entry in there where she mentions that. Then, on November 3, she sits down and writes every detail about a very vivid, very graphic, dramatic dream for her. It was Christmas time, she and Father Jim Weisner are lying there on the floor together. They kiss. She rubs his hair. I argue and contend to you he read that last entry. Then she comes home, he confronts her in the bathroom . . . and he kills her.

"That is your premeditation. That last journal entry pushed him over the edge. That's not speculation. That is a logical inference from the evidence in the case . . . I ask you, remember Elaine. Remember the kids. Don't compromise justice for Elaine Boczkowski. Do what you said you would do. Base your verdict on the evidence. Base it on the evidence and follow the law. I contend to you that when you do that, the picture is clear. Timothy Boczkowski is guilty—guilty of murder in the first degree."

CHAPTER 42

IT WAS roughly 5 p.m. on Friday, November 1, when the jury of eight women and four men began deliberating Tim's fate. Over the next two-and-a-half hours, the jurors sent Eagles several notes. They requested to see, among other evidence, the photos of Tim taken by the police after Elaine's and Maryann's deaths, a transcript of Sandy Boczkowski's testimony, copies of all of Tim's statements to the police, the photos taken during Elaine's autopsy, Elaine's and Maryann's autopsy reports, and Elaine's journal.

Shortly after 8 p.m., after learning that the jury had reached a verdict, Judge Eagles called the court to order. Randy Carroll and Detective Jim Cvetic, as they had throughout the trial, sat side-by-side at the prosecutor's table. Behind them were about two dozen friends and relatives of Elaine's and Maryann's.

Seated at the defense table were Tim, and, to his left, defense co-counsel Doug Harris and Fred Lind. The Boczkowski family sat in the second row of seats on the defendant's side of the courtroom.

"I understand from the bailiff that the jury has reached a verdict," Eagles said.

At precisely 8:22 a.m., the jury filed slowly into the courtroom. Eagles instructed the panel's foreman, a minister, to deliver the verdict sheet to a sheriff's deputy, who then handed it over to Eagles. Eagles read the verdict, then handed it to the clerk on duty.

"Madame Clerk, would you read the verdict?"

"Members of the jury, you have agreed upon your verdict in the case of the state of North Carolina versus Tim-

othy Boczkowski. In 95-CRS-20209, you say you find the
defendant guilty of first-degree murder."

"This is your verdict, so say you all?" the clerk asked.

Each and every juror, in response, nodded his or head
up and down.

Tim stared straight ahead, displaying no emotion whatsoever. But his siblings, Ron and Joan, could be heard crying. The crowd on the prosecution's side of the courtroom
exchanged smiles and hugs. "Thank you, Jesus," Maryann's
aunts, Eleanor Camp and Maggie Fischerkeller, shouted in
unison. Carroll and Cvetic shook hands.

Carroll would later say he was fairly confident the jury
was going to return a guilty verdict. "I felt I had made as
good an argument in this case as I ever had," he said. "Everything just fell into place.

"Plus," he added with a wry smile, referring to the defense mounted by Doug Harris, "I had a lot of help from
the other side."

Eagles set November 12 as the date for Tim's sentencing
hearing, then declared court in recess.

"Hang in there, Tim," Buc Boczkowski shouted to his
son as a handcuffed Tim was led from the courtroom.
"Hang in there."

Tim turned towards his father and, without changing his
expression, gave him a thumb's-up.

CHAPTER 43

NOVEMBER 12, 1996 was Todd Boczkowski's twelfth birthday. But the youngest of Tim and Elaine's three children had little reason to celebrate. That same day, his father was in a Greensboro, NC, courtroom, hours away from learning whether his conviction for ending their mother's life would cost him his.

Tim's sentencing hearing began with both the prosecution and the defense calling witnesses they hoped would convince the jury to give Tim the punishment they believed he deserved. For Randy Carroll, it was death by lethal injection. For Doug Harris and Fred Lind it was life in prison.

Carroll called Lee Cecil, the lawyer who had represented Elaine in her separation from Tim, as his first witness. Because Carroll had cited pecuniary gain as the aggravating circumstance that qualified Tim for the death penalty, he asked Cecil about the potential financial hardship Tim would have faced if he and Elaine had gotten divorced and she had retained custody of the children. Cecil testified that under the formula used in North Carolina to determine child support for the custodial parent, Tim would have had to pay Elaine $380 a month in child support, which, at the time of Elaine's death, amounted to more than a third of Tim's monthly gross income.

But under cross-examination by Harris, Cecil conceded that a certain percentage of Tim's salary would have gone to support his children regardless of whether he and Elaine ended their marriage.

"[There are expenses associated with child-rearing] whether the children are living with both parents [or with just one], aren't there?" Harris asked.

"Yes," Cecil replied.

"And so the [cost of] raising the children wouldn't [necessarily] be more because they were living with Mrs. Boczkowski alone?"

"Yes," the attorney responded again.

Kevin and Marianne Rochford followed Cecil on the witness stand. Kevin repeated some of his testimony from the guilt phase of Tim's trial, describing how Tim, less than eight hours after Elaine was pronounced dead, had asked him how soon he could collect on Elaine's life insurance policies.

"I was infuriated," Kevin said. "I said, 'Can't this wait? She's only been dead a few hours.' "

Kevin also testified he did not think Tim was aware that, under North Carolina law, it is illegal for someone to witness a will in which they are also named as a beneficiary. In other words, he said, Tim did not know at the time of Elaine's death that he would not be receiving any inheritance.

Harris, for his part, attempted to negate Carroll's argument by contending that Tim was well aware long before Elaine died that he was unlikely to profit as a result of her death because of debts they had that had to be paid.

"When the smoke cleared," Harris suggested, "there really wasn't a whole lot of money left in the estate, was there?"

"No," Kevin reluctantly agreed. "After paying off their debts, funeral expenses, et cetera, there was not a lot of money left to distribute from the estate itself."

Marianne Rochford testified that Elaine was upset not only about the fact that Tim had reached an agreement to sell King Kones without consulting her first, but about the terms of the agreement as well. According to Marianne, Tim agreed to a sale price of $120,000. But instead of paying cash, the agreement called for the buyers to sign two promissory notes—one for $52,000 and another for $34,000. The remaining $34,000, Marianne testified, was covered by a verbal agreement between Tim and the buyers

that called for the buyers to pay Tim and Elaine "with . .
cash as it [became] available to them."

When it came time for the defense to plead its case to
the jury, Doug Harris began by calling Tom Czarnomski
a friend of Tim and Elaine's from the St. Paul the Apostle
Parish to the witness stand. Czarnomski, the finance man
ager for a medical systems firm, testified that he and his
wife, Irene, joined the church around the same time Tim
and Elaine had. He said Tim had been a member of St
Paul's Family Life Commission and, in that capacity
helped recruit other church members to volunteer at church
barbecues and golf outings. Czarnomski also testified that
Tim had helped him try to get a men's club off the ground
that each year around Christmas, Tim arranged for mem
bers of the church's Young Married Couples group to sing
at local nursing homes; and that Tim had sponsored a
church youth who was preparing for confirmation.

"Describe to the members of the jury what type of per
son Tim is," Harris said.

"If I could use two words to describe Tim, they would
be *trustworthy* and *compassionate*," Czarnomski began
"Once, I was playing golf with Tim and two other friends
when a storm came up. Tim and one of our other friends
decided, because of the lightning and thunder, that they
were going to go. [But I stayed behind] because I was
having a good round. Tim had driven over to my house
that morning, so he asked to be dropped off there. I didn't
know it at the time, but when the storm hit, it knocked
down a good-sized pine tree [that was on my property]
When I got back, my wife told me that when Tim saw that
the tree had fallen, he went back to his house and got his
chain saw, then came back to my house, cut up the tree,
and took it away. I didn't even notice [it was gone] until
my wife said something. Another time, Tim and I went out
to the Greater Greensboro Open [golf tournament] and after
we parked, we got out of his truck and he threw his keys
on the floor. I said, 'Do you want me to lock the door?'
He said, 'No, I trust people. I know the truck is gong to be

ere.' Coming from New York originally, that stuck with
me."

Carroll wasn't impressed.

"*Trustworthy* and *compassionate*. Those would be ac-
urate [words] to describe Mr. Boczkowski's character?"
Carroll asked.

"Yes," Czarnomski replied.

"Well, let me ask you this. Does the death of his second
wife in Pennsylvania in any way change your opinion—"

"Objection," defense co-counsel Fred Lind interjected.

"Go ahead," Eagles instructed Carroll.

"—of the defendant's character?"

"Objection," Lind repeated.

"Overruled."

"No," Czarnomski replied.

"Was his killing Elaine and his conviction for that some-
ning that changed your opinion of his character?"

"No."

"Thank you, sir," Carroll offered. "I believe that's all."

At this point, Harris summoned his final witness to the
tand.

"At this time," he announced, "I'd like to call Rose Bo-
zkowski."

Harris began by asking Tim's mother about Tim's re-
ationship with Randy, Sandy, and Todd since his arrest.

"Their dad calls them and writes them every week," she
aid. "He's always been concerned about his children."

"Does it seem to you that the children look forward to
alking to him on the phone?"

"Yes, they do."

"Do the children write back to him?"

"Yes. They write back every week."

"Have you had occasion to read some of the letters he's
written to the children?"

"They show me the letters."

"What sorts of thing does Mr. Boczkowski express in
hem?"

"He tells them to be good, and to do good in school,

and to obey whoever watches them, and to have manners

"Are the children, in fact, doing well in school?"

"Yes, they are. Very well."

"What sort of boy was your son growing up? Was he the sort of boy that was always in trouble or was he a boy who obeyed his parents and did well?"

"Like any boy, he'd get into little things, get into it with his brother and sisters occasionally. But he was a wonderful child. He was in Cub Scouts. He was in the Boy Scouts. I had no trouble at all with him growing up."

"Did he ever get in any trouble with the juvenile authorities?"

"No."

"Was he the sort of boy who would help out his neighbors and do things for people?"

"Yes. He would cut the grass, or shovel the snow, or, if he would see a neighbor [getting] out of their car with packages, he'd be right there to help them take them into their house."

"That grass-mowing or snow-shoveling, was that for free?"

"That was free. He didn't care to be paid. Some people offered, but he said, 'No, I just do this on my own.' "

"Did he ever get into any kind of legal trouble of any variety prior to Elaine Boczkowski's death? Did he ever get arrested or go to jail or have any trouble like that?"

"No. He'd never been in any legal trouble."

"Have you ever observed him to be greedy or money hungry?"

"No, I've never, ever seen him be greedy or money hungry. In fact, he would [prefer] to give rather than take."

"Are the children fully aware of the possibility that their father may get the death penalty? Are they cognizant of that?"

"Yes. It's in all the papers and it's on the radio. We can't keep it from them. [So] we're trying to be as truthful as we can, and to explain it to them."

"Do you find that the children are very concerned by the

prospect that their father might get the death penalty?"

"Yes, they are. Todd, because he's the youngest, thinks if his dad gets the death penalty, he's going to die right away. We said, 'Todd, that doesn't mean you're going to die right away.' We tried to explain it to him. 'We just have to take it day by day,' I told him."

CARROLL, DURING his cross-examination of Tim's mother, asked her about the role Elaine had played in the children's lives, a subject Harris had ignored completely.

"Todd would always talk about how they used to go to the circus," Rose testified, "and how their mom would always get them candy and toys every time they went to K mart."

"So, that's what you remember?" Carroll asked. "That she bought them candy and toys?"

"Uh huh. Yeah."

"You don't remember other ways that she nurtured or cared for the children?"

"Well, she took care of them, just like their dad did."

"They called Maryann 'Mother,' didn't they?"

"Yes, they did."

"She adopted the children?"

"Objection," Lind interjected.

"Objection," Harris followed.

"I object to both of them objecting," Carroll said.

"I'll do the objecting and I object," Harris said.

"All right," declared an exasperated Eagles. "Overruled."

"She adopted the children?" Carroll asked again.

"Yes," Rose replied, "she did."

RANDY CARROLL began his closing argument by acknowledging to the jurors that he appreciated just how difficult a decision they faced.

"You know, it's not easy to stand up here and ask a group of twelve people to sentence another human being to death," he said. . . . But you have the hardest job of all.

You're the ones that have to make the [actual] decision."

Carroll told the panel he expected the defense would argue that Tim did not deserve the death penalty because he had no criminal history prior to his arrest for Elaine' murder, because he "had previously led an exemplary life with significant involvement in the church and the community," and because a sentence of death "would cause additional suffering to his children."

"Additional suffering?" Carroll said. "If there's any additional suffering, it's his responsibility. If it weren't for him, they would be with their mother at Thanksgiving, and on Christmas, and on their birthdays. He is responsible for every single shred of suffering that [has to do with] this case. So don't let them fool you with that."

Fred Lind spoke first for the defense.

"One thing we would argue, and contend," he said, "is that Tim Boczkowski's mere existence is of comfort to his children. He still has contact with his children. They eagerly await his telephone calls and letters. His mere presence is important to his children.

"Look at the good parts of Tim Boczkowski's life. Look at the good things he's done. You heard Mr. Czarnomski talk about him, what type of person he is. If he sees a tree down in front of a friend's house, he takes it away. He's the type of person who cares about other people.

"This is not about letting anybody off the hook," Lind added. "But what we do ask is that you consider being merciful ... because there's a lot of good in Tim Boczkowski."

After Lind concluded, Eagles called for a brief recess. When court resumed, Harris took his turn before the jury.

"Mr. Carroll said this was about punishment and I agree with that," Harris said. "And when it comes right down to it, isn't life in prison a lot of punishment? I mean, for heaven's sake, you wake up in the morning in a small cell and you spend all day in there, and you maybe get out for an hour of exercise. If you go anywhere, you're handcuffed

nd maybe your legs are shackled. You don't get outside
o be free, ever.

"Life in prison is punishment. It's no kind of life. So
ve ought not to be thinking here that a life sentence is some
ind of award, that it's a better deal than death. That's not
o. You could even make an argument that life in prison is
nore punishment than death. Indeed, there have been peo-
le who've asked for death. You could make an argument
hat the most mercy that you could give a man who is about
o [be sentenced to] life in prison would be to go over and
ill him and save him the misery of going through his life
iving like that."

Harris also implored the jury to consider Tim's children.

"How can you make them suffer more?" he asked.
There's only one way—and that's to kill their father, too.
Now, Tim Boczkowski did a bad thing. But I'll tell you
ne thing Tim Boczkowski didn't do. He didn't make those
hildren orphans. Only you can do that.

"Must you do this? Must you kill a man . . . He's not
oing to be a danger to anybody [in prison] . . . Do we have
o kill him? Is that what we have to do? Tomorrow morn-
ng, when I look in the mirror, I will see a man who did
is best to keep a man from being killed. When you look
n the mirror, will you be looking at a person who didn't
ave to kill somebody, but voted to kill them, or will you
e looking at a person who took the option of life when it
wasn't necessary to kill? Who will you be looking at in the
mirror?

"Do any of you believe that if Elaine Boczkowski could
speak, that she would say, 'Yes, kill my children's father.
That's what I want. Now that I'm dead, make them orphans. That will be even better for them'? . . . Do you believe she would say, 'Because I am dead, because my
husband killed me when he shouldn't have, that now, he
must die also, no matter what the consequences, no matter
what it does to my children . . . no matter if they are or-
phaned?' . . . I look to you as (citizens) to do the right thing.
. . I look to you to do right to protect the future. Tim

Boczkowski is going to jail for life. He's not the future . .
The future is the children. Don't hurt the children. Yo
don't need to."

At 6:34 p.m., after spending less than two hours delib
erating whether Tim should be put to death for Elaine'
murder, the jurors, having reached a verdict, ambled int
the courtroom.

Judge Eagles asked to see the verdict sheet, glanced a
it, then handed it to the clerk on duty to read aloud.

"Members of the jury," the clerk began, "in the case o
the state of North Carolina versus Timothy Boczkowski
you have agreed upon your recommendation for sentencin
in case number 95-CRS-20209. It is your recommendatio
that the defendant, Timothy Boczkowski, be sentenced t
life imprisonment."

Tim, as he had upon hearing the jury's verdict of guilt
less than two weeks earlier, showed no emotion upon hear
ing that the same panel had voted to spare his life. Ros
Boczkowski and Tim's sister, Joan, who were sitting in th
first row of seats behind the defense table, breathed sigh
of relief. Buc Boczkowski was absent. He was in Pitts
burgh, recovering from an infected gallbladder that had le
to his being rushed to the hospital only days after the guil
phase of the trial ended.

Randy Carroll was disappointed but not surprised by th
jury's decision to sentence Tim to life in prison. "I didn'
think he was going to get death," Carroll said after the trial
"Of course, that doesn't mean I don't think he didn't de
serve it."

Later, Carroll would say he thought the fact that the cas
against Tim was largely circumstantial contributed to th
jury's decision. "In my experience," he explained, "juror
want to hear good, direct eyewitness testimony before the
sentence someone to death."

On November 5, four days after Tim was convicted o
Elaine's murder, a spokesperson for the Allegheny County
District Attorney's Office had told reporters that the stat
was taking a "wait and see" position as far as trying Tim

or Maryann's murder. "We want to talk to the family and ok at the case from all angles," the spokesperson said.

What that really meant was that Tim's sentence was going to be the determining factor. If the jury sentenced Tim o death, there was a strong possibility the Allegheny County District Attorney's Office would opt against extraliting Tim to Pittsburgh to stand trial for Maryann's death. f the jury decided to sentence Tim to life in prison, the pposite would likely occur, mainly because, under a North Carolina statute in effect at the time of Elaine's 1990 murder, Tim would be eligible for parole in twenty years. But nce the jury had voted to spare Tim's life, it was all but ertain Tim would be brought back to Pittsburgh to stand rial. This suited Maryann's loved ones just fine.

"My family would like to be spared a second trial," Maryann's aunt, Ruth Schumann, told a reporter prior to Tim's sentencing hearing. "But if there's a chance he can get out, they better have one."

CHAPTER 44

AFTER BEING sentenced to life in prison for Elaine Bo czkowski's murder, Tim was transferred from the Guilfor County Jail, where he'd been held since being extradite from Pennsylvania, to Central Prison in Raleigh, North Car olina. He spent at least some of his time writing to ol friends, including Mark and Maria Crendall. Tim had bee writing to Mark for some time. A letter he had sent befor the trial for Elaine's murder was typical: He claimed h would ultimately be exonerated and that he looked forwar to getting together with Mark and Maria once he was free He sometimes mentioned people he met in jail, but neve Elaine or Maryann. Then, after being convicted of Elaine' murder, he sent Mark and Maria a letter in which he in cluded a newspaper story about a North Carolina man wh had been freed after it was discovered he had been wrong fully convicted of murder. "I think he was saying, 'This i what happened to me,' " Maria would later say.

Back in Pennsylvania, on December 11, 1996, a pane of Pennsylvania Superior Court judges heard oral argu ments regarding Allegheny County Deputy District Attor ney Christopher Conrad's appeal of Judge David Cercone' 1995 ruling that the prosecutor could introduce evidenc relating to Elaine's death at Tim's trial for Maryann's mur der only if the defense argued that Maryann's murder wa an accident.

"The odds of two wives dying in such parallel circum stances is practically astronomical," Conrad argued, addin that evidence relating to Elaine's murder "is extremely cru cial in this case. We have the responsibility to take th North Carolina trial evidence to the jury regardless o nether accidental death is raised by the defense or not."

But defense lawyer Marianne Luksik-Jarvis, an associate
James Herb, Tim's attorney since the time of his arrest,
gued that such evidence could prejudice the jury hearing
e Pittsburgh case.

Meanwhile, eleven days later, *Pittsburgh Post-Gazette*
aders found staring at them from the Sunday newspaper's
ont page, the faces of Tim and Elaine's three children.

Prior to Tim's trial for Elaine's murder, a Pennsylvania
urt had ordered the children, who had moved from Tim's
ster's home to their paternal grandparents, escorted to
reensboro by two representatives of Allegheny County
hildren and Youth Services should they be called to tes-
y. However, Buc and Rose Boczkowski instead allowed
m's sister, Pat, to bring Randy, Sandy, and Todd to North
arolina. Rose Boczkowski later claimed she was unaware
the order. She said she had been unable to attend the
aring at which the order was issued because she was sick.
t just didn't dawn on me [there was] a court order," she
stified at Tim's sentencing hearing.

Despite Rose Boczkowski's contention that she and her
mily didn't consciously violate the court order, a Pennsyl-
ania court found the Boczkowskis in contempt of court.
s a result, Randy, Sandy, and Todd were taken from their
andparents' home and placed in the care of a foster family
Franklin Park. This was meant to be only a temporary
acement. But ACCYS officials were having difficulty
ding a foster home for the children in either Ross Town-
ip or West View, where they wanted to live so they
ould not have to switch schools. So the trio, with the AC-
YS's blessing, decided to make their own public appeal.

"These are very well-behaved kids," the article quoted
e trio's then–foster mother as saying. "You couldn't ask
r three better teenagers."

The article also described how the three youths had ar-
ved at their foster home with little more than their clothes.
or space reasons, it said, they had to leave most of their
ossessions at their grandparents' house. Randy said what

he missed most were the family photographs he'd bee
forced to leave behind. Sandy said she had what matter
most to her: her two brothers.

The next day, the *Post-Gazette* published a follow-
story saying that more than twenty families had alread
called about taking the children in.

"I'm confident we will find them a home," ACCYS D
rector Mark Cherna told the newspaper.

On December 24—Christmas Eve—the *Post-Gazet*
published a second follow-up story. According to the A(
CYS, the agency had received fifty-five inquiries about th
children since the first story had run two days earlier.

ACCYS Director Cherna said he remained optimist
that the appeal would pay off. "All you need is one goo
home."

Maryann's friends' and family's hearts went out
Randy, Sandy, and Todd when they saw the *Post-Gazett*
stories. At the same time, they couldn't help but be struc
by the irony of their predicament. "One good home?" the
thought, Cherna's declaration reverberating in their ear
They'd had a good home, they pointed out, two in fact, an
it was their father's fault alone that that was no longer th
case.

Some three weeks later, on January 16, 1997, the *Pos
Gazette* ran a fourth story on the children's search, repor
ing this time that they had been placed together in a hom
in the North Hills School District. The kids chose their ne
foster family—one of ninety-six that ultimately contacte
the ACCYS—after meeting with several who had offere
to bring them into their homes. "It just felt right," Rand
said, explaining what made him and his siblings choose th
family they did.

The news for Tim, who remained in prison in Nort
Carolina, wasn't as good. About a month later, on Februar
13, 1997, the state Superior Court ruled on Conrad's appe:
of Cercone's ruling: the court voted by a two-to-one margi
to amend Cercone's decision.

"We disagree with the trial court's order which states that the aforementioned evidence may only be offered by the Commonwealth to rebut a claim that Maryann's death was accidental," noted the judge who wrote the majority opinion. "The evidence surrounding Elaine Boczkowski's death . . . [is] admissible as part of the Commonwealth's case-in-chief."

Around the same time, Tim's actions claimed yet another casualty: his parents' marriage. On February 28, 1997, at the top of the *Pittsburgh Post-Gazette*'s "Divorces Granted" listing was the following entry: "BOCZKOWSKI, Rosemary from Kieran."

Exactly when Tim's trial for Maryann's murder might begin was anyone's guess at this point, thanks to defense attorney James Herb's decision to appeal the state Superior Court's recent ruling to the Pennsylvania Supreme Court. For Maryann's family, the wait began to seem interminable. Then, in early 1998, their desire to see Tim brought to justice for Maryann's death took another blow. On January 5, Christopher Conrad, who knew as much about the case as anyone, was fired from his deputy district attorney job, a victim of politics in the battle to replace then-outgoing Allegheny County District Attorney Robert Colville, who was appointed to the bench. Eventually, the case was assigned to Ed Borkowski, another veteran deputy district attorney.

In June, word came from Harrisburg that the Pennsylvania Supreme Court had declined to hear Herb's appeal. Following the Supreme Court's decision, a start date of September 1998 was set for Tim's trial. Meanwhile, on September 15, 1998, the North Carolina Court of Appeals issued a ruling rejecting Tim's appeal of his conviction for Elaine's murder. Malcolm Ray Hunter, Jr., Tim's court-appointed appellate attorney, had argued that Judge Eagles had committed "prejudicial error" by allowing evidence relating to Maryann's death to be admitted as evidence, by allowing seventeen witnesses to testify about Maryann's death, by denying the defense's request that the instructions to the jury specifically state that Tim was on trial only for Elaine's death, and by allowing the state to introduce Sandy Boczkowski's statements to Gerri Minton the morning of Elaine's death as "excited utterances." But the appellate court ruled that: 1) evidence of other crimes, including testimony about those crimes, is admissible for purposes such as proof of motive, opportunity, intent, preparation, plan, knowledge, identity, or absence of mistake, entrapment or accident; 2) Eagles's instructions to the jury "essentially conveyed what the defense was requesting and enabled the jurors to correctly weigh and consider" evidence relating to Maryann's death; and 3) that sufficient evidence was introduced from which Eagles could conclude that Sandy's statements to Minton were "the product of spontaneous reactions to a traumatic event rather than the result of reflection or fabrication."

In the end Tim's decision to fight extradition to Pennsylvania from North Carolina prevented him from arriving in Pittsburgh until October 23, 1998. But, because the wheels of justice turn slowly, even with Tim back in Allegheny County, it remained unclear exactly when he would be tried. The fact that nearly four years had passed since Maryann's death made this uncertainty all the more frustrating for her family and friends. This was especially true for Maryann's mother, Pat, whose lingering doubts about Tim's guilt were beginning to fade.

"Is this Todd?" Maryann's cousin, Karen Schumann, asked her Aunt Pat during a Christmas visit to Maryann's parents' house, after noticing what appeared to be a recent photo sitting on a living room bookshelf. "He looks so different."

"I send them checks for their birthdays and for Christmas and they send me their school pictures," Pat explained. "They call to thank me, too. We never talk about what happened, but as soon as Tim's trial is over, I have plenty of questions I want to ask them."

*   *   *

FTER SEVERAL more months of legal wrangling, Tim's
ial was finally set for April 5, 1999. But before jury section even began, Tim's lawyer, James Herb, filed a mo-
on asking Judge David Cercone to strike down the
osecution's right to seek the death penalty against Tim.
he basis of Herb's argument was that the only aggravating
rcumstance making Tim eligible for the death penalty was
e fact that he had been found guilty of murdering Elaine.
ut according to Herb, Tim never would have been con-
cted of this crime if he hadn't been extradited to North
arolina. And that extradition, Herb claimed, was illegal
cause it violated a Pennsylvania judge's court order stay-
g any out-of-state proceedings against Tim until after he
as tried for Maryann's murder.

Cercone ruled that it "made sense" for Tim to be tried
rst in North Carolina, but agreed to take Herb's motion
nder advisement. He also said that until he reached a final
ecision, jurors should be asked whether they would be
illing to consider imposing the death penalty if the facts
f the case warranted it. Cercone, however, rejected another
erb motion: a request that the charges against Tim be
smissed because of the fact that he was tried first in North
arolina, preventing him from receiving a "speedy trial" in
ennsylvania.

Ultimately, it took seven days of questioning more than
0 prospective jurors before a jury of nine women and
ree men were seated. By this time, incidentally, Cercone
ad denied Herb's motion asking that the prosecution not
e allowed to seek the death penalty.

The gallery was packed by the time Ed Borkowski and
ames Herb delivered their opening arguments on Thursday
pril 14. Randy, Sandy, and Todd sat in the first row be-
ind the defense table, flanked by Tim's brother, Ron, and
is court-appointed appellate attorney, Jack Conflenti. Buc
oczkowski and Tim's sisters, Joan and Pat, sat in the row
ehind them. Tim's mother Rose, her new husband, Francis
ndreoletti, who she married in 1997, not long after her
ivorce from Buc was final, sat in the third row.

Pat and Lew Fullerton, who attended every day of the former son-in-law's Pittsburgh trial, sat in the first row behind the prosecutor's table, along with Maryann's brother John, and her uncle, George Schumann. George's wife Ruth, and her and Pat's other sisters, sat in the second row. The rows behind them were filled with friends of Maryann's and many other relatives.

Borkowski, echoing prosecutor Randy Carroll, his North Carolina counterpart, mentioned some of the startling similarities between Elaine and Maryann in his opening argument. Both, he began, were devout Catholics who Tim met through a Catholic singles group. Both were originally from the North Hills, both were in their mid-thirties (Elaine was 34, Maryann, 35), both weighed exactly 151 pounds at the time of their deaths, both were found unconscious in the early morning hours, both died in November, and both had unexplained head injuries.

Borkowski, however, was not allowed to tell the jury that Tim had been tried or convicted of Elaine's murder. The reason? At the time Chris Conrad appealed Cercone's ruling, prohibiting the state from introducing evidence about Elaine's death unless the defense argued accidental death, Tim's North Carolina trial had yet to take place.

The evidence would show, Borkowski continued, that Tim plotted Maryann's death. He also conceded that while "there are no eyewitnesses, no smoking guns," in this case not all of the evidence against Tim was circumstantial. Several inmates who knew Tim when he was being held in the Allegheny County Jail would testify that Tim made self-incriminating statements to them, Borkowski said, giving the jury a sneak preview of his witness line-up. "He was almost bragging about it," the prosecutor added with a sense of incredulity.

Other non-circumstantial evidence of Tim's guilt, he added, included the scratch marks the police observed on Tim's body the morning of Maryann's death.

James Herb, for his part, maintained that Maryann was not murdered. He insisted instead that she died of a heart

ttack brought on by the high temperature of the water in
he hot tub and heavy drinking.

The bruises observed on Maryann's body by rescue per-
onnel and during her autopsy, Herb argued, were the result
f efforts to revive her. He also contended that the police
gnored evidence that would have exonerated Tim, but did
ot elaborate on what that evidence might be.

"They had one goal and one goal alone in mind from
he outset," Herb said. And that goal, he insisted, was to
rrest Tim and then convict him of Maryann's murder.

"This case is not a homicide," Herb declared. "[Mary-
nn] was not strangled. There was no compression of her
eck . . . Reject this wayward and biased prosecution."

Borkowski's parade of witnesses very much resembled
he group Carroll had assembled two-and-a-half years ear-
ier in Greensboro. He began by calling Tim and Elaine's
eighbor, Wes Semple. He also called a number of the po-
ice officers and rescue personnel who arrived at the scene:
Ross Township Police Officer William Barrett, who
verheard Tim telling his mother he wished Ross Township
Detective Gary Waters was there, Waters himself, and Al-
egheny County Police Detective Jim Cvetic. Allegheny
County Chief Forensic Pathologist Leon Rozin, who per-
ormed Maryann's autopsy, again testified about the injuries
e believed were inflicted on Maryann prior to her death
nd his conclusion that she was strangled. Maryann's
riends Eileen and Chuck Datt and Gay and Bob Barbiaux
lso took the stand for the state. So, too, did a contingent
f North Carolina witnesses, including Greensboro fire-
ighter Willie Jones, Greensboro Police Officer Brenda
Gilmore-Vance, and a number of Tim and Elaine's
Greensboro friends, including Kevin and Marianne Roch-
ord. However, Marianne's sister, Gerri Minton, was not
llowed to testify in Pittsburgh. Unlike Judge Catherine Eagles, who presided over Tim's North Carolina trial, Judge
Cercone ruled that the statements Sandy Boczkowski had
made to Minton in the kitchen of Tim and Elaine's Yester

Oaks apartment the morning of Elaine's death did not qualify as "excited utterances."

Among the witnesses Borkowski called who had not testified against Tim in North Carolina was Allegheny General Hospital Nurse Linda Clemens, who told Tim the morning of November 7, 1994, that Maryann had been pronounced dead. Clemens testified that Tim didn't seem to care. Instead, she said, he began telling her how Maryann had consumed thirteen beers that day. "The first thing he said to me was that his wife was an alcoholic and that she had been drinking all day," she testified. "There was no emotion at all."

Borkowski also called a woman named Karen Habenstein, who worked in human resources at North Hills Passavant Hospital and whose testimony would solve the mystery of why Tim had insisted that Maryann be transported to Allegheny General as opposed to Passavant, even though Passavant was closer. Habenstein testified that at the time of Maryann's death, Elaine's sister, Janet, worked evenings at the hospital as a nurse's assistant. That was it. Tim didn't want to risk the possibility that his former sister-in-law might be on duty when Maryann was brought in.

Another witness who testified against Tim for the first time was Mike Minnard, an evaluation therapist for the Gateway Rehabilitation Center, the substance abuse treatment facility Maryann visited after being confronted about her drinking in Father Almade's office the February before her death. Minnard testified that he met with Maryann on March 21, 1994. He said she told him her "friends were concerned about her drinking and recommended she talk to someone."

After speaking with Maryann, Minnard concluded she did not have a dependency problem. He did, however, suggest she enroll in the center's outpatient counseling program "to head off any problems that might come up down the road." Maryann refused, Minnard said, and he never saw her again.

Sister Pat Baker testified how, at her going-away party,

ie'd seen Tim, who had professed to being concerned
bout Maryann's drinking, bringing his wife drinks. At the
ame time, the former Nativity Church choir director told
irors about having smelled alcohol on Maryann's breath
uring choir practice and about being among those who had
onfronted Maryann about her drinking in February 1994.

Maryann's friends and family couldn't understand why
orkowski had called Baker. Her testimony, they felt, only
ipported the defense's contention that Maryann had a se-
ous drinking problem. But Borkowski explained after-
ards that if he hadn't put Baker on the stand, Herb would
ave, and it might then have appeared to the jury as though
orkowski was completely ignoring the fact that alcohol,
n some level, was an issue for Maryann.

Nora Swango, whose own Noring Court house was just
o the right of Tim and Maryann's house, also took the
and. Swango said that after Tim returned from being in-
erviewed by the police the morning of Maryann's death,
ie saw him carry a heavy-duty vacuum cleaner out to the
eck behind the house. Afterwards, she saw Tim, who
new it was trash pick-up day, carry a full garbage bag
om the deck and bury it at the bottom of his garbage can.

Ultimately, no less than four former Allegheny County
ail inmates testified as witnesses for the prosecution, an-
wering questions about statements Tim had either made to
nem about Elaine's and Maryann's deaths or that they'd
verheard Tim making to someone else. The first, Claude
Gaston, Jr., had been incarcerated with Tim in 1994. "I
on't remember his exact words or nothing, but he said he
s supposed to have a body here and a body down there,"
e testified, referring to Pittsburgh and Greensboro, respec-
vely.

John Gallo, the second inmate to take the witness stand,
lso said he heard Tim make comments about having mur-
ered both Elaine and Maryann. "Another inmate said to
im it was kind of stupid to kill two women the same way,
nd [Boczkowski] said, 'Yeah, I guess it was pretty stupid'
s he was walking away."

The inmate Gallo overheard Tim talking to was obv
ously Randy Erwin, who, when it was his turn to take th
stand, repeated his testimony from North Carolina whi
adding that Tim had boasted to him that the police had litt
evidence tying him to Maryann's death.

Finally, Robert Anthony Kutchmark, another one-tin
fellow inmate of Tim's at the Allegheny County Jail, sai
that Tim had offered him $1,000 to testify that Randy E
win had admitted to him that his testimony about his con
versations with Tim was made up. Kutchmark passed.

Herb tried to discredit each of the four men who ha
served time with Tim. He branded Erwin the county jail
"father confessor." In fact, Herb noted, at various poin
during his criminal career, Erwin had shared with polic
the alleged jailhouse confessions of a total of four fello
inmates in exchange for lighter sentences. Gallo, he mai
tained, agreed to testify only because he wanted a free tri
to Pittsburgh from Florida, where he was living at th
time. Finally, Herb suggested there was a conspirac
against Tim at work here, noting that Gallo and Kutch
mark knew each other from high school and that Erwi
and Kutchmark had become friends while serving time to
gether.

As prosecutor Randy Carroll had during Tim's trial fo
Elaine's murder, Borkowski slowly but surely laid the foun
dation for what appeared to be a solid case against Tin
But ten days into the trial, the state suffered its first majo
blow when Cercone refused to allow Borkowski to preser
evidence indicating that Tim may have had chloroform i
his possession at the time of Maryann's death.

Borkowski had told the court that an assistant to D
Maryanne Davis, a dentist who sometimes hired Tim t
make dental products for her patients, was prepared to te:
tify that Tim had obtained several ounces of chlorofor
from her after telling her that Davis had okayed it. Tim ha
no use for chloroform in his business, Borkowski pointe
out. Borkowski said, too, that police theorized that Tir
might have soaked the white handkerchief found in th

hot tub in chloroform and then used it to knock Maryann out so it would be easier for him to strangle her. Borkowski conceded, though, that the police never obtained a warrant to search Tim and Maryann's house. As a result, there was no way of knowing whether there was any chloroform there. He also acknowledged that the failure of investigators to obtain a search warrant kept police from obtaining a sample of the water in the hot tub before Tim drained it.

Davis herself, however, did take the stand. The dentist testified that in July 1994, some three months before Maryann's death, she and two other professionals who also had offices in the building where Dental Smiles was located, were considering buying the property next door to theirs. When Tim found out, he approached Davis about getting in on the deal, and offered to pitch in $10,000. But because the property cost $200,000, each of the four partners, in fact, would need to contribute $50,000. That left Tim $40,000 short, and the jury, after learning this, undoubtedly wondering whether Tim might have been so desperate for money that he killed his second wife.

On Wednesday, April 28, following testimony by forty-three witnesses for the prosecution, the state rested its case. Among the last witnesses to take the stand was Liz Maple, Tim and Elaine's next-door neighbor at Yester Oaks. Maple had testified at Tim's North Carolina trial, but Judge Catherine Eagles would not allow prosecutor Randy Carroll to ask Maple about statements Todd Boczkowski had made to her only hours after Elaine was transported to the hospital. Judge Cercone did.

In what essentially amounted to a bombshell for the prosecution, Maple testified that it was roughly 3 a.m. the morning of Elaine's death when she heard Tim pounding on her front door. He explained that something had happened to Elaine, that she was being taken to the hospital, and that he was going there, too.

"Can you watch the kids?" Tim asked Maple.

Randy, Sandy, and Todd, who were in their pajamas, went right to bed at Maple's apartment, she testified. The next morning, she said, Todd told her he'd heard Elaine yelling the night before. "He said, 'Mommy was screaming so loud last night that I had to put my hands up over my ears,' " Maple testified. "He said, 'Daddy told me to get out of the bathroom. I saw Mommy. Her hands were up in the air.' Then he said he knew his mom was dead and that 'she couldn't get out of the bathroom because Daddy wouldn't let her.' "

Perhaps taking his cue from his father, who displayed as little emotion during the Pittsburgh proceedings as he had in North Carolina, Todd, who was sitting in the row directly behind the defense table, did little but blink as Maple told her story.

Herb, in presenting Tim's defense, made many of the same arguments Doug Harris and Fred Lind had during Tim's trial for Elaine's murder. In an attempt, for instance, to negate the prosecution's argument that financial gain was among Tim's motives for killing Maryann, he called an employee of a Pittsburgh brokerage firm who testified that in 1993 and 1994, Tim made monthly deposits of between $200 and $300 in accounts he had opened in each of his children's names. Tim clearly had gotten back on his feet money-wise, Herb contended.

Among the witnesses Herb called to testify about Maryann's alleged drinking problem were Joe Baranowski and Jackie Wainwright, the Nativity Church choir members who had mentioned to Sister Pat Baker that they had smelled alcohol on Maryann's breath during choir practice. He also called Dr. Robert Tippin, Maryann's fertility doctor, who said Maryann had told him she drank up to five beers a day. Tippin also testified that during one office visit he found Maryann's blood pressure to be slightly higher than normal, a possible sign of alcohol abuse.

On Friday, April 30, the courtroom was abuzz over Herb's declaration that Tim was leaning toward testifying in his own defense. Herb told Judge Cercone that although he had advised Tim against doing so, Tim was considering taking the stand. Tim, however, had also said he wanted to

vait until after Herb had called his final witness, which
Herb said he expected to do the following Monday, before
making his final decision.

Herb's final witness turned out to be Dr. Glenn Larkin,
who had served as Allegheny County's chief forensic pathologist from 1979 to 1982. Larkin testified that the fact
hat water was found in Maryann's sinuses indicated that
she was submerged at some point," and that drowning
was, "more likely than anything," the cause of her death.
I saw no significant signs that she was strangled," he in-
isted.

Larkin said the fingerprint marks that Rozin said he
found on Maryann's neck appeared to him, when he examined photos taken during Maryann's autopsy, to be not
on her neck but directly below her jaw line. Moreover, he
said, the marks could have been made by a paramedic tilt-
ing Maryann's head backward during efforts to revive her.

As for the petechia, the pinpoint hemorrhages Rozin said
he found in Maryann's eyes, Larkin contended that "in all
probability," they were caused by the needle used to extract
liquid from Maryann's eyes during her autopsy.

Finally, because Maryann's liver was found to have the
kind of fat deposits often found in the livers of heavy drink-
ers, Larkin suggested there was a possibility that her liver
could have failed suddenly and that that caused her death.
People who die in this manner, he explained, "die unat-
tended, unexpectedly, and [without any] witnesses."

After Larkin, Dr. Abe Friedman, a cardiologist from
Pittsburgh's Shadyside Hospital, was called by Borkowski
as a rebuttal witness. Friedman, contradicting Tippin, testified that Maryann did not suffer from high blood pressure.

Despite all of Tim's claims over the years that he had a
bad heart, Herb never called a cardiologist to support these
assertions. This made Maryann's relatives wonder just how
serious a heart problem Tim had, if he had one at all.

AFTER FRIEDMAN finished testifying, Cercone instructed
Tim and Herb to approach the bench.

"Do you still wish to testify on your own behalf?" the judge asked Tim.

Tim said no, that he'd changed his mind.

Detective Jim Cvetic, among others, was hardly surprised. "Tim would have been crushed by Borkowski," he said. "If he wanted to beat the charge, he had to keep his mouth shut."

CHAPTER 45

ON TUESDAY, May 4, Allegheny County Deputy District Attorney Ed Borkowski, in his closing argument, scoffed at the defense's characterization of Tim as a good father.

"What good father kills his children's mother while they're in adjacent rooms?" he asked rhetorically. "What good father strangles to death the woman that not only opened her heart to him but gave her heart to his kids?"

Borkowski implored the jury to keep Tim from making a mockery of the criminal justice system. "Stop his laughing," Borkowski begged the twelve-member panel. "Stop his lying. Stop his killing. Convict him of first-degree murder."

Defense attorney James Herb, for his part, labeled the authorities' handling of the case a "fiasco" and had no qualms about spreading the blame. The police, he said, mishandled evidence. The District Attorney's office, he maintained, was overzealous in its pursuit of Tim. Dr. Leon Rozin, he suggested, bowed to pressure from the Allegheny County Police Department and ruled a death that was obviously a drowning a homicide. His initial notes, Herb said, indicated that he'd concluded Maryann had drowned, but he eventually "caved in" to the police and altered his findings.

Herb, too, attacked a specific prosecution witness. He called Randy Erwin a "dirtball" who simply did whatever Allegheny County Detective Jim Cvetic told him to do. "The prosecution lies down with dogs and gets up with fleas," the defense attorney sniffed.

As far as the bruises Rozin testified he found on Maryann's body, Herb contended they could have occurred when Maryann was lifted out of the hot tub and placed on the wooden deck or when she was being treated at the scene by paramedics.

Finally, Herb characterized Elaine's death as a "red herring," dismissing the fact that she died under similar circumstances as Maryann. "It proves nothing," he said. "It is something totally irrelevant to this case."

It was roughly 4 p.m. on Tuesday when the jury began deliberating. Cercone, in his instructions to the panel, said it had three options as far as a verdict: guilty of first-degree murder, guilty of third-degree murder, or not guilty.

Shortly thereafter, Borkowski met briefly with Maryann's family. Pat Fullerton had asked the prosecutor if she could see some of the photographs that were taken during Maryann's autopsy. He agreed. So after the jury exited the courtroom to begin its deliberations, Borkowski brought Pat over to the prosecutor's table and showed her several shots. With her husband, Lew, and son, John, huddled around her, Pat looked longingly at each of the photos. She then ran her hand across one showing Maryann's bruised and swollen face, and began to cry.

Maryann's friends and family knew better than to take a conviction for granted. At the same time, they felt confident that this jury would reach the same conclusion as the one that had convicted Tim of Elaine's murder two-and-a-half years earlier. They felt even stronger after talking with one of the jury's alternates, who was dismissed after the panel began its deliberations.

"Do you think he's guilty?" Maryann's aunt, Ruth Schumann, asked the woman after stopping her on the sidewalk outside the courthouse.

"He's guilty as sin," she said with no hesitation, "and I hope they give him the death penalty."

At 8:30 p.m., after four-and-a-half hours of mulling over the evidence, the jury informed Cercone that it had yet to reach a verdict. Cercone told the panel they could continue deliberating the following morning and sent its members

ho had not been sequestered during the trial, but were
ow, to a local hotel for the night.

Deliberations resumed at 9:30 a.m. on Wednesday.
ome two hours later, the jurors informed Cercone that they
d reached a unanimous decision.

As he had when the verdict was read at his North Car-
ina trial, Tim displayed no emotions upon hearing this
ry's verdict: guilty of first-degree murder. Randy and
odd also were expressionless. Sandy, however, bowed her
ad and began to sob. Friends and relatives of Elaine's
d Maryann's, meanwhile, exchanged hugs. They were
o for two.

Outside the courtroom, Maryann's mother, Pat Fullerton,
oke her four-and-a-half year silence to the press. "No one
ins in a situation like this," she said. "The Boczkowski
mily lost their son. I lost my daughter, who lost her
ance to live. The district attorney did a good job, and
s, we're happy with the outcome. It's in God's hands
w."

HE FOLLOWING day, Thursday, May 6, the jury returned
 Cercone's courtroom to hear testimony in the sentencing
ase of Tim's trial.

Borkowski, now permitted to tell the jury that Tim had
en tried and convicted of Elaine's murder, offered a sim-
e and straightforward argument. Tim had killed two wives
 a similar manner. He deserved to be put to death by
thal injection for his crimes.

Defense Attorney Jack Conflenti, on the other hand,
ade an impassioned plea imploring the jurors to spare
m's life for the sake of his and Elaine's children. "These
ildren have unresolved issues," he contended. "If you
ntence their father to death, they won't have a chance to
ok into his eyes [ever again]. There's no chance for re-
mption or resolution."

Conflenti, too, stressed to the panel members that Tim,
 they could see to let him live, would still, under Penn-
lvania law, be facing life in prison with no chance of

parole. "Prison is hell," he assured the jurors. "Myself? I'
rather be dead."

Randy, Sandy, and Todd also pleaded with the jury n
to sentence their father to death.

Randy, Tim and Elaine's first-born, intimated how ha
it would be to lose someone else close to him, especial
his father. "Please don't put him to death," an emotionle
Randy begged the panel.

Todd, meanwhile, talked about how close he felt to h
father.

Both boys managed to maintain their composure whi
being questioned by Conflenti. Their sister, Sandy, on t
other hand, began crying the moment she took the witnes
stand. At one point, Sandy, a bunch of tissues clenched
her hand, shared some advice her father had given he
advice she clearly hoped would strike a chord with the jur
too. "He says treat others how you'd want to be treated
she said, clearly missing the irony that undoubtedly wa
not lost on the adults scattered throughout the courtroon
Sandy also described how she kept in touch with her fath
through letters, phone calls, and occasional visits. "H
means a lot to me," she said, struggling to get each wor
in the sentence out.

Conflenti then asked Sandy to read a letter she'd broug
to court with her that day, a letter she'd written to Ti
telling him how proud she was of him and how glad sh
was that he was her father.

She held the letter in front of her and began to read
aloud. But before she finished even the first sentence, sh
stopped, unable to finish through her tears.

"I can't do it," she sobbed.

There were but two dry eyes in the courtroom by th
time the teenager climbed down from the witness stan
They were Tim's. Apparently, he was more concerned wit
other matters than he was with the fact that his daughte
had just broken down in front of him. As she walked bac
to her seat in the gallery, Tim, rather than offering som

ords of comfort to his daughter, turned instead to Con-
enti.

"Don't forget to bring me my sandwich tonight," he re-
inded his attorney.

CHAPTER 46

THE CHILDREN'S testimony had clearly struck a nerve with the members of the jury. Ed Borkowski, too, could feel Randy, Sandy, and Todd's pain. But Borkowski, at the same time, knew he had a job to do. In his final words to the jury, the prosecutor railed against Conflenti's contention that Tim's life should be spared because his children need him now that they don't have their mother or stepmother any more. Tim, Borkowski reminded the jury, was the reason the children had only one surviving parent, and had no one but himself to blame for that fact.

"He took away the two people who meant the most to these children and could have given them a normal life," he argued. "He made the choice to kill the two mothers of these children. He made the choice when he murdered Elaine. He made the choice when he choked the life from Maryann."

The jury that found unanimously that Tim had murdered Maryann took less than two hours to reach a unanimous decision as far as a sentence. Having committed the premeditated murders of both his first and second wives—of his children's biological and adoptive mothers—Tim, the panel agreed, deserved to die.

There was little doubt that some of the jurors had struggled with the decision. At least three cried, and a few sniffled as the verdict was read. Randy and Sandy were visibly shaken as well. Randy, after tears began to well in his eyes, buried his face in his hands. Sandy fell into her Uncle Ron Boczkowski's chest. Todd wasn't there. He had gone to school instead.

Tim, meanwhile, responded to the verdict by turning to

Conflenti and asking him two questions: "Can we appeal?" and "Is there any way I can speak to my parents?"

Judge Cercone imposed the jury's sentence immediately, after which Tim was led from the courtroom in handcuffs. Before long, he would be on his way to the State Correctional Institution at Greene in Waynesburg, Pennsylvania, the maximum-security prison where the state houses all of its male death-row inmates.

A short time later, during an impromptu press conference outside the courtroom, Borkowski told reporters he believed the jury had meted out an "appropriate sentence." "He took the heart and emotions of two families and destroyed them," the prosecutor said of Tim. Tim, he added, was responsible for "a path of emotional devastation that read like a phone book."

Conflenti, in his comments to reporters, continued to stress that the children were being punished as much as Tim was for his crimes. "The kids are victims for a third time," he maintained. "They lost two mothers. Now they are losing a father."

When asked to play Monday morning quarterback as far as the jury's verdict, Conflenti suggested that Tim's lack of emotion during his children's testimony "may have left a negative impression on the panel. I think the jury was paying attention to him when the children were on the stand," he said. "In fact, I noticed them looking around me to look at him."

Meanwhile, Pat Fullerton, after regaining her composure, faced the media for the second day in a row. She explained that she was torn over her desire for retribution and her concern for the three children her daughter couldn't have loved any more had they been her own. "I go back and forth," she said. "One day, I hate him and want him to pay for what he did. Then there are the children. Maryann loved and cared about them, and we know they are hurting, too."

Gay Barbiaux, Maryann's friend of nearly twenty years, was decidedly less diplomatic. "He's a cold-blooded killer," she declared. "Maryann was a wonderful person. She didn't deserve to die. No one deserves to die the way she did."

Later that day, Maryann's cousin, Joan Zappa, drove out to St. Anthony's Cemetery and attached a sign she had composed on her computer to Maryann's flat tombstone. It read: "Justice for Maryann: May 6, 1999." At the same time, her sister, Jean Zappa, covered the word "Boczkowski" with tape. That evening, a group of Maryann's aunts and cousins assembled at her Aunt Maggie Fischerkeller's house. There, they ate a celebratory cake and sang—to the tune of *"Happy Birthday"*—"Happy justice to you . . ."

CHAPTER 47

ONCE THE governor of Pennsylvania signs a death warrant for an inmate on the state's death row, and an execution date is set, the inmate is placed in a cell where he or she is kept under around-the-clock observation by a specially-trained guard. The inmate is allowed to keep legal papers inside his or her cell, but most other items—from televisions to toothbrushes—are prohibited. At this point, non-contact visits are limited to the prisoner's immediate family, spiritual advisor, and attorney.

If the inmate's execution is not stayed, he is transferred to the execution facility just outside the State Correctional Institution at Rockview, in Bellefonte. A guard and a state trooper remain with the inmate around-the-clock, until he is strapped to a gurney and wheeled into the death chamber. Once there, the inmate is issued brown pants, a white T-shirt and short-sleeved shirt, socks, and terry-cloth slippers and held in one of three cells located a short distance from the death chamber. He is then briefed by prison officials on the execution procedure and chooses his final meal.

A lethal injection of poisonous drugs is administered intravenously by an individual the Pennsylvania Department of Corrections will identify only as "technically competent by virtue of training or experience to carry out the lethal injection procedure."

Twelve people—six citizens and six representatives from the media, are allowed to witness the execution. The citizens are picked from a list of 350 volunteers and may include the inmate's relatives.

Such is the fate that awaits Tim Boczkowski should he exhaust all avenues of appeal of his death sentence for the first-degree murder of his wife, Maryann Fullerton Boczkowski.

On October 28, 1999, Tim's attorney, James Herb, filed a notice of appeal with the Supreme Court of Pennsylvania. The court has yet to hear Tim's case.

TIMOTHY BOCZKOWSKI remains incarcerated today in a restricted housing unit at the State Correctional Institute at Greene in Waynesburg, PA. Like all death-row inmates, he is held in a single cell twenty-three hours a day. He is allowed only non-contact visits from people on an approved list.

Pat and Lew Fullerton still live in the Shaler Township home where Maryann Fullerton Boczkowski spent most of her childhood. They continue to struggle daily with the void her murder left in their lives, especially Pat. For all intents and purposes a part of her died, too, on November 7, 1994.

Rose Boczkowski lives with her second husband, Francis Andreoletti, in Pittsburgh. Buc Boczkowski lives near his daughter, Joan, in Cranberry, PA, about twenty-five miles north of Pittsburgh.

Friends and relatives of Elaine's and Maryann's say they run into Randy, Sandy, and Todd Boczkowski, who still live with the North Hills foster parents who took them in following Tim's conviction, from time to time. "They're friendly, well-spoken, and intelligent," says Maria Crendall, who remains married to Tim's boyhood friend, Mark Crendall. "They remind me of Elaine, and they would have made Maryann so proud."

"They seem to be okay, considering everything they've gone through," Tim and Maryann's one-time neighbor, Wes Semple, adds. But according to Maryann's longtime friend, Eileen Datt, there continues to be a subject the children studiously avoid whenever she runs into them—Tim. "They'll say whether they've seen him or talked to him recently," she says, "but they never mention what he did."

Mark Crendall, who has known Tim for more than thirty years, exchanges letters with Tim a few times a year. "Our friendship goes way back," he says, "and I remember too many good things about Tim to just abandon him. Whenever I needed him, he was there."

Mark refers to himself as "the last hold-out," explaining that he refused to believe until Tim was convicted of Maryann's murder that his childhood friend could be guilty of killing both his first and second wives.

"I just thought, 'This all has to be a big mistake,' " he says. "I didn't think he was capable of hurting someone like that. He was always trying to help people. He was the one who was always getting me out of fights."

Mark says he's never asked Tim about the murders. "I don't think I have the courage to do that," he concedes.

But he does lie awake some nights wondering what made his best friend commit two heinous murders—slayings that stole his children's mother from them not once, but twice. "I'll stay up trying to make sense of it all," he says. "But I haven't figured it out yet, and I don't think I ever will."